THE HUNTER'S BIBLE

BY W. K. MERRILL

THE HUNTER'S BIBLE

A HANDBOOK FOR THE TYRO AND THE EXPERIENCED

HOW TO BAG UPLAND BIRDS, DUCKS AND GEESE

AND HUNT SMALL AND BIG GAME

DOUBLEDAY & COMPANY, INC., GARDEN CITY, NEW YORK

ISBN: 0-385-01533-X

Library of Congress Catalog Card Number 68–22523
Copyright © 1968 by W. K. Bill Merrill
All Rights Reserved
Printed in the United States of America
20 19 18 17 16

Contents

ing Game. Taking Care of Your Firearms. Storing Arms. Free
Gun-Cleaning Guide.

Horns. Wild Boar. How They Are Hunted. Peccary, the Little
Pig. Pig Hunting. Caliber?

Who May Need It. First Aid if Injuries Do Occur. General Direc-
tions. Shock—the Killer. Wounds with Severe Bleeding. Overcome
by Smoke, Asphyxiation, Stoppage of Breathing. Poison—Internal.
Burns. Burns of Limited Extent. Extensive Burns. Broken Bones
or Dislocations. Sprains. Wounds, Bleeding Not Severe. Wilderness
Treatment of Venomous Stings and Bites. Recommended Reading.
Poison Ivy—Poison Oak—Sumac—Nettles, and Other Plants. Blis-
ters. Heat Exhaustion. Heat Stroke. Sunburn. Snow Blindness.
Prolonged Exposure to Cold. Heart Attacks. Rescue Breathing.
Emergency Oxygen. Wilderness Camp Medicine. Basic Medical
Supplies for a Small Expedition. Cold Weather and General Sur-
vival Techniques. Emergency Shelters. Bivouac Sheet. The
Lean-to. Hole-in-the-Snow or Tree Shelter. Snow Dugout. Desert
Hunting and Survival. If You Do Get into a Desert Survival Situ-
ation. If You Become Lost—What to Do. Sense of Direction. Lost-
in-the-Woods Experience. Your Survival Fire. Useful Fire Hints.
The Art of Keeping Warm. How to Keep Warm and Keep Your
Sleeping Bag Dry. Checklist for Cold-Weather Survival.

A Few Simple Forest Rules. Suggestions for Safe Boating.
Sportsmanship Needed in the Outdoors.

Sources of Emergency Rations and Dehydrated Foods. Outfitters
Catalogs for Hunters and Campers. Where to Write for Hunting,
Camping, and Boating Information.

PREFACE

Within this small handbook I am not attempting to embrace every aspect of hunting upland birds, ducks, geese, small and big game. Many volumes could be and have been written by experts on these subjects and the equipment and weapons necessary to bag these prizes. The modern nimrod is not necessarily a new or inexperienced hunter. I am merely attempting to point out the pertinent facts I have observed during my thirty-six years' experience in the field as a State Game Warden and Ranger—tips and facts that will be helpful for the hunter with limited time so that he will know how to plan in advance, take the right equipment, be more comfortable, and have a better chance of being successful.

Approximately 90 percent of nimrods entering the field are weekend hunters from nearby towns in areas where game is more or less abundant. About 5 percent will drive several hundred miles to reach their goals. The other 5 percent are nonresident hunters who travel out of state to the big-game hunting grounds of the West—Alaska, Canada, and Mexico.

To the "old-timers" who have worn "The hunting moccasins of experience," I hope that the information I am about to present will be tolerantly accepted. And the tips and new material in this book will make the neophyte and old-timer alike enjoy a more successful hunting adventure.

I owe thanks to many individuals and veteran hunters whose suggestions contributed to the preparations of this little handbook, and to:

The U. S. Bureau of Sports Fisheries and Wildlife Service, Department of the Interior; The California Fish & Game Department; The U. S. Forest Service; The U. S. National Park Service; The National Rifle Association; The National Shooting Sports Foundation; The Olin Mathieson Chemical Corporation, Winchester-Western Division; The Poly Choke Company; W. R. Weaver Company; Shakespeare Company; Bear Archery Company; Ben Pearson Company; to the Tuolumne Country Research Librarian, Mrs. Robert Hooe and staff; Brig. General J. B. Sweet, U.S.A., Retired; Colonel R. S. Gunderson, U.S.A.F., Retired; Colonel Frank R. Wilkinson, Commandant, U. S. Marine Corps Mountain Warfare Training Center; Lieutenant Colonel Burton Miller, U.S.A.F., Retired; and that Dean of Outdoorsmen—Clyde Ormond.

To each of these and to the many others who have helped but are not named, my sincere appreciation.

And to all you hunters, please remember: Once a bullet has been triggered, no power on earth can bring it back. Only the hunter behind the gunsights can determine its mission. Only his eyesight, his reflexes, and his judgment can control its direction. This great responsibility is his alone. He is the conscience of that bullet!

W.K.M.

THE HUNTER'S BIBLE

The Alaska Highway, in Canada's Yukon Territory, leads the hunter to new adventures.
CANADIAN GOVERNMENT TRAVEL BUREAU

Chapter 1

THE ADVENTURE OF MODERN HUNTING AND WHERE TO GO

Why do many men and women enjoy going hunting? The answer is simple! In all of us lies a latent instinct to heed the Call of the Wild. The thrill of the chase has been inherited from our primitive ancestors, who had to obtain their food, clothing, and shelter by hunting. Modern man, too, often experiences this urge—especially in the fall when hunting season nears.

The right of Americans to own and use firearms is a cherished part of our heritage and has kept us a strong and free people. In much of the world owning firearms is a rare privilege, even for hunting or protecting one's home and family.

The true sportsman realizes his duty to handle firearms properly. And he gladly teaches the younger generation the responsibilities of gun ownership. The finest example of democracy in action is that millions of Americans are free to keep firearms and enjoy recreational hunting.

Today more people engage in this thrilling and exciting form of recreation than any other personal sport. It has become a national pastime. With a shorter work week and longer vacation, a hunter can enjoy twice as much opportunity for hunting than he did a decade or so ago.

The wilderness that witnessed the birth of our nation and nourished its growth no longer spreads across the land as our pioneer forefathers knew it. Neither has it been tamed. Wildlife still roams the primitive regions of the continent— lands that embrace the desert country and brushlands, virgin timber stands, great valleys and alpine meadows, and some of the loftiest mountains. These contain countless streams and natural lakes, and great quantities of pure water flow from their glaciers. They abound in small animals and upland game, ducks and geese, and big-game animals so dear to the heart of the hunter such as deer, elk, moose, antelope, caribou, peccary, wild boar, mountain goat, and the nimble-footed big-horn sheep. Some are the province of the musk-ox, the polar, black, brown, and grizzly bear, which must have wilderness habitat to survive.

The Secret of Where to Hunt Many writers continue to state that there are very few places left to hunt. This just isn't the case as you will learn shortly, and I do not agree with them! It is just a simple matter of knowing what public and private land is open to hunting and then deciding where you want to go.

One method of finding out how far you live from a hunting area is to use your town or city as a hub, then on a road map draw a circle out from it—one hour driving time, fifty miles out; one hundred miles, two hours; 150 miles, three hours; and two hundred miles, four hours' drive, and so on as far as you want to go. You will be suprised, for there is very likely to be some type of hunting within these circles close to home that you may be interested in—

The immensity, vastness, and mobility of birds and game beyond Canada's border urge the hunter northward. CANADIAN GOVERNMENT TRAVEL BUREAU

upland, small- or big-game, and perhaps water-fowl.

The Wilderness Areas To better your odds, try one of the Wilderness Areas in our national forests. National Forest Wilderness Areas total 22,656 square miles of scenic hunting terrain in fourteen states. This is a bonanza for the rifle-man or bow hunter. Here competition is at a minimum and your chances to collect game will be greatly enhanced.

These areas range in size from the 8.4-square-mile Great Gulf Wild Area in New Hampshire to the two-thousand-square-mile Selway-Bitter-root Wilderness in Idaho and Montana, an area the size of Delaware.

All areas are open to hunting in season under state laws. However, all motorized vehicles and equipment are prohibited, and travel must be on foot or by saddle and pack outfit. Fortunately, vehicles can travel through most other sections

of the national forests where most hunting is carried on, and the Forest Service has set aside places for "off-the-road" travel for those hunters using "back country" types of transportation. This is a boon to the handicapped hunter who is unable to hike very far from camp. He can find a good spot near camp in the shade close to a game crossing and still have nearly as good an opportunity to shoot as his more rugged companions.

USFS Grasslands the Upland Bird Mecca Other vast public shooting areas where all sportsmen own hunting rights (yet few are aware of it) are our nineteen National Forest Service Grass-lands. These areas comprise nearly six thousand square miles—a region populated by a growing concentration of quail and other upland birds, many of them underhunted. Here is a list of these upland game bonanzas:

Game-Bird Resources of Our Grasslands

National Grasslands	Location	Administrative Headquarters	Bird Hunting Available
Cedar River	North Dakota	Custer National Forest Billings, Montana	Sharptail grouse, sage grouse, pheasants
Little Missouri	North Dakota	Custer National Forest Billings, Montana	Sharptail grouse, sage grouse, pheasants
Grand River	South Dakota	Custer National Forest Billings, Montana	Sharptail grouse, sage grouse, pheasants
Cheyenne	North Dakota	Chippewa National Forest Cross Lake, Minnesota	Sharptail grouse, pheasants
Buffalo Gap	South Dakota	Black Hills National Forest Custer, South Dakota	Sharptail grouse
Cimarron	Kansas	San Isabel National Forest Pueblo, Colorado	Scaled quail, bob-white quail, pheasants
Comanche	Colorado	San Isabel National Forest Pueblo, Colorado	Scaled quail, bob-white quail, pheasants
Port Pierre	South Dakota	Black Hills National Forest Custer, So. Dakota	Sharptail grouse, prairie chickens
Ogalala	Nebraska and South Dakota	Nebraska National Forest Lincoln, Nebraska	Wild turkeys
Pawnee	Colorado	Roosevelt National Forest Fort Collins, Colorado	Pheasants
Thunder Basin	Wyoming	Medicine Bow National Forest Laramie, Wyoming	Sage grouse
Black Kettle	Texas	Panhandle National Grasslands, Amarillo, Texas	Scaled quail, bob-white quail
Caddo	Texas	Panhandle National Grasslands, Amarillo, Texas	Bob-white quail
Cross Timbers	Texas	Panhandle National Grasslands, Amarillo, Texas	Bob-white quail
Kiowa	New Mexico	Panhandle National Grasslands, Amarillo, Texas	Scaled quail
McClellan Creek	Texas	Panhandle National Grasslands, Amarillo, Texas	Bob-white quail
Rita Blanca	Texas, Oklahoma, New Mexico	Panhandle National Grasslands, Amarillo, Texas	Scaled quail, bob-white quail, pheasant, prairie chickens
Curlew	Idaho	Caribou National Forest, Pocatello, Idaho	Sharp-tailed grouse, sage grouse
Crooked River	Oregon	Ochoco National Forest, Prineville, Oregon	Valley quail, chukars, Hungarian partridges

Where to Write for Full Details For full information on National Forests, Primitive, Wild, Wilderness Areas, and National Grasslands, write to the Chief, Division of Information and Education, United States Forest Service, Department of Agriculture, Washington, D.C. 20250, or one of the regional offices near you.

Region 1 (Northern): Federal Building, Missoula, Montana 57801

Region 2 (Rocky Mountain): Federal Center Building No. 85, Denver, Colorado 80225

Region 3 (Southwestern): New Federal Building, 517 Gold Street S.W., Albuquerque, New Mexico 87101

Region 4 (Intermountain): Forest Service Building, Ogden, Utah 84403

Region 5 (California): 630 Sansome Street, San Francisco, California 94111

Region 6 (Pacific Northwest): 729 N.E. Oregon Street, Portland, Oregon 97208

Region 7 (Eastern): Center Building, 6816 Market Street, Upper Darby, Pennsylvania 19082

Region 8 (Southern): 50 7th Street N.E., Atlanta, Georgia 90323

Region 9 (North-Central): Carpenter Building, Milwaukee, Wisconsin 53203

Region 10 (Alaska): Fifth Street Office Building, Juneau, Alaska 99801

Be specific with your questions—where you want to go, species of game you are interested in, closed areas, forest and fire regulations, etc.

The Primitive Weapons Area Here is fun for the bow-and-arrow and cap-and-ball enthusiasts. Old-time weapons are required if you want to hunt the varied game found in the 7300-acre Primitive Weapons Area in the Cumberland National Forest. The area has been set aside by the U. S. Forest Service in cooperation with the Kentucky Department of Fish and Wildlife Resources for the sportsmen who like to hunt game under the same conditions that existed in Daniel Boone's and Davy Crockett's time.

The only weapons permitted here are muzzle-loading rifles and shotguns, longbows and crossbows. This is one of the few places where the crossbow is a legal weapon. The PWA is in Bath and Menifee counties, in the northern section of the forest, fifteen miles southeast of Moorehead, Kentucky. Modern methods of game management have produced an abundance of small game on the area—grouse, quail, dove, squirrel, rabbit, and larger game such as deer. For full details about the area write to the Forest Supervisor, Cumberland National Forest, Winchester, Kentucky 40391, or the Department of Fish and Wildlife Resources, Frankfort, Kentucky 40601.

TVA'S Land between the Lakes This 266-square-mile area is still being developed, and lies between Kentucky Lake, biggest of the TVA impounds, and the newly filled Barkley Lake in western Kentucky. For full details on hunting conditions write: TVA, P.O. Box 27, Golden Pond, Kentucky 42231.

The Little-Known BLM Hunting Areas Who says there isn't any place to hunt any more? Besides the 354,698 plus square miles contained in our national forests, much of them open to hunting, there are the vast BLM lands!

From the deserts of Arizona to the tundra of Alaska, there are over 718,750 square miles of public lands. You'll find room to roam here, wide open space where you can camp and hunt your fill—and really get away from the nervous strain of urban living. This is the public domain, that part of the original public lands of the United States still in federal ownership, lands which haven't been set aside for national forests, parks, and other special uses. You will find variety, from deserts to forests, sagebrush canyons to snowcapped mountains with excellent hunting in many sections. These lands are under the jurisdiction of the Bureau of Land Management, an agency of the Department of the Interior. For full details, write to the Division of Information, United States Bureau of Land Management, Department of the Interior, Washington D.C. 20240.

Hunting in National Parks All hunting in national parks is prohibited with the exception of Grand Teton National Park, where a special elk permit hunt has been allowed the past few years. However, hunting is allowed in some of the more recent recreational areas of the Park System. For information regarding them, write to: The Division of Information, United States National Park Service, Department of the Interior, Washington D.C. 20240.

Army Engineer Facilities Don't overlook Army Engineer facilities. Write to Conservation and Recreation Planner, Building T-7, Washington D.C. 20315.

Indian Reservations Some Indian reservations such as the Southern Ute in Colorado, and the Jicarilla Apache in New Mexico are open to hunting. Mule deer and black bear in this territory have always been outsize. Their increase in numbers has become a problem for the state and federal game authorities. The policy on the Southern Ute Reservation has been to allow three deer of either sex per hunter, and in the balance of the area two deer have been allowed.

There is good javelina shooting on the San Carlos Reservation near Globe, Arizona. Bow season is open all of January, with a gun season following. A state hunting license is required plus a special tribal permit from the Indian Council.

For information on these and other Indian reservations, write to the Department of Indian Affairs, United States Department of the Interior, Washington, D.C. 20240.

Maine deer. Who says there isn't any place to hunt any more? MAINE DEPARTMENT OF ECONOMIC DEVELOPMENT

Recreation on Reclamation Land Write to Information Officer, United States Bureau of Reclamation, Department of the Interior, Washington, D.C. 20240.

Shorelines for the Waterfowl Hunter The ORRRC reports that the forty-eight conterminous states have approximately sixty thousand miles of shoreline. About one-third of these can be considered possible waterfowl recreation waters. These include beaches, marshes, bluffs, and points of land where numbers of waterfowl gather.

Inland fresh waters within the original forty-eight states cover some ninety-five thousand square miles, an area comparable to the state of Oregon. This water is in almost a million miles of streams and rivers and more than one hundred thousand natural lakes; ten million surface acres of it is in artificial impoundments; and over half of the total area is in the Great Lakes. Moreover, wildlife habitat is near water!

Public Shooting in Refuges Yes, you can hunt in vast areas of our game refuges! Where are these areas? They are scattered all over the nation. One may be near your town! Portions of some of the larger of the migratory waterfowl areas provide public shooting, for instance, the Bear River Refuge in Utah. The Mattamuskeet, in North Carolina, has become one of the famous goose-shooting areas of the Atlantic coast. Here the State Fish and Game Department manages the public shooting under a cooperative agree-

Oregon offers a variety of game in a land of scenic beauty. OREGON GAME COMMISSION

ment with the U. S. Fish and Wildlife Service. Portions of the Bowdoin and Medicine Lake in Montana, Deer Flat in Idaho, Havasu and Imperial along the Arizona and California borders, Lower Klamath and Tule lakes in California, Ruby Lakes, Nevada, the Snake River in Idaho, and the Upper Mississippi extending through Minnesota, Wisconsin, Illinois, Iowa, and Missouri furnish public shooting for waterfowl.

The Upper Mississippi Refuge, extending through five states, has set aside approximately 20 percent of the area as a refuge, while the balance is open to waterfowl and upland game shooting.

There are over 350,000 square miles of United States land available to the responsible hunter. COURTESY OF THE AUTHOR

Upland bird shooting and small- and big-game hunting is permitted under state game laws and in accord with state seasons on Desert Game Range in Nevada, the Hart Mountain Antelope Refuge in Nevada, Pend Oreille in Washington, Lostwood and Lower Souris in North Dakota, Necedah and Trempeleau in Wisconsin, San Andreas in New Mexico, Seney in Michigan, and other refuges.

The Arrowwood Refuge in North Dakota, the Necedah in Wisconsin, and Blackbeard Island off the coast of Georgia have produced some excellent bow-and-arrow hunting for many years. For further information write to the Information Division, United States Fish and Wildlife Service, Department of the Interior, Washington, D.C. 20240.

State Game Refuges and Private Preserves Write to the Information Officer, Fish and Game Department of your state for refuges that have been opened to hunters; also request a list of the private hunting preserves.

Private Timberlands Open to Hunting Don't overlook this vast area where game is abundant! Private timber owners and the logging industry are also opening land for public camping and hunting. The lumbermen have joined the ranks to relieve the hunting pressure in our national forests by opening over eighty thousand square miles of privately owned land containing over forty thousand miles of streams. Hunters, too, know that deer and other game thrive in cutover land. However, much of this can be withdrawn if hunters do not respect private property.

Vandalism Some vandalism has already been noted. Initials have been carved in camp tables, benches, signs, and trees; comfort stations have been left unsightly and filthy, and signs have been split up for kindling. Padlocks have been shot off gates in some closed areas. Holes have been shot into gasoline and diesel storage tanks in the woods. Logging equipment has been stolen, and some hunters have endangered the lives of loggers operating logging "shows" by indiscriminately shooting at targets and game nearby. Any sportsman worth his salt observing acts of this sort should make it his personal duty and responsibility to report these persons to the nearest law-enforcement officer. Otherwise, a few may spoil hunting privileges for many, and owners will start putting up more and more "No Trespassing" signs in self-defense.

The Hunting Land North of Our Border The awe-inspiring beauty of the Canadian prairies provides a perfect background for small game, upland birds, and waterfowl shooting. There are wide open spaces sweeping to far horizons . . . endless miles of grain stubble . . . and oceans of grasslands studded with potholes that waterfowl favor. These are the bountiful gamelands that confront the upland bird hunter over the provinces of Manitoba, Saskatchewan, and Alberta. The immensity, the vastness, and the mobile type of birds and small-game hunting it offers the deskbound nimrod are sure to plant

Banff Jasper Highway, Jasper National Park, Alberta, Canada. CANADIAN GOVERNMENT TRAVEL BUREAU

the urge for those of us living below the Canadian border to head north. And, don't forget, Canada also has some of the finest big-game hunting in the world. For full details, write to the Director, Canadian Government Travel Bureau, Ottawa, Ontario, Canada, and to the Game Department at the province capital of the area you wish to hunt in. In turn you will receive border crossing information, maps, game regulations, and a pack of other material to ease your way along. The Canadian officials really do a bang-up in public relations for tourists and hunters.

South of the Border The southernmost country of North America, Mexico, is a land of con-trasts. Towering mountains alternate with broad plateaus and scenic highlands giving way to unexplored jungles. Its 758,259 square miles offer excellent hunting opportunities for the sportsman. Its primeval forests and mountain passes abound in varied fauna such as black or silver-tipped bear, several species of deer, puma, wild boar, lynx, badger, and coyote; wild turkey, quail, duck, snipe, goose, pheasant, and dove. For full particulars, write to one of the nearer Mexican consulates, with offices in our larger cities.

The National Shooting Preserve Directory Shooting preserves across the nation have be-come year-round outdoor recreation centers with

The Trans-Canada Highway through Glacier National Park opens up this virgin area to mobilized hunters. CANADIAN GOVERNMENT TRAVEL BUREAU

Hunters in high alpine areas, like Mt. Baker National Forest in Washington, can obtain early licenses before winter weather makes hunting impossible. U. S. FOREST SERVICE PHOTO BY ROBERT J. DE WITZ

hunting, rifle, and pistol ranges, and clay-target shooting. For a free copy of the directory, write to the National Shooting Sports Foundation, Inc., 1075 Post Road, Riverside, Connecticut 06878.

The Future of Hunting Despite increasing hunting pressure in certain areas, creeping urbanization, and the diversion of lands for agri-culture uses, the future looks bright unless you let a few misinformed legislators pass laws to disarm you.

No doubt certain species of game have been affected by the encroachment of civilization; others have prospered; but game management has helped retain good hunting and promises its perpetuation. Hunting is going to be more plentiful and better in the near future—so, CHEER UP, MR. SPORTSMAN!

Chapter 2

PLANNING YOUR HUNTING TRIP

The Importance of Advanced Planning and Organization Plan your hunting jaunt now. Use the summer months to get prepared. The successful hunts do not "just happen." They are the direct result of advance preparation. There are many things you need to know before you hop a train or plane for the North Woods or load your pickup camper with hunting and camping equipment before sunup and set out for the tall timber. The smart hunter who plans ahead will not drive long miles to find on his arrival that his favorite hunting spot has been closed due to high fire danger or for other reasons. Again, he won't make a long trip from home to a hunting mecca only to discover that the outfitter retired last year or that the resort operator's duck boats have all been booked for the season.

Hunting Logistics Logistics is the science concerned with transportation, supplies, and equipment. The hunter will need to know in advance what to take, where he is going, and when and how he is going; amount of food needed, camping equipment necessary, ammunition and caliber or gauge gun required to kill the species of game to be hunted.

The first consideration, of course, is financing the trek. How much this will amount to depends on many variables: distance to the hunting grounds, transportation, number of days you will be away from home, type of accommodations, food, ammunition, license, and entrance fees if you have to travel through a national park to reach hunting terrain on the other side. If you hire a guide or pack outfit, expenses can mount rapidly.

If you are in business for yourself, plan for someone to take over while you are away. If you are employed, make arrangements for taking time off during the hunting season.

Planning ahead need not be complicated. A simple letter or telephone call in advance of your trip may save time, money, and dissappointment. Many major newspapers have outdoor experts in their sports departments who will assist you without charge. You can also write to the editorial departments of several of the national outdoor magazines. Their staff members can give you expert advice on planning a hunting-camping trek. The back pages of these magazines are filled with information about outdoor and hunting equipment and services.

Hunting Intelligence To be successful, the hunter must be able to outsmart his cunning woods quarry if he is to fill his bags. Furthermore, he is going to have to obtain all the information about the particular species of winged or four-legged animal he intends to lock up in his home freezer.

How to Make Your Summer Camping Trip Pay Off Many successful hunters take their summer vacation by camping with their families in the area they plan to hunt in the fall. In this manner they can enjoy the scenery, do some fishing, observe game conditions, locate the best deer crossings, and become acquainted with the surrounding terrain.

If possible play it safe by going back into the area a few days before the opening of the season to look over the lay of the land to check if game conditions have changed since your summer exploring jaunt. If the area should be barren of fresh droppings and other spoor you still have time to reconnoiter another region. If

Many successful hunters take their summer vacations by camping with their families in the area they plan to hunt in the fall. U. S. FOREST SERVICE PHOTO BY ROBERT J. DE WITZ

tracks and droppings are plentiful, map out and plan your strategy so that when you arrive a day or so ahead of shooting time you will be able to set up a comfortable camp and gather enough dry firewood so that no hunting time will be lost doing these camp chores.

After making a reconnaissance, you will be able to determine if you will stalk your game by still hunting, driving or taking a stand, or by a combination of these methods. This of course depends on how many companions are in your party or if you will decide to hunt alone. Generally, the lone hunter has a much better chance.

Tips on Accommodations If you do not plan on setting up a hunting camp, but are going to use motel or hunting lodge facilities instead, to save time, try to get accommodations as close to your hunting area as possible. It is wise to get your reservations months in advance of the opening of the season—otherwise you probably won't find a place to sleep and have to stay miles out of the way. Be sure to inquire if cooking facilities are available in the units, or if there is an all-night restaurant close by, or one that opens early and closes late so that you can eat and get on your way to hunt before the sun rises too high.

I have found it convenient to take an alarm watch or clock along in my "stampede" bag so that I can set it for an early rising either at camp or other lodgings. Once the management at a motel failed to call me, and I lost several hours of good pheasant hunting.

Lunches in the Bag Arrangements should be made the night before to have lunches prepared and ready to go at breakfast time, unless you have purchased lunch material in town and plan to make your own lunch early in the morning on opening day. A word of advice on lunches: Don't take food that will spoil quickly; food poisoning can result. Ham sandwiches, potato salad, and cream pies are not recommended. Cheese, peanut butter, jelly, honey, roast beef, and egg sandwiches are safer. Cookies and fruit add to the lunch. Keep sandwiches and other lunch articles wrapped separately. Hunting and hiking burns up a lot of energy, so in addition to my lunch, I carry a small bag of nuts mixed with chopped chocolate bars or suck on hard candy for a quick energy builder. Added to my kit is a small bottle of water-purifying tablets for the field.

Hunting Camp Cookery There is no place where cooking and food mean so much as it does

There is no place where cooking and food mean so much as it does in a wilderness camp. U. S. FOREST SERVICE

in a wilderness hunting camp. There is something about the outdoors that seems to whet the appetite. It may be the change of environment, the fresh air plus the vigorous activities of hunting, the smell of the woods, or a combination of all. Whatever it is, it adds zest to the meals you prepare in the hunting camp in the desert, along the waterfowl areas of the coast, or in a big-game camp in the mountains. You just naturally eat more in the open—so don't stint or cut yourself short on camp rations in your planning. It even pays to have an extra day's supply, in case of a forced layover, or if you invite the game warden or another hunter to join you for a meal. Buy food that will keep. Any supplies left over can be divided between your companions and consumed at home.

Well in advance of your hunting jaunt, figure out the number of days you will be eating in camp, and then make up a menu that will be satisfactory to all concerned. Meals in camp can be just as tasty as at home if you have the right ingredients and a little knowledge of camp cookery.

Where transportation problems are difficult, use dehydrated or quick-freeze foods, especially where temperatures have a wide range. When weight is a problem, as it certainly is for the "go-light" hunter, and those using canoes and other watercraft on float or aircraft hunting trips, dehydrated subsistence is indicated. This costs a little more, but when the cost is divided up it is not too expensive, and will serve from two to four persons.

It is wise to include a couple of emergency rations in your hunting jacket or pack. Chuck Wagon Foods make besides civil defense survival kits, a small pocket-size food kit weighing only a few ounces, and a Woodsman's Emergency Kit containing American pemmican, tropical chocolate bars, candy-coated gum, a fire starter, moistureproof matches, water-purification tablets, a plastic water bag, a razor blade, several small fish hooks and line, and Band-Aids. The price is only $1.98, and the address is 176 Oak Street, Newton, Massachusetts 01355.

The Federal Recreation/Conservation Permit There will be no charge for hunters using Forest Service roads or primitive campsites. However, there will be a charge on entering a national

The dedicated hunter often takes advantage of "bush taxis." BEAR ARCHERY COMPANY

park to reach a hunting area on the national forest outside of the park.

What is this annual Golden Federal Recreation Area Entrance Passport? The passport is a gold-colored wallet-size card that provides admission to designated federal recreation areas. It sells for seven dollars. When signed by the purchaser, it is valid from April 1 to March 31 of each year.

The annual passport will admit the purchaser, regardless of his mode of transportation, to all federal recreation areas at which entrance or admission fees are charged. In addition, it will admit all persons who accompany the purchaser in a private, noncommercial vehicle to the designated federal recreation areas commonly entered by private, noncommercial vehicles.

Persons 16 years or older not wishing to purchase an annual card may pay a daily or sea-sonal fee valid only at individual designated federal recreation areas. The daily fee varies from twenty-five cents to one dollar. It does not cover any special fees that may be charged within an area for use of sites, facilities, equipment, or service provided by the government; nor are they usable in state parks or private campgrounds.

The annual passport can be purchased at most entrance points to federal recreation areas where it is valid for entrances, at offices of federal land management agencies and at local offices of the American Automobile Association, or at Forest and Park Service offices. It can also be purchased by writing to Operations Golden Eagle, P.O. Box 7763, Washington, D.C. 20004 or to the Bureau of Outdoor Recreation, Department of the Interior, Washington, D.C. 20044.

Hunters Who Fly the Airlines Carrying weapons on aircraft:

"The airlines, in conjunction with their federal regulatory agencies, ask that hunters traveling as airline passengers package their sporting weapons in strong, well-padded shipping cases, caddies or trunks which are suitable for normal airline baggage handling, and check their gun cases as baggage rather than carry them aboard the airliner into the passenger cabin. Sportsmen are urged to provide suitable weapon containers which will not only protect their equipment but also permit inspection of the weapon by airline personnel at the airport to insure that the weapon is unloaded and safe for storage aboard the aircraft. This suggestion applies to most scheduled airline operations and is not intended to apply to the bush-type operations where small aircraft are used in such places as Canada and Alaska."

Forest Campgrounds If you plan on hunting from a campground, you will encounter several types in the national forests; ones operated by a concessionaire where you pay one dollar or so per night, and hot and cold water, toilet, and other facilities are furnished; the improved campground with rustic tables, stone fireplace, flush or pit toilets and pure water are available for which a daily charge is made or your annual Golden Passport will admit you without charge; and the primitive back country campsite where you set up your tent, and build your own latrine and garbage pit at no cost.

Campsites like these are available in our national forests. U. S. FOREST SERVICE

After choosing the campsite and pitching the shelter, assign each member of the hunting party a specific chore. U. S. FOREST SERVICE

Campsite Checklist Play it safe and follow this advice:

Your health and safety should come first. Don't camp under dead snags, tall trees which might attract lightning, or where wind, snow, or rain may cause limbs or trees to fall on you or your shelter. These are called "widow makers" by outdoorsmen.

Don't camp in tall grass nor near thick brush fields or near swamps, for there is a fire danger ever present in the former and insect pests in the latter.

REMEMBER, pure water is essential to your health and well-being! Never take it for granted that lake and stream water in the wilderness is pure. Always boil it or treat it with purification tablets!

Never pitch camp in a gully or canyon where a sudden flash flood beginning miles away might wash you and your gear away.

If you camp or hunt in a coastal area, pitch your camp well above high tide. Be sure your boat (if you have one) is well above high water mark when not in use.

Never camp under an overhanging cliff or bluff where a rock slide or avalanche may endanger you or your camp.

Your camp or shelter should be located, if possible, on higher ground away from beach, lake, or stream edge where it will be protected from high winds, but so that it will receive some breeze for coolness and assist in keeping insects away.

Pitch your tent or fly on a level knoll or slight slope so that the ground will drain away from the front of your shelter. Try to keep away from marshy or clay soils where mud and rain may collect.

The tent or fly should be pitched to take advantage of favorable exposures. It should be faced toward the southeast to get the morning's warming sunlight, but it should be located so that you will get some shade in the afternoon.

Most outdoorsmen and hunters like to have their tents or tarp shelters faced away from any other campers who might be nearby. If they are camped near a highway or in a public campground face the front away from it; also camp away from the public washroom, if any, so pedestrian traffic will not be disturbing.

Make it a point to remove all rocks, sharp sticks, and other hard objects from the spot you pitch your camp. Don't forget, any sharp objects may puncture your tent floor or sleeping bag air mattress.

TENTS: 1 Forester— 2 Mountain— 3 Pup with a wall— 4 Pup — 5 Baker — 6 Trail — 7 Wedge 8 Cruiser — 9 Miner —10 Wall

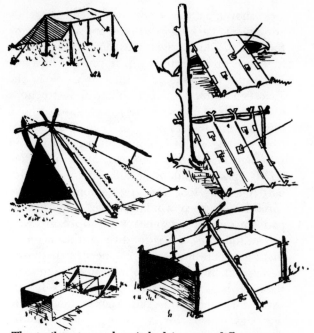

The trail tent may be pitched in many different ways

The selected campsite will often determine the type of shelter used. COURTESY OF THE AUTHOR

If using a trailer, pack for comfort but remember the last things to be removed should be the first stowed away. BEAR ARCHERY COMPANY

Place your campfire so that the prevailing breeze will not waft or blow smoke into your tent or where sparks may damage your home away from home.

As soon as you have chosen your campsite and pitched your shelter, assign each member of your party some specific camp chore; when breaking camp, strike your tent as soon as the dew has dried.

Generally, most of us are limited to the car trunk and possibly a car-top carrier or a small two-wheel utility trailer for stowing our hunting and camping gear. If so, you will want to think about packing the most comfort for all concerned in the least space. Otherwise you may cramp a hunting partner forced to sit in the back seat with most of the gear. *And* don't forget when packing that the last things to come out of your vehicle should be the first stowed in. And *don't* pile gear on top of the spare tire, tools, jack, shovel, ax, skid chains, or other emergency equipment. Pack them so they are handy. Some thought should be given regarding storage space for game on the return trip if you are lucky to bag some (You should if there is game in the area you hunted in and followed instructions given in this hunter's bible!). Few hunters give this the consideration it deserves. One or two deer or a bear plus hunting, camping gear, and passengers can load a car down dangerously low on its springs, making it difficult to steer. It's hard on tires, too! You are cautioned to drive carefully on steep winding curves, especially if you are driving a top-heavy pickup camper.

The following list is for two outdoorsmen. If there are more hunters or campers in the party, perhaps another vehicle is indicated. Additional sleeping bags, tableware (camp chairs if you use them), and extra grub! Your summer sleeping bags will do for fall camping and hunting if you add a couple of warm wool blankets inside the bags, unless you want to go to the expense of buying a feather bag.

Checklist for Automobile Camping—Two Hunters:

Air mattresses (2)

Air pump (1) or use car tire pump (Some people get a severe nosebleed when they blow up their air mattress at high elevation!)

Aluminum griddle (1), optional

Aluminum or canvas folding camp chairs (2), optional

Ax, full size, single-bit (smallest size, not less than 2¼-lb. head)

Ball hitch for trailer (1), optional

Broom, small size (to sweep dirt out of tent)

Buckets (2), one plastic and one folding canvas

Bug bomb or insect repellent; small bottle per person

Camera, film, filters, flashbulbs, etc., optional

Camp stove (gasoline or canned gas type, two-burner), optional

Camp stove, wood or folding type using charcoal briquettes, optional

Canteen (1), gallon size; water bag (1)

Canvas windbreak or tarpaulin for sun or rain, 10×12 ft., optional

Chain, tow chain for car, or steel cable, hook at each end—15 ft.

Charcoal briquettes for grill, optional

Cleaning material, detergents, soap, steel wool, etc.

Coffeepot if one in nested cook kit isn't large enough, optional

Compass with adjustable declination and sighting line (2)

Cook outfit, nested 2-man or 4-man type

Firearms, ammunition, hunting licenses, cleaning gear for guns

Fire extinguisher, Du Gas or CO_2 (carbon tetrachloride not used any more!)

Fire permit where needed (Look out for closed fire areas!)

Flashlights (2), extra bulbs and batteries

First aid kit (1). Add any personal prescriptions, laxative, snake bite kit, metal wound clamps, water-purification tablets, etc.

Funnel with strainer for filling gas stove or lantern (Fill outside cabin or shelter for safety!)

Gasoline, white gas for outboard motor, stove or lanterns, 5 gals.

Gasoline can, leakproof w/strainer and nozzle attached

Icebox, insulated type (1), optional

Jack, bumper type (1); hydraulic type (1)

Jacket, warm type, and extra clothing for each member

Kits, toilet, sewing bags, duffel bags for tents and sleeping bags

Knife, skinning knife, BSA pocket knife w/whetstone

Lantern, canned gas, gasoline or electric, extra mantles, wrenches, filters, generators, etc.

Maps, road and Geological Survey contour, large-scale of area

Matches, large kitchen type. Keep in waterproof container!

Mattress or cot ticks (2), optional

Mirror, steel or nonbreakable type (2), optional

Night clothes, flannel; or use sweatsuit, which is warmer

Oven, camp stove, folding or reflector type

Pick and shovel, folding Army type

Pillows, optional

Plastic washbowl

Portable folding toilet or old-fashioned "highboy," optional

Pressure cooker, optional

Saw, folding or Swede type (1)

Shovel, "O" or Forester type (1)

Sleeping bags (2). Warm type!

Tarpaulin, 8×10 ft., optional

Checklist for Small Travel Trailer:

Flags, red road signal type (3)

Flares (3) red glass road reflecting type

Flashlight, electric w/flashing red light and white spotlight (1)

Funnel for filling water tank, w/strainer

Funnel for filling gas tank, w/strainer

Hose, sewer hose, carry in four-inch-diameter hose carrier under trailer

Hose, short piece for draining into "gopher hole" near trailer (1)

Hose, sink hose, largest size that will fit standard fittings (1)

Jacks (2), screw type for under trailer axle while parked

Jack blocks to chock wheels to keep trailer from rolling (2)

Light cord, electric, heavy-duty type for plugging in trailer lights (1)

Stepup Pullman type steps (1)

Tires, spare for car and trailer; tool kit, four-way lug wrench, extra tire valves, butane or propane tank connectors, washers, rubber electrician's tape, extra fuses for car and trailer, extra light bulbs

Be sure your car and trailer insurance is valid and still in force!

Be sure to check off all needed supplies before you take off for the tall timber. You may be a long way from supplies!

Wet-Pack Provision List for Heavy Camping—Car or Pack Train

TWO PERSONS—TWO WEEKS

Fruit

2 cans applesauce
2 pkgs. dried applesauce
1½ lbs. dried apricots
1 can fruit cocktail
1 dozen lemons
1 dozen oranges
1 can peaches
1 can pears
1 can pineapple
1 lb. dried prunes
1½ lbs. seedless raisins
2 jars Tang (orange)

Vegetables

1 can corn with peppers
2 cans creamed corn
1 toe garlic
2 cans peas
6 lbs. potatoes
3 lbs. onions
5 cans tomatoes

Starches

1 pkg. Bisquick flour mix
1 pkg. blueberry muffin mix
3 bread (large size)
1 pkg. cornbread mix
1 lb. cornmeal
1 lb. soda crackers
1 lb. graham crackers
1 pkg. gingerbread mix
1 pkg. macaroni (small, with cheese)
2 pkgs. dehydrated potatoes
1 pkg. pancake flour (large)

½ lb. minute rice
1 pkg. Ry Krisp (large)
1 pkg. spaghetti (small)
1 pkg. dehydrated spaghetti sauce

Meat—Fish—Fowl

3 lbs. bacon
3 lbs. Canadian bacon
1 can corned beef
1 pkg. dried chipped beef
1½ lbs. ground beef (1st day)
1 lb. bologna
1 can boneless chicken
1 can boneless turkey
1½ dozen eggs
1 can precooked ham (6 lbs.)
1 can pressed pork meat
1 salami (small)
1 can white tuna
2 cans wieners

Dairy Products

2 lbs. butter or margarine
1 lb. cheese (choice)
1 lb. processed cheese
2 cans evaporated milk
1 med. size pkg. powdered milk

Sweets—Nuts—Candies

5 lbs. cookies
24 chocolate bars (non-melt type)
1 pkg. cake mix
1 fruit cake
1 can peanut brittle (large)
1 lb. hard candies

1 jar strawberry jam
1 jar raspberry jam
7 pkgs. pudding mix
1 can maple syrup (large)
1 lb. brown sugar
1½ lbs. granulated sugar

Miscellaneous Food

1 jar peanut butter
1 can bouillon cubes (small)
1 bottle catsup
1 can cinnamon
1 jar instant coffee
2 lbs. coffee
1 pint mayonnaise
1 can mixed salted nuts
1 jar pickles
1 can pepper
½ lb. salt
1 box tea bags (50)
1 can tomato paste (small)

Camp Kitchen

1 dozen paper bags (small)
1 dozen paper bags (large)
1 box waxed sandwich bags
2 rolls 12-inch aluminum foil
1 roll heavy aluminum foil
2 pkgs. paper napkins
1 bar Ivory soap (large)
1 dishcloth
2 dish towels
2 face towels
1 container detergent
1 box kitchen matches (large)
1 set kitchen cutlery

A heavy pack train hunting trip must be well planned for a bag as successful as this one. U. S. FOREST SERVICE PHOTO BY ROBERT J. DE WITZ

Provision List for Two Persons for Two Weeks

Item	No. Meals	Quantity	Lbs.	Ozs.
			WEIGHT	
Apricots (dried)	8	3 lbs.	3	0
Bacon (Canadian)	9	5 lbs.	5	0
Bacon (smoked)	6	3 lbs.	3	0
Bisquick (prepared)	12	4 1½-lb pkgs.	6	0
Bread (large size)	9	3 loaves	3	0
Brown sugar	6	2 lbs.	2	0
Butter or oleo	14	2 lbs.	2	0
Cheese	4	2 lbs.	2	0
Chipped dried beef	5	1½ lbs.	1	8
Cocoa (instant)	14	1 lb.	1	0
Coffee (instant)	14	2 4-ounce bottles	0	8
Corned beef hash	3	3 ⅜2 cans	3	6
Dehydrated potatoes	12	6 5-oz. pkgs.	2	14
Deviled ham	3	6 3-oz. cans	1	2
Eggs	4	1½ doz.	1	12
Jam (strawberry)	7	2 1-lb. cans	2	0
Jelly	7	1 jar or can	1	0
Ham (smoked)	3	6 slices	2	8
Hard candies	14	1 jar or can	1	0
Lemon extract	4	1-oz. bottle	0	1
Mapeline extract	6	3-oz. bottle	0	3
Milk (evaporated)	7	4 14½-oz. cans	3	10
Milk (powdered)	7	1 large pkg.	3	4
Nuts (salted)	7	1 1-lb. can	1	0
Onions	4	2 lbs.	2	0
Pancake flour	6	2 1¼-lb. pkgs.	2	8
Pilot crackers	4	2 1-lb. pkgs.	2	0
Prunes (dried)	7	2 lbs.	2	0
Quaker Oats (1-min.)	6	2 1¼-lb. pkgs.	2	8
Raisins (seedless)	7	2 lbs.	2	0
Ry Krisp	4	2 lbs.	2	0
Salami	3	1 lb.	1	0
Salt	14	¼ lb.	0	4
Roast beef	4	4 12-oz. cans	3	0
Soup	13	13 3-oz. pkgs.	2	7
Tea	14	30 tea bags	0	3
Triscuits	9	9 5-oz. pkgs.	2	13
Sardines	3	3 cans	1	3
Veal loaf	3	3 7-oz. cans	1	5

Food List—Two Persons—Ten Days

Staples
1 lb. shortening
1¼ lbs. Bisquick
1 lb. corn meal
5 loaves bread
1 pkg. Ry Krisp
1 pkg. Triscuit
2 lbs. butter
5 lbs. sugar
1 bottle Mapeline
8 ozs. instant coffee
8 ozs. Tang (orange)
8 ozs. chocolate mix
16 tea bags
1 lb. dry milk
½ lb. salt
1 can pepper
1 lb. raisins
1 bottle catsup
2 bars Ivory soap
2 dish towels
2 dishcloths
1 roll toilet paper
3 candles
1 box matches

1 bug bomb
1 "Chore Girl"

Breakfast
5 lbs. bacon
3 lbs. pancake flour
3 lbs. dried fruit
1 lb. oatmeal
1½ doz. eggs

Lunch
½ lb. dried beef
1 lb. cheese
1 jar jam (large)
1 jar peanut butter
1 lb. cookies
3 cans pork and beans
3 cans sardines
1 lb. sausage
6 pkgs. Kool-Aid
20 candy bars
1 lb. hard candy
½ lb. nuts
1 lb. lunch ham
12 lunch bags

Supper
2 8½-oz. Rice-a-Roni
1 lb. weiners
1 can beefsteak
1 can corned beef
1 can Spam
1 can chicken fricassee
1 can beef stew
1 can meatballs
2 Kraft Dinners
1 can chili
1 can carrots
1 can peas
2 cans corn
1 can beets
1 can mixed vegetables
1 can string beans
4 cans tomatoes
9 pkgs. hash brown potatoes (8-oz. servings)
2 pkgs. powdered potatoes
2 pkgs. dried soups
½ pound onions
6 pkgs. powdered desserts

Menu for Two Weeks—Two Campers

Breakfast 3 days: bacon, eggs, bread, and beverage.
6 days: Canadian bacon, oatmeal, cream, sugar, and beverage.
6 days: bacon, pancakes, butter, syrup, and beverage.

Lunch 3 days: salami, bread, jam, nuts, and beverage.
4 days: soup, cheese, Ry Krisp, raisins, jam, and beverage.
3 days: deviled ham, Triscuit, jelly, nuts, and beverage.
3 days: soup, sardines, pilot crackers, jam, and beverage.
2 days: soup, veal loaf, Triscuit, jelly, nuts, and beverage.

Dinner 3 days: ham, potatoes, bread, prunes, peanut butter, and beverage.
4 days: roast beef, potatoes, onions, biscuits, jam, and beverage.
5 days: creamed chipped beef, potatoes, biscuits, apricots, and beverage.
3 days: corned beef hash, biscuits, jelly, prunes, and beverage.

There will be a small amount of food left over from the provision list. This should take care of emergencies and laying over a day or so in case of necessity. Ration out the candies and nuts or they will all be gone the first few days. People crave sweets in the outdoors.

Desert Camping Checklist—Two Persons

THREE-DAY SUMMER EXPLORING TRIP

Air mattress and pillow (2)
Air pump, optional (1)
Ammunition, optional
Ax, 2½-lb. single-bit (1)
Bags, sleeping (2)
Box, food, ratproof (1)
Box, ice, 25-lb. capacity (1)
Bucket, metal, plastic or canvas (1)

Bug bomb (1)
Camera, film, filters, optional (1)
Camp lantern, LP gas w/extra cans (1)
Camp stove, LP gas or gasoline (1)
Canteen, 1-gal. (2)
Canteen, belt type, 1-qt. (2)
Compass with sighting line (2)
Cook kit, nesting, 2-man (1)

Dish and hand towels (2)
Dishes, cups and saucers, ea. (2)
Flashlight, pen type, w/batteries (2)
Flashlight, 3-cell type, extra bulbs (1)
Duffel bags, canvas (2)
Firearms, optional (2)
Flares, red reflector type (3)
Flares, red signal type (3)

First aid kit (1)
Food, 4 days, dehydrated type
Gasoline cans, 15-gal. capacity (2)
Gasoline for Jeep, 30 gals.
Insect repellent (2)
Jacks, car (2)
Jeep with four-wheel drive (1)
Knife, BSA type (2)

Map, large-scale of area (1).
Matches and safe, boxes (2)
Shovel, Forester type LHSP (2)
Snake bite kit, antivenin (1)
Snake bite kit, suction (1)
Spare tire and tube (2)

Spark plug, power-pump type (1)
Sunglasses and cases (2)
Tent, floored (1)
Thermos jug, 1-gal. capacity (1)
Tire tools, cement and patches kit (1)
Tool kit for car (1)
Tow cable, hooks at both ends (1)
Water cans, Jeep type, 5-gal. capacity (2)

NOTE: Vehicles used for desert side roads should be in excellent mechanical condition, preferably four-wheel-drive type with six-ply tires. Several pounds of paper-wrapped Dry Ice should be placed in the bottom of the icebox. When the wet ice melts, the Dry Ice will refreeze the melting ice for a minimum of three days.

Snow Camping Checklist

	WEIGHT			WEIGHT	
	Lbs.	Ozs.		Lbs.	Ozs.
Air mattress, plastic	2	0	Knife, BSA type with blade, screwdriver, leather punch	0	6
Air pillow, optional	0	8	Map, topographic, large-scale of area	0	2
Air pump, optional	1	8	Match case, waterproof	0	1
Aneroid barometer for high-elevation climbing records, optional	1	0	Matches, waxed or waterproofed	0	1
Anti-fog stick for sun- and snowglasses	0	1	Mittens, 2 pair wool inners, ski cloth outers	0	6
Bag, sleeping, eiderdown, mummy type	4	0	Moccasins, high-ankled or other type of camp shoe	1	6
Balaklava wool helmet, optional	0	4	Muffler or wool scarf, headband optional	0	6
Bandana handkerchief, large size	0	2	Notebook and pencil	0	2
Bar soap, hotel size	0	1	Parka, close-weave, wind- and water-repellent, fur collar	0	12
Belt or suspenders	0	4	(Parka should be hip length with zipper opening full length. Wolf fur preferable for collar.)		
Blanket, wool	4	0			
Camera, film, filters, case	2	8	Poncho or plastic ground cloth	2	0
Camp cook kit, one-man aluminum, nesting type	1	4	Rucksack, Kelty, Gerry, Trailwise, or other lightweight model	2	6
Camp cook kit, four-man aluminum, nesting type	6	8	Sewing kit, Army type, optional	0	4
Camp stove, knapsack model or Primus type	1	4	Shirts (2), lightweight wool	2	8
Can, leakproof fuel, plastic type with strainer and spout	0	8	Ski socks (2 pairs), heavyweight, ½ size larger than usual size	0	6
Can, leakproof fuel, with strainer and spout	1	8	Ski pants, loose-kneed, wind- and water-repellent	2	0
Can opener, twist-turn type	0	2	Ski poles, steel type	2	0
Canvas bag, waterproof, for fuel can	0	4	Ski socks (2 pairs), lightweight	0	4
Compass, adjustable for declination with sighting line	0	4	Skis, good grade, laminated with good grade bindings	3	8
Dish and hand towel	0	4	Sno-Pacs, insulated type for snow shoe travel or camp boot	2	8
First aid kit, small size	0	8	Snow shoes, bear-paw type for steep mountain climbing	4	8
(Add a mild laxative, codeine, sulfa, aspirin, water-purification and salt tablets, and personal prescriptions.)			Snow shoes, cross-country, Alaska model w/bindings	7	2
Handkerchief, white (2)	0	1	Sunburn lotion for sun- and windburn	0	2
Hat, alpine type or ski cap	0	10	Sunglasses with case	0	8
Headnet for mosquito country	0	1	Sweater, wool	2	2
Hot water bag, rubber type for sleeping bag comfort	1	8	Tent, Army Arctic model with aluminum stakes	6	6
(Water can be stored overnight to keep it from freezing, and it insures water for breakfast liquids; saves fuel.)			Tent, mountaineer type, Gerry, Trailwise, or Abercrombie model	2	14
Insect repellent	0	4	Thermos bottle for hot drink on trail or to keep water from freezing	1	12
Knapsack, Army frame or Bergan-Meis	4	8	Toilet kit, optional	1	2

NOTE: Don't forget that you must be in good health for winter snow camping!

	WEIGHT	
	Lbs.	Ozs.
Underwear, wool or U. S. Navy thermal type, two-piece	1	6
Underwear, wool, loose-weave, 2-piece long johns	2	12
Watch, water- and shockproof	0	10
Whisk broom, for brushing snow off clothing and from inside tent	0	10

NOTE: For Sno-Cat or Sno-Weasel travel camping ex-peditions, use snow camping checklist. Bring only dehydrated foods. This type of food will not freeze. However, more stove fuel will be necessary for melting snow for water to soak the dry food. Use the same provision list for dog-team sledge camping. For dog-team rations, see section on Backpack Camping. Add dried salmon or prepared dog food to last the trip. Be sure that the dogs are in good health and that the mechanical equipment is in good working order. Take a portable radio along for insurance.

These backpack hunters in Oregon had to decide what provisions were essential. OREGON GAME COMMISSION

Backpack Camping Checklist—One Person

	WEIGHT				WEIGHT	
	Lbs.	Ozs.			Lbs.	Ozs.
Air Mattress, ¾ length, plastic or rub-berized, optional	2	0	Camp cook kit, 1-man aluminum nesting mountaineer model		1	4
Air pillow, optional	0	8	Camp stove fuel container, plastic model		0	4
Ax, Hudson-Bay type w/sheath, optional	3	0	Camp stove, knapsack model, optional		1	4
Bag, sleeping, eiderdown, mummy model	3½	0	Can opener, twist type		0	2
Belt or suspenders	0	4	Canteen, 2-quart capacity, plastic model		0	8
Binoculars, 6×30-power with case, optional	0	12	Carborundum stone		0	2
Boot wax, optional	0	2	Compass, declination adjustable with sighting line		0	4
Boots, hiking or mountaineer model with nailed sole	5	4	Detergent container, plastic		0	2
Boots, hiking or mountaineer model with Vibram type soles	3½	0	Dish- and hand towel, 1 each		0	4

	WEIGHT	
	Lbs.	Ozs.
First aid kit; add snake bite kit and personal medicines	0	12
Fishing gear, fly rod, flies, reel, line, and aluminum case	1	8
Flashlight, pen type, w/extra batteries and bulbs	0	4
Glasses, prescription, and/or sunglasses with case	0	4
Handkerchief, large-size bandana	0	1
Hat or cap, large-brimmed or long-billed	0	10
Headnet for mosquito country	0	1
Helmet, wool	0	3
Insect repellent	0	2
Jacket, windbreaker, water-repellent, zipper front	1	6
Knapsack, lightweight model, Kelty, Trailwise, or Gerry	2	4
Knife, BSA type, w/leather punch, can opener, blade, screwdriver	0	6
Knife, hunting type, BSA or Marble 4-in. blade, skinning type	0	8
Map, large-scale USGS topographic	0	1
Margarine or butter container, plastic or aluminum	0	2
Match case or container, waterproof	0	2
Matches, waterproof, plus cigarette lighter	0	3
Mittens or woolen gloves	0	4
Moccasins or tennis shoes for camp or emergency	0	8
Muffler or wool scarf	0	5
Notebook and pencil	0	1
Nylon boot laces	0	1
Nylon cord, 50 ft.	0	3
Pants, poplin or blue jeans	1	14
Parka or windbreaker, water-repellent	1	6
Poncho or ground cloth	1	3
Rucksack, Army frame or Bergan-Meis	4	8
Salt and pepper container, aluminum	0	½

	WEIGHT	
	Lbs.	Ozs.
Scotch tape, small roll	0	½
Sewing kit, small Army type	0	2
Shirt, heavy wool	1	4
Shirt, string type, open weave	0	9
Shirt, wool, lightweight	0	14
Shorts, lightweight, underwear	0	3
Shorts, poplin hiking, khaki type	0	6
Snake bite kit, antivenin type, optional	0	6
Soap, hotel size bar	0	1
Socks, lightweight wool, 2 pairs	0	7
Socks, heavyweight wool, 2 pairs, ½ size larger than usual size	0	10
Spare knapsack fittings	0	4
Sugar container, plastic or aluminum	0	2
Sunburn lotion	0	2
Sweater, lightweight wool	2	2
Tent, Army Arctic model, with aluminum snow stakes	6	6
Tent, lightweight mountaineer model w/stakes	2	11
Toilet kit, optional	0	14
Toilet tissue, small roll or package	0	7
Underwear, lightweight wool or U. S. Navy thermal type	1	6
Underwear, lightweight wool, 2-piece long johns	2	12
Watch, wrist type, water- and shock-repellent	0	10

NOTE: Use backpack and general camping equipment list for outfitting; plane, swamp-buggy, Tote-Goteing, canyoneering. A pilot or guide is usually a must for this type of camping. Plan on one pound of dehydrated food per person per day. For mountaineering, ski-mountaineering, dog-team and snow camping, figure on 2–2½ pounds of dehydrated food. Check sections on provisions, menus, and emergency rations. Better have too much food than too little!

Checklist for Pack Outfit

Personal gear
Toilet kit
Hunting and fishing licenses
Compass and maps
Washcloths and towels

Clothes—Inner
Lightweight wool shirt
Heavyweight wool shirt
Medium-weight wool pants
Wool underwear (2)
Socks, 6 prs., wool
Bandana handkerchiefs (2)

Clothes—Outer
Saddle slicker
Hunting cap with ear flaps
Red hunting hat with brim
Down jacket
Wool cruiser coat

Mountain-climbing boots
Barker or Sno-Pac boots
Rain parka and pants
Leather work gloves
Wool mittens
Suspenders
Camp moccasins
Sunglasses (yellow lens)
Binoculars
Spotting scope with small tripod
Extra inner soles
Extra bulbs and batteries
Flashlight
Pocket knife BSA model
Sheath knife 3½-inch blade
Battery-powered shaver
Hot water bag or bottle
Thermos bottle, qt. size
Sharpening stone

Boot waterproofing
First aid kit
Personal medicines
Smoking gear and tobacco
Pocket warmer
Flannel pajamas
Hooded sweatshirt and pants
Air mattress
Down sleeping bag
Bedroll
Air pump
Camera and extra film and gear
Duffel bags
Saddle bags
Snake bite kit
Waterproof match safe
Waterproof matches

Firearms gear
Rifle, scope-sighted

Rifle, iron sights
Hooded leather scabbard
Rifle cleaning kit
Ammunition
Scope hoods

Camp gear
Light canvas fly 12×12 ft.
Tarpaulin, canvas, 10×10 ft.
Coleman lantern
Ax, single-bit, 3-lb. head
Camp saw, folding type
White gas, square type, 5-gal. can
Strainer
Shovel, Forester type, 3 lbs.
Extra generators, mantles for lantern
50 ft. ¼-inch rope

Ball twine
Toilet tissue
Pliers, lineman type
Aluminum grill
Wire grill
Reflector oven
Pressure cooker, optional
Cooking pans
Kettles
Kitchen gear—knives, forks, spoons, pancake turner, etc.
Tableware
Bottle and can opener
Aluminum foil
Lunch gear, wax paper, sacks
Salt and pepper shakers

Soap and dish towels, detergents
Kitchen Maid, S.O.S. pads
Pot holders
Paper towels
Large cooking fork
Dutch oven
Large iron frypan
Nesting cook kit
Coffeepot
Dishpan
Wash pan
Oil cloth
Plates
Cups
Butcher knife
Paring knife
Insect repellent

Automobile Camping Checklist—Two Persons

Air mattress (2)
Air pillow (2)
Air pump (1)
Ax, 2½-lb. head (1)
Bags, sleeping (2)
Box, food, mouseproof (1)
Box, ice, 25 lbs. capacity (1)
Bucket, plastic (1)
Bug bomb (1)
Camera, film, filters (1)
Camp lantern, gas or LP canned gas (1)
Camp stove, wood or gasoline (1)
Canteen, 1-gal. capacity (1)
Chairs, folding canvas or aluminum (2)
Compass with sighting line (1)
Cook kit, nesting, 4-man (1)
Dish and bath towels (2)
Dishpan (1)

Duffel bags, canvas (2)
Dutch oven (1)
Fire extinguisher, dry type (1)
First aid kit (1)
Fishing gear and tackle (2)
Hot water bag, rubber type (1)
Ice bag, rubber (1)
Insect repellent (2)
Knife, B.S.A. type (2)
Match safe, waterproof (2)
Matches, waterproof (100)
Paper towels and napkins
Pillow, blankets, sheets
Plastic dishes, cups, saucers
Portable radio (1)
Portable TV (1)
Pots and pans

Rope, 100 ft. ⅜-inch, coil (1)
Rubber slicker or poncho (2)
Spare tire and tube (1)
Sponge or Kitchen Maid (1)
Sunglasses and case (2)
Tableware for 2
Tarpaulin, 10×10 ft. (1)
Tent, umbrella or other type (1)
Toilet tissue, rolls (1)
Twine, heavy, ball (1)
Water can, Jeep type, 5-gal. (1)
Flares, red road type (3)
Flashlight, bulbs, batteries (2)
Food to last trip
Hammer, claw type (1)
Water-purification tablets (100)
NOTE: Car in good shape, basic tools, tow cable, necessary extra parts.

House Trailer

Ax, single-bit with 28-inch handle, 2½-lb. head (1)
Ball hitch for front of car (1), optional
Buckets, canvas or plastic (2)
Canteen, 1-gal. capacity (1)
Canteens, 1-qt. size (2)
Canvas awning for windbreak, 6×18 ft. (1)
Canvas tarpaulin for shade or rain 10×10 ft. (1), optional
Chain, tow chain or cable, 15 ft. with hooks at each end (1)
Cleaning equipment, detergent, soap, dustpan, sponges, mop, broom
Cook kit, nested aluminum, 4-man type, add knives, forks, and spoons (1)
Dish, plastic, sets (1)
Fire equipment, Du Gas, CO_2 or dry-powder type (1)
First aid kit, add personal medicines, vitamins, aspirin, codeine, sulfa

Flares, red glass reflector road type (3)
Flares, stick road type (3)
Flashlight, electric, white-spot and red-flasher (1)
Flashlight, extra batteries, bulbs (2)
Funnels, with strainers, for filling gas and water tanks, 1 ea. (2)
Gasoline can, 5-gal. with spout and strainer, filled with gas (1)
Hose, sewer hose, carried in 4-in. hose carrier under trailer (1)
Hose, short piece for draining water into "gopher hole" nearby (1)
Hose, sink hose, largest size that will fit standard fittings (1)
Hose, 25 ft.—rubber lawn hose for filling water tank (1)
Icebox, 25-lb. size, large enough to hold wrapped Dry Ice underneath (1)

Jacks, 1 hydraulic and 1 bumper (2)
Light cord, electric, heavy-duty, 50 ft. (2)
Map, large-scale topographic of area (1)
Pick, Army type, small size (1)
Radio, portable type (1)
Shovel, "O" or Forester type, sharp point, long-handled (1)
Snake bite kit, antivenin type, optional (1)
Snake bite kit, suction type (1)
Stepup, Pullman type or sturdy box (1)
Stove, LP gas or small wood type (1), optional
Tire gauge (1)
Tire pump, manual type or spark plug motor type (1)
Tire tools, patches, rubber cement, extra valves
Tire tubes, 1 for car and 1 for trailer (2)
Tires, spare tire, 1 each for car and trailer (2)
Tool kit, basic auto kit, hammer, pliers, screwdriver, lug wrench, socket wrench, monkey wrench, nails, screws, extra valves and washers for butane tank and connectors; be sure not to forget electrician's and friction tape!
Water can, Jeep type or a wide-mouth milk can (1)
Wheel chocks, 2 ins. square, 6 ins. thick, with one end tapered to fit against car or trailer tire

a) Make certain that car and trailer insurance is valid.
b) Check on trailer and speed laws in states in which you travel.
c) If outfit isn't paid for, be sure to have lien owner's permission if you leave the United States for Canada or Mexico.
d) Have necessary fire permits, and hunting and fishing licenses.
e) Be Sure to turn off gas at tank for safety reasons in case appliances leak at night while you are asleep. Have ample ventilation when using them!

Chapter 3

THE WEAPONS-RIFLES AND SHOTGUNS

Statistics have proven that the majority of hunters are weekend nimrods. They disappear from town so fast after work Friday that one might believe the sheriff is close behind them. (Very likely he is—with his pet Deerslayer). They hunt all day Saturday and Sunday and return home Sunday night.

Some of these gunners are lucky and bag a bear, deer, or elk and return home the first day.

In the West and Northwest (and in the East to some extent), where towns are surrounded by woods or are in mountainous terrain where game is abundant, many local sportsmen hunt from their homes—they hunt all day and return that night—these are the "lucky guys." I'll have to admit that I have done the same thing plenty of times myself. However, in this manner you miss the pleasant adventure of camping out in the big woods and sitting around a flickering campfire at night swapping stories in "bullfests" with fine hunting pals. I have at times even had some Davy Crockett type "city slickers" from a nearby camp who wanted to stay up half the night trying to win my pet cannon in a game of draw.

The Average Hunter There are thousands of once-a-year hunters who own one rifle and buy one box of ammunition. They shoot once or twice in the woods, and either miss their quarry or down a deer; and that ends it for the season. Others may own a battery of fine rifles and shotguns and hunt some species of animal or waterfowl during open season. However, the

Shotgun or rifle? It's the hunter's choice. SAVAGE ARMS PHOTO

average hunter who can hunt only on weekends —the majority, generally—owns a .22 rifle for plinking, target shooting, and to use on pests and small animals such as rabbits and squirrels, plus a "deer rifle" which must serve regardless of the game hunted. Very likely he also owns a shotgun for waterfowl and upland game shooting. And again, he may own just a scattergun. However, in some thickly populated states where shotguns only may be used, a hunter can use his smoothbore for upland game birds, wa-

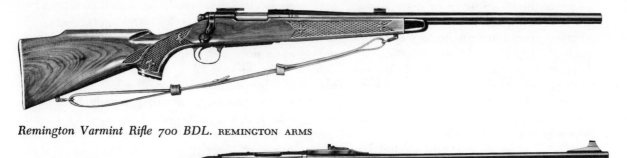

Remington Varmint Rifle 700 BDL. REMINGTON ARMS

Bolt Action Center Fire Rifle 788. REMINGTON ARMS

Remington Carbine Model 600. High-power bolt action rifle. REMINGTON ARMS

terfowl, and small game. And at short ranges, if he uses buckshot or slugs, he can down big game too!

Owning one big-game rifle or a shotgun has its advantages, in that the rifleman or shotgunner will become better acquainted with it. On the range and in the field he will discover all its good and bad traits—how it handles and sights, its weight, balance, trigger squeeze, and recoil.

The trend these days is for lighter-weight firearms with shorter actions and barrels. Because of its faster action, autoloaders (semiautomatic) are gradually overtaking the lever, pump, and the single-shot break-open actions. However, it is a matter of choice—whichever handles the quickest and smoothest for you.

The lightweight, short-barreled rifle or shotgun in a large caliber or gauge, shooting high-base high-velocity loads, will naturally have a heavier recoil and muzzle blast. This can be relieved or overcome somewhat by installing a recoil pad on the stock and adding a compensa-

tor on the muzzle. Adding a leather or web sling can be helpful for long open-range shots when the animal hunted is presenting a standing broadside shot. Where there is time, a sitting or prone position will be more steady than an off-hand shot. Moreover, it is an aid in carrying the arm when one tires.

Arms for the Budget-Minded Hunter There are several economical rifles and shotguns sold by Montgomery Ward & Company, Sears, Roebuck and Company and other mail order and retail sporting goods houses that have brand-name guns—shotguns under sixty dollars and rifles under seventy dollars that will do the trick. I personally would rather have one of the more economical arms than some of the junk military items I have observed while patrolling various hunting areas. However, there are a few American surplus rifles and shotguns found in surplus stores that can be sporterized, and it can be fun restocking and working them over to fit individual need and use. Added fun can be obtained by reloading your own ammunition, and this will cut costs in half. If you do purchase a used firearm, be sure to have a gunsmith check it for head space before you shoot it. Also if you want to reload, be sure, for safety reasons, to study up on the subject before attempting the game.

Selecting a Big-Game Rifle The major mistake most often observed by wardens and forest officers is that the novice rifleman enters the field over- or undergunned.

The largest group of big-game hunters are deer hunters. Bear, antelope, moose, elk, and other game are bonus animals sought only occasionally by the average deer hunter—trophy hunters excepted.

For long-range shooting at mule deer and antelope, a flat-shooting, telescope-equipped rifle is needed. For whitetail deer and bear in heavy cover, a short-barreled gun shooting a heavy brush-cutting bullet is required to get results. Most state big-game regulations specify rifles of .25 caliber or larger—so guide yourself accordingly. (A .30-caliber or larger bullet makes a better brush pusher than the smaller .25-caliber.)

Average Shooting Let us examine some of the actual elements of average shooting, on stand, driving, or stalking in typical deer terrain. Gen-

erally, the shot will be at less than a hundred yards—fifty yards being about average—with the exception of open range country common to mule deer and antelope.

The chance of a shot will come suddenly which precludes a deliberate target range stance. Moreover, it will generally have to be a snap shot taken offhand, usually at a running target. Because of this, more and more quick-swinging, lightweight, short-barreled, carbine-style rifles such as the new Remington 600 series are showing up in the field.

The Long and Short of It A rifle for average short- or long-range deer shooting should possess three basic factors: portability, speed of aiming and getting off the shot, and accuracy. Needless to say, rifle balance and weight go hand in hand. They give you a fast-handling gun to take advantage of the split second you have in making a snap shot. At times you may be fortunate and able to take a more deliberate shot at a standing target, but not often.

As mentioned before, a big-game hunter is confronted with four types of actions from which to choose in selecting a suitable rifle; thus he will have to determine which works best for him.

The Old Reliable Brush-Cutters The .30-.30. That old deerslayer, the thirty-thirty, or as some

Remington Carbine Model 600 Magnum. High-power bolt action rifle. REMINGTON ARMS.

Bolt action center fire rifle. Model 700 ADL deluxe. REMINGTON ARMS

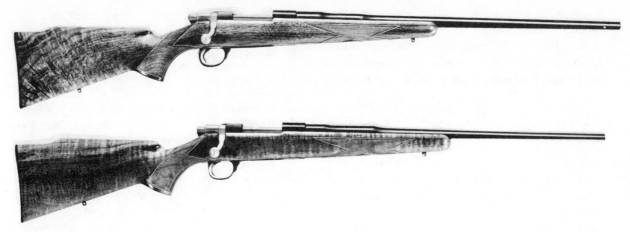

Browning high-power rifles. BROWNING ARMS COMPANY

old-timers called it, "the ol' thurty-thurty"—has probably killed more deer and other game than any other rifle to date.

For best results, as we have seen, the deer rifle should be light and handy, with a fast action. The bullet should be fairly large in diameter and be easily expanded. Furthermore, the rifle should be equipped with fast iron sights or a low-power wide-angle scope or both as an aid in seeing deer or other game through thick brush as well as in aiming.

At moderate ranges in the hands of a fairly good shot, the .30-.30 is plenty potent for most thin-skinned game. Most .30-30s sell for under $100. The model 840 Springfield bolt action is priced at $54.50; Savage sells their model 340 bolt action for $71.50; Winchester's model 94 at $84.95; Marlin's model 336 carbine for $89.95; Ruger's single-shot at $275; and Harrington & Richardson, their single-shot model 163 at $41.95 according to Stoeger's Shooter's Bible.*

How to Become a Crack Shot The most important thing is to start right, and for a good start you must have a good weapon. No matter how hard you try, you cannot become an expert marksman with an inferior rifle or shotgun which will not shoot accurately.

Any experienced sportsman will tell you that, no matter what the game of skill is—upland bird shooting, waterfowling, or small- or big-game hunting—it always pays to get the best equipment. Daniel Boone, Kit Carson, and Buffalo

* Prices subject to change.

Bill were crack shots—for they used only the finest weapons that could be obtained in those days. And they practiced with them! Those pioneers recognized the value of quality and made the most of it. These days, rifles and shotguns are much more efficient, and good weapons are within the reach of most sportsmen's pocketbooks.

Today, good weapons are within the reach of most sportsmen's pocketbooks. SAVAGE ARMS PHOTO

So in picking your firearm, remember that quality means better shooting, and therefore more game in the bag. Get a weapon famous for its accuracy (most American-made firearms are) and you can depend on its functioning properly and shooting as true as you can hold it. Here is the way to pick the best:

See that the gun feels right in your hands, that it comes up to your shoulder quickly and easily, and that it can be carried and handled without unnecessary effort. Then you know it has proper balance, and you can soon learn to "make it a part of you." Test the action and see that it works smoothly and without friction. See that the lines are clean and graceful. Examine the sights. Make sure they are the type which will help you aim and shoot quickly and accurately.

Selection of Ammunition   A firearm will shoot only as true as the ammunition used in it. After you have decided you really want to become a crack shot you must be just as careful in choice of ammunition as with the selection of your rifle or shotgun. To shoot true and hit the bull's-eye or game, cartridges and shotshells must be made exactly uniform. Therefore, the next time you go out into the woods, field, or down to the target range, load up your "shooting iron" with the right ammunition!

Ammunition   A rifle or shotgun is no more effective than the ammunition it uses. Cartridges, bullets, and shotshells are scientifically designed and manufactured to do a certain job on various species of game. The following chart may be helpful in choosing the right combination:

For rabbits, squirrels, crows,
and other small pests—
.22 Short
.22 Short Hollow Point
.22 Long
.22 Long Rifle
.22 Long Rifle Hollow Point
.22 Winchester Automatic
.22 W. R. F.
.22 Magnum Rimfire

Gunning for coyotes, peccary,
chucks, ground squirrels, etc.—
.22 Magnum Rimfire 40 grain
.218 Bee 46 gr.
.22 Hornet 45 or 46 gr.

.220 Swift 48 gr.
.222 Remington 50 gr.
.243 Winchester 60 gr.
.244 Remington 90 gr.
.25-20 W. H. V. Win. 60 gr.
.250 Savage 87 gr.
.256 Winchester Mag. 60 gr.
.257 Roberts 87 gr.
.264 Winchester Mag. 100 gr.
.270 Win. or Rem. 100 gr.
.280 Remington 125 gr.
.284 Winchester 125 gr.
.30 Carbine 110 gr.
.30-06 Springfield 110 or 125 gr.
.308 Win. or Rem. 110 or 125 gr.
.32-20 W. H. V. 80 gr.

For deer, bear, boar—
.250 Savage 100 grain
.257 Roberts 100 or 117 gr.
.264 Winchester Mag. 140 gr.
.270 Win. or Rem. 130 or 150 gr.
.280 Remington 165 gr.
.284 Winchester Mag. 125 or 150 gr.
7 mm Mauser (7×57) 175 gr.
7 mm Mauser Rem. Mag. 150 or 175 gr.
.30 Remington 170 gr.
.30-30 Win. or Rem. 150 or 170 gr.
.30-06 Springfield 150 or 180 gr.
.30-40 Krag 180 gr.
.300 Savage 150 or 180 gr.
.303 Savage 180 gr.
.303 British 190 gr.
.308 Win. or Rem. 150 or 180 gr.
.32 Winchester Special 170 grain
.32 Remington 170 gr.
8 mm Mauser (8×57 or 7.9) 170 gr.
.338 Winchester Mag. 200 gr.
.348 Winchester 200 gr.
.35 Remington 200 gr.
.351 S. L. 180 gr.
.350 Remington 200 or 250 gr.
.44 Magnum H. P. 240 gr.
.444 Marlin 200 or 250 gr.

These are the long-range flat-
trajectory calibers for open or
plains shooting of antelope,
caribou, sheep, goats, etc.—
.243 Winchester 100 grain
.244 Remington 100 gr.
.250 Savage 100 gr.
.257 Roberts 100 gr.
.264 Win. Mag. 140 gr.
.270 Win. or Rem. 130 gr.
.280 Remington 125 gr.
.284 Win. 125 or 150 gr.
7 mm Rem. Mag. 150 gr.
.30-06 Springfield 150 or 180 gr.
.300 Winchester Mag. 150 or 180 gr.

.300 H & H Mag. 180 or 200 gr.
.300 Savage 150 gr.
.308 Win. or Rem. 150 or 180 gr.
.338 Win. Mag. 200 gr.

For large game (including moose, grizzly, and Alaska brown bear)—
.270 Winchester 150 grain*
7 mm Rem. Magnum 175 gr.*
.30-06 Spring. 180* or 220 gr.
.30-40 Krag 220 gr.
.300 Win. Mag. 180 gr.
.300 H & H Magnum 180 or 200 gr.
.308 Win. or Rem. 180† or 200 gr.†
.338 Win. Mag. 250 or 300 gr.
.358 Win. 200† or 250 gr.
.375 H & H Mag. 510 gr.
.458 Winchester Mag. 510 gr.

* Excerpts from Winchester-Western Division Ammunition charts.
† Not for grizzly or Alaska brown bear. The last three calibers listed are suitable for any large animal on the North American continent.

The Essential Ballistic Factor The point is that the essential ballistic factor a hunter must keep in mind is that ultra-high velocity cannot be used effectively in short-range brush shooting. These high-speed bullets are too easily deflected or blow up.

For brush penetration, a velocity between 2000–2500 f.p.s. (feet per second) gives the least deflection with seldom a blow up. Therefore, a bullet weight in the neighborhood of 150 grain, or heavier, is indicated. For example, a 150–180-gr. bullet driven at 2000–2500 f.p.s. is excellent for heavy cover. Moreover, this velocity would handle the occasional longer-range shot across open terrain where there may be openings around 250 yards, more or less. There would be less bullet drop over the longer distance, even with the rifle sighted in for a hundred yards, as it should be for hunting in heavy cover.

Generally, a hunter needs two rifles—one for short-range, heavy brush cover shooting one meets in the hardwoods of the East, and one for shooting at the longer ranges across open cutover land or the wide open spaces found in much of the West.

The Best All-Around Rifle For the person who needs other hunting and camping gear but who doesn't feel like putting out hard-earned cold cash for a second big-game rifle, there is a com-promise—the famous .30-06 and the recent .308 comes to mind, with ammunition loadings from 110-, 125-, 150-, 180-, and 220-gr. bullets. The 110-gr. bullet can be used on varmints; the 150-gr. driven at 3000 f.p.s. can be used for long-range open-terrain shooting, and the 180-gr. bullet at 2400 f.p.s. for short-range brush work.

The best part of it is, both calibers can be purchased from most sporting goods stores under brand names. The .30-06 and .308 can be purchased from Montgomery Ward & Company, and Sears, Roebuck and Company retail and mail order houses for under $70. Ward's have an excellent Western Field in .308 caliber with a 3X–9X Zoom scope and mounts for just $99.84. Klein's of Chicago sells a .30-06 with deluxe custom features—a sporterized Enfield for $69.95. Other brand names will run from $100 on up the scale to over $200 or more, and are well worth the price.

No one needs to go without hunting arms, for they may be purchased on the layaway or time payment plan.

Iron versus Scope Sights What sights are best, you may ask—open, peep, or scope? On my pet "muskeet" I use a 4X scope backed by a peep sight. Why? Because I slipped and damaged my scope on some rocks while hunting elk in the Olympics several years ago, but didn't have to abort the hunt because I had "secondary" iron sights to fall back on. Generally, most rifles arrive from the factory equipped with open sights because they are cheaper. However, open sights are only useful at relatively short ranges. The poorest of these is the "buckhorn," sometimes referred to as the "Rocky Mountain," with large "ears," and it is still favored by a few hill people who use what they call "Kentucky windage" because adjustments are not available on this type of sight. In other words, they guess at the amount of windage necessary and take either a fine or coarse bead for elevation. I will have to admit, however, that these hill boys do meet with considerable success, for they have venison on the table—sometimes the year around.

The disadvantage of this type of sight is that the average eye, while using open iron sights, attempts to focus upon three separate objects

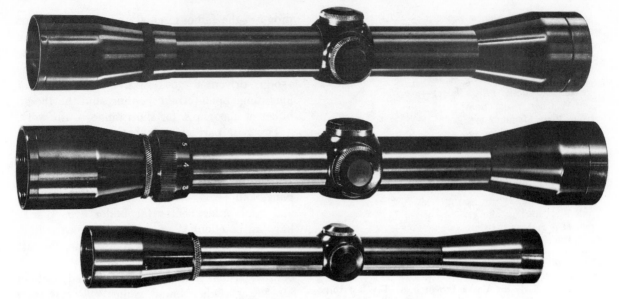

Telescopic sights not only help identify and sight game, but can take the place of a binocular if the hunter wishes to save the extra weight. BROWNING ARMS COMPANY

When purchasing a scope, it is important to consider price, lightness, and best power for the intended game. SAVAGE ARMS PHOTO

at once—the rear sight, the front sight, and the target.

The hunter whose eyesight isn't up to par often encounters difficulty in making quick visual adjustment when using a flattop, buckhorn, or semi-buckhorn rear sight. The peep sight is more accurate for target shooting and hunting and is used by more hunters than any other type of sight. While hunting, the large target cup disk should be removed to give a larger aperture. This will give a quicker lineup on the animal or target. In use, the front sight is aimed at the target and the eye naturally "centers" the aperture of the rear sight automatically without actually seeing it. Most peep sights are adjustable for elevation and windage.

Remember, when adjusting the rear sight for windage or moving the point of impact on the target, the sight must move in the direction in which you wish to shoot.

What to Look for in a Telescopic Sight More and more hunters are using telescopic sights.

Even though they are more expensive, they are the finest sights obtainable. A few of the cheaper models have the disadvantage of lens fogging in damp regions, especially in the Northwest coastal and rain forest areas. The more expensive brands are fogproofed by a nitrogen process, and have coated lenses complete with lens caps. The telescope sight has the added asset that the shooter focuses upon only one object—the target. The scope also assists one quickly to identify man or game, and can take the place of binoculars if the hunter wishes to save the extra weight.

When purchasing a scope, it is important to consider price, lightness, and best power for the intended game. A scope must have a wide field, high luminosity, and be waterproof. It should resist recoil, mount close to the receiver, attach and detach easily, and once adjusted, stay so indefinitely. It is best to have a mount which permits the use of open sights when the scope is attached so that the iron sights may be used in case the scope becomes disabled.

For average use, the 4X glass is preferred by many hunters. BROWNING ARMS COMPANY

For most big-game hunting, scopes of 2½ to 6 power are used by most experienced nimrods. For average use, many hunters prefer a 4X glass. At present, the scope with cross-hair reticule is most popular. In the poor light of heavy wooded terrain, or for shooting at running game, many prefer a post reticule, or a dotted cross-hair with a 2½ power glass. The variable scope may, by turning a graduated collar, be changed in power, usually from 2 to 8X or more. The higher the magnifying power the more difficult it is to hold on a target; therefore a steady hold or support is necessary. Target shooters and varmint hunters are more apt to use the higher powered glasses—shooting from a bench rest or from a prone position.

Boresighting Your New Rifle   Your new rifle should be boresighted before you try it out in the field. Boresighting is done primarily to make certain that the bore and the sights are in line. Sights sometimes get out of line in shipping, or by leaning the gun against hard objects, and sometimes they get knocked helter-skelter by being carried in a car. When not in use the weapon should be cased, and it is a good idea to put a "hooded" clamp on the front sight to protect it.

This is one way to boresight your gun: With a bolt action weapon, remove the bolt and place the rifle in a padded vice or rigid stand. Sight through the bore at a target 25 yards away (a .22 caliber fifty-foot small bore target will do); when the "bull's-eye" of the target is centered in the bore, sight down your iron sights to make certain that both are in line; if they are, you are in business. If your iron sights are slightly off, adjust the rear sight right or left (windage) as necessary. The rear sight may also have to be adjusted for elevation—higher or lower so that the bore and sights are "right on" target. When all adjustments are made, you are ready to sight in with live ammunition.

Targeting versus Sighting in   Targeting and sighting in are not the same! However, they are closely related. As a part of testing a new firearm, manufacturers target a gun by firing it a number of times on their range to determine whether there is sufficient remaining sight adjustment to meet the needs of the individual shooter. In testing, the rear sight is raised a small amount; a number of shots are then fired at a specified distance. If the group of shots fired doesn't fall within a specified area in relation to the aiming point, sights are replaced or modified to give the correct results.

Sighting in refers to the precise adjustment of sights causing the center of impact and point of aim to coincide at a particular distance. To be accurate it must be done by the individual, as there are no two persons who hold the weapon or aim exactly the same way. In other words, sighting in is a follow-up to the targeting procedure to insure accuracy in the field.

The Importance of Sighting in   It is important that you sight in with ammunition you will use in the field. Many riflemen make the mistake of doing this by using military metal-jacketed cartridges—then use soft-nosed, factory-made ammo on game. Each brand of ammunition has a different point of impact on the target, and that is one of the reasons some misses occur. Bullets do not travel in a straight line, but in a long curve called the "trajectory." As a consequence the bullet tends to drop below the line of the bore the moment it emerges from the muzzle. By adjusting and raising the rear sight for elevation, the muzzle is thus pointed up slightly so that the bullet will rise above the line of sight. The bullet crosses the line of sight twice—near the muzzle and again at some distance from the muzzle. Where the bullet crosses the line of sight the second time is the range for which the rifle is "sighted in."

Trajectory Chart for Some Popular Cartridges
EXAMPLE ONE   For instance, take the .30-06 Springfield Super-X 180-grain cartridge with a bullet speed of 2700 f.p.s. Its velocity at 100 yards is 2330 f.p.s.; at 200 yards it is 2010 f.p.s., and at 300 yards the velocity has slowed down to 1740 f.p.s.

MIDRANGE TRAJECTORY   The highest point of the arc reached by the bullet is called the "midrange trajectory," and is the center point between where the bullet crosses the line of sight the first and second times. At 100 yards the midrange for this particular cartridge is 0.7 inch; at 200 yards it is 3.1 inches, and at 300 yards 8.3 inches.

TRAJECTORY CHART

The bullet's flight in relation to the line of sight is pictured at the top of the page. The bullet leaves the barrel below the line of sight, crosses it at a short range, rises above it, then drops below the sight line at longer ranges. The figures in the trajectory chart show how high or low the bullet will strike at ranges of 100, 150, 200, and 250 yards, when your rifle has first been zeroed at 25 yards.

The information shown in the trajectory chart is based on data for standard commercial ammunition. The figures can only be approximate, due to variation in barrel length, type of bullets, barrel bedding, and other factors. For these reasons your rifle should be checked at one of the longer ranges after zeroing at 25 yards.

CENTER FIRE CARTRIDGES	BULLET WEIGHT	25 YARDS	100 YARDS	150 YARDS	200 YARDS	250 YARDS
.22 Hornet	46	0	+1¾	+ ½	—3½	—9
.220 Swift	48	—½	+1½	+1¾	+1½	+ ½
.222 Remington	50	0	+2¼	+2	+ ½	—2½
.222 Remington Magnum	55	0	+2¾	+3	+2¼	0
.225 Winchester	55	—¼	+2	+2¼	+1½	—1
.243 Winchester	80	—¼	+1¾	+2	+1¼	— ½
.243 Winchester	100	0	+2	+2¼	+1¾	— ½
6mm Remington	100	0	+1¾	+2¾	+2	0
.244 Remington	75	—¼	+1¾	+2	+1¾	— ½
.250 Savage	100	0	+2¼	+2¼	+1½	—2
.257 Roberts	100	0	+2¼	+2¼	+1	—2
.264 Winchester Magnum	100	—¼	+2	+2¼	+2	+ ½
.264 Winchester Magnum	140	0	+2½	+2¾	+2	0
.270 Winchester	130	0	+2½	+2¾	+2	0
.270 Winchester	150	0	+1¾	+1¾	— ½	—4
.280 Remington	150	0	+2¼	+2¼	+1¼	—2
7mm Remington Magnum	150	—¼	+1¾	+2	+1¼	— ½
7mm Remington Magnum	175	0	+2¼	+2¼	+1¼	—1½
.30-30 Winchester	150	0	+2¾	+2¼	— ¾	—5
.30-06	150	0	+2¼	+2¼	+1¼	—1½
.30-06	180	0	+2¼	+2¼	+ ¾	—2½
.30-06	220	0	+1¾	+ ½	—2	—7
.300 Savage	150	0	+1¾	+1¾	— ½	—4
.300 Winchester Magnum	150	0	+2¼	+2½	+1¾	0
.308 Winchester	150	0	+2¼	+2	+ ½	—2½
.308 Winchester	180	0	+1¾	+1¾	— ½	—4
.375 H & H Magnum	270	0	+2¼	+2¼	+1	—2

RIM FIRE CARTRIDGES	BULLET WEIGHT	25 YARDS	50 YARDS	75 YARDS	100 YARDS
.22 LR-HS	40	0	+ ½	+ ¾	—4
.22 WRF	45	0	+ ¾	— ½	—3
.22 Magnum	40	0	+ ¾	+ ½	0

COURTESY OF W. R. WEAVER COMPANY

Suppose you are sighting in the .30-06 mentioned above. You have a target at 100 yards, and the pattern of a three-shot group shows that the group is two inches high and two inches to the left of the bull's-eye. If your sight is adjustable, then correct by moving the rear sight down and to the right. Receiver sights are generally graduated in ¼ minute of angle for target and range shooters, and in ½ and 1 minute of angle for hunting sights. If your sight clicks in ½ minute of angle, you will have to change your sight 4 clicks to the right and lower the sight 4 clicks to be able to strike the center of the bull's-eye.

EXAMPLE TWO Take the .270 Winchester cartridge with the 130-grain bullet. You decide that you want to sight the rifle to hit the point of aim at 250 yards. The bullet first crosses the line of sight at 20 yards. At 125 yards it is 3 inches high. At 250 yards it is at point of aim, and at 300 yards it is 4 inches low. This method of sighting in gives a more or less point-blank range of 300 yards. Aimed at game, the bullet is never more than four inches above or below that point out to a distance of 300 yards, and isn't sufficient to miss a vital part of an animal.

EXAMPLE THREE *The Four Simple Steps to Adjust Micrometer and Telescopic sights*

On request, many sporting goods stores will give you one or more 100-yard correction targets without charge. These are approved by the Sporting Arms and Ammunition Manufacturers' Institute.

Measure off a 100-yard range with a safe backstop. Next, your rifle should be shot from a well-padded rest, under calm wind conditions, resting forearm, not barrel, on pad.

1. Locate on the target chart the exact center of at least three carefully aimed and carefully fired shots, using the same hold and sight setting. For example, suppose the center of the group is a small circle in the first upper-right-hand quarter of the target.
2. Following the vertical line we come to the figure 3L. This means that to bring the next group onto the vertical line requires that you move your rear sight 3 minutes of angle to the *left*. If your sight reads in minutes of angle this means you must give it 3 clicks to the *left;* if calibrated in ½ minute of angle, 6 clicks, and if in ¼ minute of angle, 12.
3. Now follow the horizontal line to the edge of the target and we come to the figure 3D. This means that you must move *down*

the sight 3 minutes of angle to bring your next group onto the horizontal center line.
4. If your aim was steady and correct on the first group and no puff of wind blew any of your shots out of the group, your next group will be in and around the 10 ring or bull's-eye. Your rifle is then sighted in for the range and ammunition used.

Don't Forget the Minute of Angle Changing your sight 1 minute of angle makes a change where the bullet strikes on the target: ½ minute of angle at 50 yards, 1 inch at 100 yards, 1½ inches at 150 yards, and 2 inches at 200 yards. Be sure to fire your groups slowly, and let your rifle cool for a few minutes between groups. Simple, eh?

Wind Drift All bullet flight is affected by wind drift. Little effect on bullet trajectory and point of impact is given a bullet traveling directly up- or downwind. However, a crosswind, particularly one at right angles to the bullet's flight, may drift the bullet a noticeable amount at long range. However, at short ranges, with high-velocity cartridges, the effect is generally small and need not be taken into account when hunting.

Here is what a 10-mile-per-hour wind will do to a .22 Long Rifle Super-X bullet, with a muzzle velocity of 1335 f.p.s. It will be blown downwind approximately five inches at 100 yards and seventeen inches at 200 yards. An identical wind will blow a .30-06, 180-grain Silvertip bullet off its flight course approximately eight inches (depending if the wind is steady or variable); a thirty-mile-per-hour wind will triple this effect.

For all practical hunting purposes, at normal hunting ranges up to 300 yards in a fairly heavy blow, only a small allowance is necessary for wind drift—just lead the animal slightly more.

.22-caliber pump action rifle. Model 572 BDL deluxe. REMINGTON ARMS

At longer ranges, say at 400 or 500 yards, and at up to 1000 yards, ranges ordinarily shot by target shooters, the wind drift must be carefully "doped out." Wind estimating requires long practice and a great amount of skill and judgment on the part of the rifleman, because the wind is rarely constant.

Accuracy   No gun will put all its bullets through exactly the same hole on a target. Instead, the bullets striking the target form a pattern known as a "group." The size of the groups is generally measured by the distance between the center of the group and the center of the outermost bullet hole.

An ordinary sporting rifle is considered accurate for hunting purposes if it will shoot into 3 minutes of angle—or a 3-inch circle at 100 yards.

Normally it is the practice to sight in a big-game rifle for the longest practical range that will not cause misses at midrange. Generally, a rifle shooting 3 inches high at 100 yards is a good bet. It will put you right on at 225 yards —a long shot for the average hunter!

Again, don't forget this rule when making sight adjustments: The point of impact (the spot where the bullet strikes) moves in the direction that the rear sight moves. If you move the rear sight up for elevation, the point of impact moves up. If moved right, the point of impact moves right. Moved left, the impact is left.

After making the correct adjustments and you find that you are hitting where you want, set the sight screws tightly and leave them there!

If you have a shotgun and don't wish to purchase a hunting rifle, don't overlook the shotgun as a short-range big-game gun for deer and bear. Used with rifled slugs it is accurate enough and carries effective knock-down power at 100 yards. Properly sighted in, the shotgun can be brought into action quickly and effectively.

A Handy Sighting-in Guide   A handy little plastic gadget for the rifleman is the Marlin Sighting-in Guide for all the latest and most popular cartridges. It works on the same principle as a slide rule. The data is based on figures supplied by ammunition manufacturers and by field shooting by Pete Kuhhoff, Gun Editor for *Argosy* magazine in cooperation with the Marlin

Firearms Company's research department. The price is $1.

Shooter's Range Guide   This little plastic "slide rule" will deflate the egos of some hunters who claim 300- and 400-yard shots at deer. A deer at 300 yards isn't much larger seen through the rangefinder than the end of a pencil eraser! Mighty small target, I would say! Of course, you rarely have time to check the range of your target when you are out hunting. This Range Guide is meant for use during the off season to help you learn how to judge distance by the eye. It is not necessary to locate deer to practice estimating ranges: a post or any object 60 inches high will do as well. It is a product of G. A. Company, 14 East 34th Street, New York 10010. The price is $1.

Estimating Ranges   One way to become proficient in estimating range distances is to learn how to pace. A pace is two natural steps. The average-height man steps off 2½ feet when taking a natural step forward when he walks. Set up two stakes 100 feet apart and see how many steps it takes between them. Next, pace off the distances between various objects. Practice this a week or so before opening season and you will be able to judge how far off an animal is with fair accuracy. At least it will be more accurate than the educated guess of most hunters.

Shooting Positions   Don't forget—that crafty old buck or other game isn't going to stand still and wait until you can get into a perfect shooting position before busting out of his bedding area and hightailing it for parts unknown. Unless you are gunning from a blind, you will probably be caught flat-footed and off balance—so here is where practicing snap shooting pays off. If caught at a disadvantage, shift to the best stance in which you can aim, squeeze, and fire, and very likely you will be eating liver for your supper. For sudden surprise shots, you will likely take an offhand snap shot. For standing or slowly grazing animals at short range, you will very likely take an offhand shot. However, at longer ranges where it is possible, you will be more successful and have a more steady aim if you drop to a sitting or a prone position. If your

The game won't wait for you to get into a perfect shooting position. Practice snap shooting whenever possible. SAVAGE ARMS PHOTO

piece is equipped with a sling and there is time, use it. It will give you added support and steadiness in aiming.

That Thing Called Leading Some sportsmen never shoot at a running animal, others only at game running parallel to them. Some will empty their magazine at a panicked deer heading directly away from them. Probably it is a good thing that submachine guns are barred, or some of these characters would spray the woods with lead! However, under certain circumstances shooting at moving game is justified.

Hitting a running animal or any game, particularly in a vital spot, is by no means easy, but it isn't as difficult as it might seem. A running animal offers just as large a target as though it were standing. Naturally, the animal will look smaller as it takes off and the range increases. Here is where leading game comes in! The hunter who has practiced on running rabbits and other small game with a rifle or smoothbore will more likely connect with running game. The unskilled nimrod will very likely miss and drop some of his bullets or shot into someone's camp over the hill.

Generally, the same techniques apply to shooting running game as to potshots at flying waterfowl with a scattergun. The chief difference is that the rifleman must place his one shot in a vital area at a greater distance instead of a hail of shot at short range. Depending on circumstances, the gunner who is forced to shoot at running game or not at all, will have to take a quick chance on a snap shot. This means using a "fast swing" with a sustained *lead*, a technique where sights follow behind the animal, catch up with it, and the trigger is squeezed off just as the sights pass its nose. This is called "pointing out."

Here are a few pointers that may be helpful: If the animal is climbing out of a gully going directly away, hold slightly above it. If it is angling away as it climbs the other side, hold slightly above and to one side so that it will be running into the bullet. If the animal is on the same level as you, and going directly away, take a deliberate shot down its back and try to break the spine. If your shot goes slightly high, you may down the beast with a neck or head shot. If you are low, you may shoot between

the hams or damage the loin meat or even puncture the bladder and contaminate some good meat.

In short-range heavy cover brush shooting, the distance will be short, the angle gentle. Under these circumstances the hunter should aim where he wants to hit and squeeze off the shot the *instant* the sight picture looks right. If he doesn't, he will likely gut shoot the animal or shoot behind it. If the angle is great, the shot must be taken with a moving gun, just as a crossing waterfowl must be led with a scattergun.

A Few Pointers to Remember When Leading Game

At longer ranges, when game is moving directly across the line of sight, the hunter should swing his rifle with the animal and fire when his lead picture looks right. If the animal is moving at a walk at, say, 100 yards, the lead should be a bit ahead of the brisket. If the game is running, swing a full length ahead of the animal.

At 150 yards a lead of 3 or 4 feet is called for. If the animal is really moving, swing out 6 to 8 feet.

At 200 yards swing out 8 to 10 feet, depending how fast the critter is traveling. Wind, terrain, and other variables will have to be taken into consideration. A running deer at 200 yards is a mighty small target. Maybe you had better let this one go!

Every individual must discover his own *leads* by practicing at moving targets on the home range, by watching spurts of dust if he misses an animal, and by recalling how far a lead he took when he did connect with game. Practice and experience with rifle and shotgun will have to be your guide!

Last: A good stalker who can still hunt and gets out in the woods early enough so that game is still feeding and moving around may often get a standing shot and won't have to bother with this leading stuff. Try it sometime!

Chapter 4

WHAT YOU SHOULD KNOW ABOUT SHOTGUNS

The Versatile Shotgun We are supposed to be a nation of riflemen. Maybe so. However, many people in this country and Canada hunt with a shotgun. Why? Because the smoothbore is so versatile. It can be used on small and big game, upland birds, and on ducks and geese—and for the sport of skeet and trap-shooting. At close range it remains the most deadly weapon of all. The same scattergun that fires a load of No. 9 shot pellets to bring down a small bird without completely demolishing it will also fire a load of buckshot or a rifled slug and knock over the largest North American game animal more effectively (at 50 to 100 yards) than the average high-velocity rifle cartridge.

Another point: very likely, the new shooter will be more involved with the shotgun than the rifle for most of his shooting pleasure.

Double, Pump, or Autoloader? Like rifles, shotgun actions come in bolt, pump, or autoloading. At present the pump or slide action appears to be the most popular. However, because of its faster action, the autoloader is quickly overtaking the pump as the basic American smoothbore.

The 12-gauge is, for practical purposes, the largest bore size now made in the United States. Due to its throwing a larger number of pellets, the new gunner will probably do a better job with it than with a shotgun throwing a lesser number of shot. An added incentive is that the 12-gauge shells can also be obtained in magnum

The versatility of the shotgun has made it the most popular gun among hunters. SAVAGE ARMS PHOTO

loads to produce practically 10-gauge results.

The little 20-gauge is less powerful and has less recoil, and for that reason is a favorite weapon for women and for the young shooter, and some upland hunters swear by it. However, most sportsmen will agree that the 12-gauge is more versatile and effective for all-around shooting than the 16-gauge or "20."

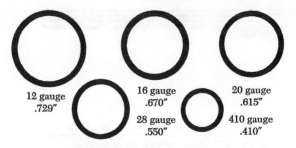

12 gauge
.729″

16 gauge
.670″

20 gauge
.615″

28 gauge
.550″

410 gauge
.410″

Selecting a Shotgun Right now there is no mistaking the fact that sportsmen are becoming very conscious of gun weight, over-all length, and trimness of stock design. They are demanding firearms which are lighter, shorter, and slimmer in stock and forearm, and bores and ammunition that will throw the best patterns.

The Upland Game Gun First, decide if you will use it on small game and upland birds, or just on waterfowl. The upland game hunter doesn't want to lug a heavy duck or goose gun

over hill and dale all day, so he prefers a lightweight 16- or 20-gauge gun. But if he can only afford one shotgun, what action and gauge should he purchase? The answer is, one of the new lightweight short-barreled 12s. Why? Because the pumps and automatics in 12-gauge are as light as the 16s and 20s used to be (in fact, some are even lighter), and they will throw a denser pattern than the smaller bored shotguns at slightly longer range.

With its denser pattern, the lightweight 12-gauge automatic with its faster action is becoming more popular than the pump, or double-barrel guns of smaller gauge, and is outselling the big-bore 12s in the latter actions.

The Intermediate 16-Gauge The 16-gauge is an excellent all-around gauge for the person who doesn't demand absolute maximum range from a scattergun. When shooting low-base shells and using Nos. 7½ and 8 shot, it makes a fair upland game gun. And a full choke 16 shooting

Browning Lightning *Trap Model.* BROWNING ARMS COMPANY

Remington Model 1100 deer gun. 12-gauge automatic shotgun. REMINGTON ARMS

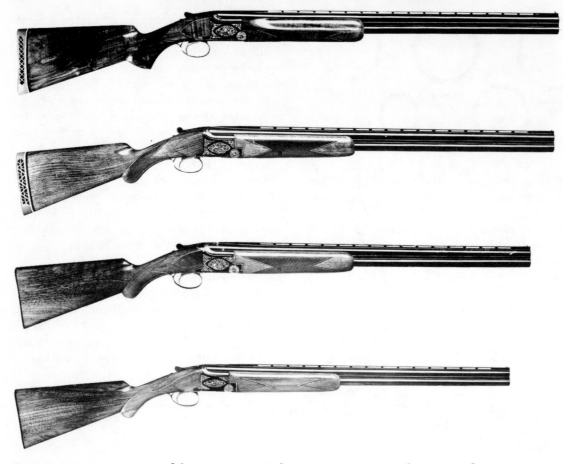

Browning 12-gauge trap model; 12-gauge, 3-inch magnum; 12-gauge hunting and skeet; 12-gauge hunting and skeet. BROWNING ARMS COMPANY

1⅛ ozs. of No. 6 shot over decoys should take ducks out to 40 or 50 yards, whereas a full choke 12 using 1¼ ozs. of No. 6 shot will take them reliably from 45 to 55 yards; and a Magnum 12 in the hands of an expert using a 1⅝-oz. shot may drop birds at 55 to 65 yards if he leads properly.

The Little 20-Gauge The little 20-gauge is popular with many wing-shooters, especially when shooting the 3-inch magnum load. Women seem to shoot better with the low-base shells, and the "little 20" is the one for the young shooter and the senior nimrod who tramps the hills all day. Packing a heavy weapon long distances can become tiring at times.

To sum up, the 12-gauge has more pellets and more range to put on the target than the 16-gauge, the 16 has more range and shot than the 20; but the lighter 20-gauge gets on the tar-

get faster and thus the handicap is more apparent. Moreover, a full-choked 20-gauge using the 3-inch magnum shell loaded with No. 6 shot has about all the range the average bird shooter can handle, even on waterfowl.

The Duck and Goose Muskets Most of the 12-gauge scatterguns will do the trick. However, many waterfowlers want to gain a few extra yards for high-flying birds. These are the big boys: the brand-name 12-gauge magnums weighing from 8 to 12 pounds in double, over and under, pump and autoloader, and the super skyscrapers: the long-barreled 10s, like Stoeger's double-barrel Magnum Goose Gun shooting a 3½-inch magnum shell through a 32-inch barrel. This young cannon weighs in oil-wet at 10 lbs., 11 ozs. I only hope that no gunner packing one of these cloud busters will break loose with one near my duck or goose blind! Some of us short-

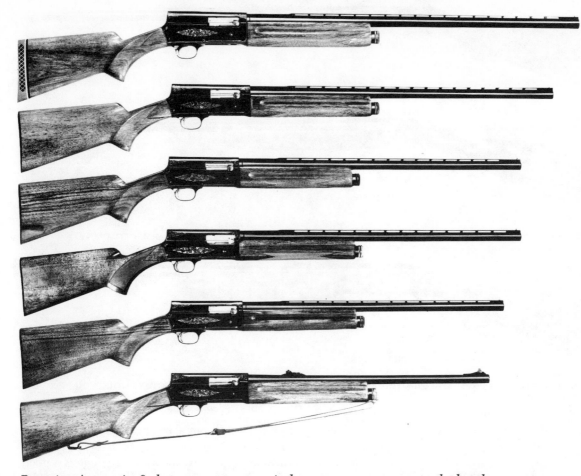

Browning Automatic—6 shotguns. 12-gauge, 3-inch magnum; 12-gauge, standard and lightweight; 16-gauge, lightweight; 20-gauge, 3-inch magnum; 20-gauge, lightweight; 12-gauge, Buck Special. BROWNING ARMS COMPANY

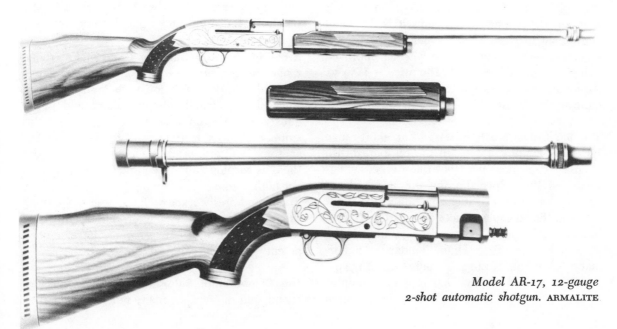

Model AR-17, 12-gauge 2-shot automatic shotgun. ARMALITE

Browning double automatic shotgun. Twelvette; twenty weight. BROWNING ARMS COMPANY

Remington Model 1100-SA skeet gun. Automatic shotgun, 12-guage, 5-shot. REMINGTON ARMS

barreled guys like our birds to come in to our decoys a little closer.

The Super Lightweight 12-Gauge One of the popular lightweights on the market is the superb Model AR-17, 12-gauge 2-shot automatic weighing only 5 lbs., 6 ozs. When taken down, it is only 24 inches long. This means it is light and convenient to pack when traveling. Three interchangeable choke tubes come with it: improved cylinder, modified and full. The price is $159.50. Armalite also makes the .22 cal. AR-7 Survival Gun at their Costa Mesa plant in California.

The Big-Game Brush Busters For short-range big-game hunting, there are the big-bore brush busters! Browning has the rifle-sighted sling-equipped Buck Special using the standard 12-gauge slug; the 12-gauge magnum, the light 16-, and the 20-gauge. Prices range from $179.95 to $189.95. Franchi's light and heavy model slug guns sell for $196.95. High Standard's "Supermatic" deer gun (12-gauge only) for $154.95, and Hi Standard's "Flite-King 12-gauge pump at $124.95. Ithaca's Model 37 Deerslayer in three

gauges is still popular at $119.95. Remington Model 1100 Deer Gun may be had for $174.95, and Remington's Brushmaster 12-gauge is a good buy at $99.95. The smoothbore operator who doesn't want a special slug shooting arm can have his pet shotgun equipped with rifle sights and do as well. The brush busters can also pinch-hit for duck and upland game hunting.

Army Surplus Riot Guns for Game? For short-range field work these economical 12-gauge smoothbores do a fair job with both buckshot, slugs, and shotshell. These military and police guns may sometimes be picked up at surplus stores and are sometimes sold for less than $50 at some military establishments that advertise them as surplus military equipment. I have tried out both automatic and pump purchased for $25. The open bores worked well on close-range quail shooting. However, I suggest that if you ever do obtain one of these weapons, have a competent gunsmith check it for head space.

The Combination Rifle/Shotguns The farmer's friend, and the weapon many ranch boys learned

Remington Model 1100-TB automatic trap gun, 12-gauge. REMINGTON ARMS

to shoot with is the "little" Savage over and under rifle/shotgun. It comes in several models: The standard Model 24-S (.22 LR with .410 or 20-gauge shotgun barrel) and Model 24-MS (.22 WMR with .410 or 20-gauge). These little plinking "gems" sell for $52.50. In the deluxe models, 24-DL and 24-MDL for $67.50. The newest model—24-V—comes in .222 or 20-gauge at $79.50. The latter model could be used on deer-size game by using slugs in the 20-gauge barrel for short range and have the .222 to back it up.

The Hege Combination Rifle/Shotgun Unlike most German-made guns of this type, the Stoeger-imported Hege gun is made in standard American calibers and may be obtained in either standard 12-gauge or 20-gauge magnum shotgun barrel in combination with the .222 Remington or .30-06 rifle. This immigrant can be scope sighted by the manufacturer. However, it is a wee bit heavy for this old Ranger to pack, and a little too rich for my pocketbook.

The All-Around Shotgun Many riflemen, bow hunters, and new hunters wanting to take up the "smoothbore" for the first time, want to know what is the best "all-around scattergun" for deer and waterfowl. The answer is simple: There just isn't any! However, there is a compromise: If you have a rifle and want a shotgun too, but feel you can't afford two shotguns—one for upland game and one for waterfowl—the slide action or autoloader, to which has been fitted a choking device such as the Cutts Compensator, Poly Choke, or one of the other brands, will come close.

Shotgun Fit Is Important The standard dimensions in factory shotguns are a pull length of 14 inches; a drop at the comb of 1½ inches; a drop at the heel of 2½ inches; and a "pitch" of 2 or 3 inches depending on the barrel length.

Factory guns are designed for the average person. So before buying a scattergun, consult your local game warden or an experienced shotgunner and ask him about choke and other pertinent facts about the smoothbore. Then rent and try out several different models and actions for fit, balance, quickness, and ease of handling. For a better fit you may have to have the stock shortened or a recoil pad added to lengthen it. This should be done by a competent gunsmith if necessary. Having a good rubber recoil pad placed on the stock butt and a compensator installed on the muzzle for a brake can improve your shooting considerably.

How to Pattern Your Shotgun When you have decided which shotgun you can handle best and have purchased it, or if you already have a scattergun but haven't patterned it, take it out and pattern it. About the best paper shotgun targets are large newsprint. Your local newspaper publisher will have on hand what is known in the trade as "end rolls." These are the last yards of paper remaining on the cardboard core, and cost very little. The targets should be cut out lifesize. Birds may be simple outline silhouettes, or cardboard cutouts pasted on the target. When using animal targets, you can cut them rough size or order them from Stoeger's Shooter's Bible, 55 Ruta Court, South Hackensack, New Jersey 07606, or from some sporting equipment stores. For birds, set your target stand at 40 yards against a safe background. Set the animal target at 50 and 100 yards for slugs.

When testing for pattern, wear the same jacket or coat you will wear while hunting. Be sure that it has plenty of shoulder room and does not bind or bunch up when you swing and point the gun. Try to duplicate field shots. To accomplish this, move off several yards at an angle to the line of fire. Carry the gun in the crook of your arm, or in a safe position usual in hunting. Walk up to the firing point. At the

Good fit, balance, quickness and ease of handling must all be considered in choosing a shotgun. SAVAGE ARMS PHOTO

moment you come to the spot from which to shoot, suddenly slip the safety off, swing, point, and fire at your target. When you finally are able to hit the target, draw a 30-inch circle around the shot imprinted on the target. This will indicate if you have any blown or open patterns. If you do, try out various size shotshells until you find the brand and shot size that your particular gun patterns best with. For a starter, use Nos. 2 and 4 for goose-size targets, Nos. 4 and 6 for duck, and Nos. 6 and 8 for quail-size birds. It may be that No. 5 and No. 7½ shot will pattern best in your piece. You alone will have to determine which brand and shot size works best for you. One thing to keep in mind is that the smaller size shot used, the more dense the pattern. However, the finer or smaller shot will not carry as far as heavier shot.

For example, my old hunting pal, Forest Ranger Clyde Werley and I would hunt quail occasionally on his cattle ranch below Fish Camp near Yosemite National Park. Clyde owned a battery of fine smoothbores, but did a better job of shooting with his father's old beat-up Winchester Model 97 full choke 12-gauge pump hammer gun with the pump handle well taped to hold it together. It would only pattern well with No. 6 shot, and Clyde would drop his birds at longer range to keep from de-molishing them. To top it off, he would collect his limit before any of the rest of the party.

My pet scattergun, a 12-gauge lightweight Savage autoloader with a Poly ventilated choke, would only pattern well with Nos. 6 and 8—so I would load the first two shells with No. 8 shot and back these up with a load of No. 6s in case I was lucky enough to get off a third shot. It is perhaps needless to say—use the weapon and shot size that bring you the best results.

Approximate Number of Pellets to the Ounce

No. 9—585; No. 8—410; No. 7½—350; No. 6—225; No. 5—170; No. 4—135; No. 2—90.

Buckshot Loads per Shell

12-gauge	3 inch mag.	No. 00	15 pellets
12	2¾	No. 00	12
12	2¾ reg.	No. 00	9
12	2¾	No. 0	12
12	2¾	No. 1	16
12	2¾	No. 4	27
16	2¾	No. 1	12
20	2¾	No. 3	20

Rifled Slug Loads

12-gauge	2¾ max.	1 ounce
16	2¾	⅞
20	2¾	⅝
410	2¼	⅕

Suggested Choke and Shot Size for Birds and Beasts

TABLE 1
Shotshell Loads

Gauge	Shell Length	Powder (dr.-eq.)	Shot (oz.)	Shot Sizes	Muzzle Velocity
10	3½	5	2	2, 4	
10	2⅞	4¾	1⅝	BB, 2, 4	1330
12	2¾	3¾	1¼	BB, 2, 4, 5, 6, 7½, 9	1330
12	2¾ magnum	4	1½	2, 4, 5, 6, oo buck (12)	1315
12	3 magnum	4	1⅜	BB, 2, 4, 6, oo buck (15)	1315
12	3 magnum	4¼	1⅝	BB, 2, 4, 5, 6	1315
12	3 magnum	4½	1⅞	BB, 2, 4, 5, 6	1255
12	2¾	3	1	4, 5, 6, 8	1235
12	2¾	3	1⅛	4, 5, 6, 8, 9	1200
12	2¾	3¼	1⅛	4, 5, 6, 7½, 8, 9	1255
12	2¾	3¼	1¼	7½, 8	1220
12	2¾	2¾	1⅛	7½, 8, 9	1145
12	2¾	3	1⅛	7½, 8, 9	1200
16	2⁹⁄₁₆	3	1⅛	2, 4, 5, 6, 7½	1240
16	2¾	3¼	1⅛	2, 4, 5, 6, 7½, 9	1295

Gauge	Shell Length	Powder (dr.-eq.)	Shot (oz.)	Shot Sizes	Muzzle Velocity
16	2¾ magnum	3½	1¼	2, 4, 6	1295
16	2⁹⁄₁₆	2½	1	4, 5, 6, 8, 9	1165
16	2¾	2¾	1⅛	2, 4, 5, 6, 7½, 8, 9	1185
16	2¾	2½	1	9 (skeet load)	1200
20	2¾	2¾	1	2, 4, 5, 6, 7½, 9	1220
20	2¾ magnum	3	1⅛	2, 4, 6, 7½	1220
20	3 magnum	3¼	1¼	4, 5, 6, 7½	1220
20	2¾	2¼	⅞	4, 5, 6, 8, 9	1155
20	2¾	2½	1	4, 5, 6, 7½, 8, 9	1165
20	2¾	2¼	⅞	9 (skeet load)	1200
28	2¾	2¼	¾	4, 6, 7½, 9	1295
28	2¾	2¼	¾	9 (skeet load)	1200
28	2¾	2¾	1	6, 7½, 8, 9	1220
.410	2½	Max.	½	4, 5, 6, 7½, 9	1135
.410	3	Max.	¾	4, 5, 6, 7½, 9	1135
.410	2½	Max.	½	9 (skeet load)	1200
.410	3	Max.	¾	9 (skeet load)	1150

TABLE 2
Buckshot Loads

Gauge	Shell Length	Shot Size	Number of Pellets	Muzzle Velocity
12	2¾	oo buck	9	1325
12	2¾ magnum	oo buck	12	1325
12	3 magnum	oo buck	15	1250
12	3 magnum	4 buck	41	1225
12	2¾	o buck	12	1300
12	2¾	1 buck	16	1250
12	2¾	4 buck	27	1325
16	2¾	1 buck	12	1225
20	2¾	3 buck	20	1200

TABLE 3
Rifled Slugs

Gauge	Load	Slug wt.	Velocity					Energy				
			Muzzle	25 yds.	50 yds.	75 yds.	100 yds.	Muzzle	25 yds.	50 yds.	75 yds.	100 yds.
12	3¾	1	1600	1365	1175	1040	950	2485	1810	1340	1050	875
16	3	⅞	1600	1365	1175	1040	950	2175	1585	1175	920	765
20	2¾	⅝	1600	1365	1175	1040	950	1555	1130	840	655	550
28	2¼	½	1600	1365	1175	1040	950	1245	905	670	525	440
.410	2¼	⅕	1830	1560	1335	1150	1025	650	475	345	255	205

Courtesy of Olin-Mathieson

Patterning Isn't All There Is to It There is another important factor which doesn't show up in the "test" pattern, and that is the controlled shot string. With due allowances for size and style of gun bores, all that is asked of the shot charge at moderate ranges is satisfactory speed, pattern, and penetration. But at longer ranges, the length of the shot string usually is important.

Only the shell which combines short shot string with high pattern percentage maintains a dense enough concentration of shot to produce long-range, clean kills. High-velocity, dense-patterning, short-shot shells backed by skillful gun pointing mean fewer cripples, and more game to divide with friends.

When an expert wingshooter talks about a good "pancake" pattern, he naturally means a short shot string, in which *most* of the pellets reach the target area in time to provide effective shock killing power. The average velocity of a shot charge is approximately 10 times faster than the speed of a fast-flying duck (50 to 65 miles per hour). For example, let's take two full choke guns which provide exactly the same pattern—an ideal 74 percent. Perhaps they are both perfect. It's entirely possible, however, that the shot string from the first gun may be as much as 30 percent shorter than the shot string produced by the second gun. The payoff? The entire shot string from the first gun reaches a fast-flying duck, and gives a perfect kill. But when the second gun is fired at the bird, only part of the shot string reaches it—the other part or section catches up but after the duck has flown past.

Patterning a scattergun on paper can be extremely helpful in determining the density and uniformity of the shot pattern fired at a stationary target. It is well to remember that *the third-dimension factor of shot string length does not show up on paper.*

It is interesting to note that the average shot string produced by a 3¾-dr., 1¼-oz. No. 6 duck load, shot from a 12-gauge full choke gun, is approximately 12 feet long at 40 yards. Extensive testing by independent ballistics laboratories has proved that choke devices reduce shot string length considerably from that produced by a normal fixed choke gun. One thing to remember is that the greater the choke constriction, the longer the shot string will be.

Choke Devices An important phase of selecting shooting equipment is choice of choke. Waterfowl shooting generally requires a full choke, while a more open bore is suitable for smaller upland game.

Choke is the bore constriction of a shotgun, located at the end of the muzzle, and is the means by which the charge of shot is concentrated for its flight through the air. Choke gives a relatively small and dense pattern instead of a widely scattered one. The degree of choke is measured by the approximate percentage of pellets in a shot charge which hits within a 30-inch circle at 40 yards. The following gives percentages obtained with various degrees of choke:

Full choke: 65–75 percent (full); improved modified: 55–65 percent (¾ choke); modified: 45–55 percent (½ choke); improved cylinder: 35–45 percent (¼ choke); cylinder: 25–35 percent (no choke). Choke will vary slightly in each individual gun.

In order to give the shooter owning a single-barrel scattergun a variety of chokes so he doesn't have to change barrels or choke devices for different species of birds, several variable-choke devices have been perfected. The type with or without the compensator-ventilated slots or holes to let gas escape is based on the principle of the collet, an instrument which may be screwed down by degrees to give the desired choke constriction. The "one-gun man" who invests in a variable choke has a better opportunity to use his smoothbore for all kinds of gunning throughout the year.

What You Should Know about Leading Unfortunately, it is impossible to compile a definite chart or table of how far to lead your birds. There are just too many variables involved. The distance of the target from the shooter, the angle of flight, the wind, the speed the bird is traveling, the quickness of your swing, combined with your reflexes and shooting position will govern the lead at the time. The problem is to send out a load of shot in a direction and angle to meet the bird at a preconceived point. That is to say, the shot charge should intercept the game somewhere along its line of flight before it can get out of range. You must learn to swing with the target in the same line of flight in order to shoot ahead of the target. A load of shot placed behind the bird will never catch up, but a pattern placed well ahead has the best chance of connecting!

To snap shoot means to throw the gun to the shoulder, but to pause just long enough to make sure of the target instead of squeezing off the trigger the instant the butt of the stock strikes the shoulder. The idea, of course, is to shoot for the spot you expect the charge and bird to meet.

That Thing Called Swing If you shoot at upland game, ducks or geese flying at approximately (your educated guess) 40 m.p.h. at a crossing angle of, you estimate, 30 yards, you should lead the bird by 6 feet, the distance the bird would fly in the tenth of a second it took the shot to reach it. Since a bird's speed is variable, depending on the situation at the time, many hunters are apt to overestimate the bird's speed by 5 to 15 m.p.h., its angle of flight by several degrees, its distance from the gun by 5 or more yards, and then they might forget to allow for a possible 10- to 20-m.p.h. tailwind.

What should you do about it? Generally, you will know if the bird is flying with or against the wind. If it is flying with a tailwind, add a foot or two to your lead. (A study of wind speed with a Beaufort Wind Scale can help you judge wind velocity.) In practice it isn't too important to figure how much to lead a bird in feet and inches; the important thing to know is lead it you must, and to do so you have to swing the gun ahead of the bird and keep swinging it until the shot has cleared the muzzle. With practice, most wing and pass shooters acquire a sort of conditioned reflex about swinging, and automatically adjust their swing speed to the estimated wing speed of the quail, duck, or whatever species of bird they are shooting. Swing fast on crossing shots, slower on incoming birds, or those flying out at an angle. Whatever method you use, remember you have to see your gun barrel in relation to the bird when you fire! Doing that with a shotgun is precisely the same thing as calling a shot with a rifle. No matter whether you use the fast swing or sustained lead method, you have to *keep the gun swinging!* Likewise, you will miss if you don't *keep your face down* on the comb of the stock.

It can be comforting to remember that an ounce of No. 9 shot contains about 585 pellets, which will spread out and cover an area of about 3 feet in diameter at average shooting distance on quail. No. 6s contain only about 225 pellets.

Just swing your smoothbore and I'll bet you'll likely see feathers fly! If you miss the first shot, you probably haven't lead enough; double the lead and try again on the next bird. Only practice will improve your shooting. One of the best methods is to spend some time at trap and skeet shooting. If you do not belong to a club,

there are some economical hand traps for sale, and with a box of clay birds and someone to throw them for you, you can get in some preseason practice that will benefit you in the field when the hunting season opens.

Bird Dogs Every sportsman who can should own a good bird dog. It not only adds to hunting pleasure, but contributes to game conservation. Every hunting season, from 30 to 50 percent of birds that fall before gunners are lost. Having a trained retriever will reduce this waste. It is beyond this handbook to include bird dogs—it would take a volume to cover the subject.

Recommended Reading *The American Shotgunner*, $6.95; *Shotguns*, $5; *Fun with Game Birds*, $7.50; *Modern Dog Encyclopedia*, $10. The Stackpole Company, Kelker and Cameron streets, Harrisburg, Pennsylvania 17105.

Every sportsman who can should own a good bird dog. SAVAGE ARMS PHOTO

Chapter 5

HUNTING INDIAN STYLE-WITH BOW AND ARROWS

The Challenge of Bow Hunting Bow hunting goes back centuries. Today the number of bow hunters is increasing by the thousands. To the modern archer, his form of taking game offers a real challenge. To be successful he must have an intimate knowledge of the habits and habitat of the game in which he is interested and its food and range. He must know the terrain, and how to stalk it. And if he will keep his broadheads sharp, he'll have one of the most effective weapons for hunting known to man.

Two Hunting Seasons Many riflemen and shotgunners have joined the ranks of the archer—especially the sportsman who enjoys a double season. If the double-weapons enthusiast fails to bag game during bow season, he increases his chances to connect with game during the general open rifle season.

Too, there are many other reasons why many guntoting deer hunters are attracted to bow hunting. In thickly populated, heavily hunted areas, the safety angles have lured many "muskeeters" to bow hunting. There's also the consideration that the competition is not as widespread, since there are far more riflemen afield during the general open season.

Bow hunting is recognized as a safe sport, and the archer can practice it in his backyard without the noise of his shot disturbing his neighbors; and he can shoot arrows over and over without concern about ammunition costs if he takes reasonable care of his archery equipment.

The shooting and hunting sports are family sports. Brawn, size, sex, or weight have little influence on the final score. Practice and an earnest desire to improve are the factors that really shape the bow hunter's skill.

Costs of Archery Archers need only a simple list of equipment. A hunting bow, arrows, quiver, armguard, glove, and to be reasonably successful, a camouflage suit, hat, gloves, and face mask.

The requirement over which the bow hunter has most control is this equipment, but many archers arm themselves with gear that is not suitable for jackrabbits, let alone bear- or deer-size game. The hunting bow should be of good quality. Expensive models won't kill any more game than the moderately priced ones, but cheap models and offhand brands should be avoided.

Needless to say, the occasional or once-a-year bow hunter doesn't need to spend as much for his equipment as does a top-notch tournament or serious bow hunter who is after a record size game head. Like firearms, some of the medium-price hunting bows are just as powerful and deadly, and pull just as smoothly and will cast an arrow just as fast and far as a higher price weapon. However, it is best to get the best bow and arrows you can afford. You will be better satisfied in the long run and the outfit will give longer service.

Selecting a Bow and Arrows A good hunting bow should have maneuverability, with longbow smoothness and accuracy. It should cast

Bow hunting today offers the hunter a real challenge with a real reward. BEAR ARCHERY COMPANY

Archery is as effective under the water as it is in the woods. BEAR ARCHERY COMPANY

an arrow flat, hard, and far, from any shooting position—without stacking, torque, or kick.

Generally, bowmen use a draw weight from 35 to 70 pounds. However, it doesn't pay to get a bow with a draw pull so stiff that you can't enjoy or handle it properly. You need one that will permit the steadiest aim and smoothest release possible for maximum accuracy.

The average hunting bow requires about a 45- to 55-pound pull. Some states require a minimum limit on bows for deer hunting, usually around 45 pounds.

If your bow doesn't come with an arrow plate— that point on the side of the bow across which an arrow shaft passes—glue on a small piece of buckskin or moleskin. Anyone who has lost game because a slight sound resulted when his arrow was drawn realizes the importance of a silent draw. On a quiet day, a nearby deer or bear will generally pick up any unusual noise, however slight. Too, the loud twang of a bow string has "spooked" many animals.

On one hunt, I missed a standing deer by overshooting, and was unable to get off another shot due to bowstring noise putting the critter into high gear. After that experience I added string dampeners or silencers to deaden the twang noise. Later I found out why I was over- or undershooting and hitting a foot or so to one side. I was not nocking (seating my arrow nock on the bowstring) in the exact spot each time and I was canting the bow off and on, causing my misses. To overcome this I added "nocking points." These allow you to spot your arrow nock correctly for each shot. Adding a bowsight and no-cant reticule has kept my misses to a minimum, and a bow quiver has increased my speed in stringing an arrow for a possible second shot. For extra arrows, I use a Browning Hip Pocket quiver. In this manner I do not have a side quiver slapping my thigh as I move through brush cover. A shoulder quiver may give you trouble.

Arrows   The best bow in the country, matched with inferior arrows, won't produce much game. But a fairly good bow teamed up with a set of

Camouflage is sometimes most important to the bowman. BEAR ARCHERY COMPANY

perfectly straight spined arrows will give you a combination likely to score.

Arrows must be matched in spine, or stiffness, to the weight of the bow. Most experienced bowmen prefer shafts made from aluminum tubing or tubular fiberglass. They cost more than wood shafts, but they are worth the slight difference in price.

Both arrows and bow should be toned down in color. A hunter wearing head-to-toe camouflage may frighten game when he raises a highly polished bow loaded with a bright-colored shaft that reflects sunlight. Many bow hunters prefer dark fletching (feathers), while others want white feathers so they can see the arrow's flight in dim light. The latter is sometimes called archer's "tracers." Waterproofing feathers will not only help to preserve them, but will help them from becoming matted when wet.

Basic Bow Technique   There is only one way to learn to shoot a bow, and that is the right way! Try to get an experienced bowman to teach you the proper fundamentals and techniques. Target shoot every chance you get on a regular bow range if possible. If none is available, set up your own.

As soon as you are able to hit regular archery bull's-eyes, arrange to shoot at animal-size targets through light foliage, uphill and down, point-blank and at long bow ranges. Learn to shoot from different positions and at various angles. Deer or other game "bust out" of brush or other cover from many directions. To be successful you must be alert and ready!

Don't Make This Mistake   Even some experienced hunters, under stress, will shoot at the whole animal. Aim at one vital point. Let the arrow go the instant you are lined up! Don't hesitate hoping for a better shot—you may not get one.

For practice, deer-size paper targets may be obtained from sporting goods or equipment stores, and these can be mounted on heavy cardboard or other backing material and fastened to a bale of hay for a backstop.

The Five Elements for Accuracy   The elements for archery accuracy are as follows: 1. standing stance; 2. nocking; 3. drawing; 4. holding aim;

Archery practice on field targets is the first step toward game shots. BEAR ARCHERY COMPANY

5. releasing and following through. For target practice, one must use the same form for each shot. The arrow must always be nocked at the same spot on the bowstring. The bowstring must be pulled back the same distance each time, and the bow held the same for each shot if accuracy is to be obtained.

Preseason Practice Hunting and stalking rabbits and "chucks" is one of the best ways to practice for whitetail and mule deer. These fast-moving smaller targets give you plenty of sport. Shoot your bow every chance you get from now until the bow season opens.

The Two-Bow Hunter A spare bow is a must when you are on a hunting trek in some remote wilderness. Many riflemen pack an extra weapon just in case something happens to their one and only means of collecting game.

Many bowmen use an old or beat-up bow for shooting carp in muddy flats or when cruising in salt water for sharks, stingrays, or other non-game fish. It can also be used to teach some member of the family to learn archery.

Six Pointers That Can Help Here's how to avoid mistakes:

1. Check your nocking. The arrow must be at

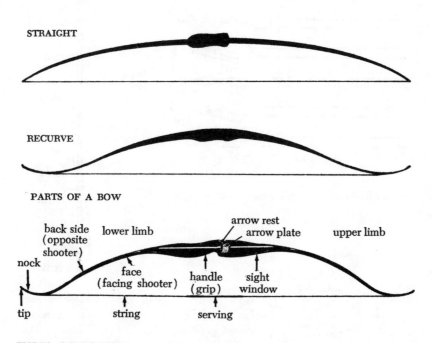

STRAIGHT

RECURVE

PARTS OF A BOW

back side (opposite shooter)   lower limb   arrow rest   arrow plate   upper limb

nock   face (facing shooter)   handle (grip)   sight window

tip   string   serving

TYPES OF BOWS

There are basically two different types of bow designs. (1) A straight bow is exactly as name implies when it is unstrung. (2) The recurve bow has limbs which curve opposite to its strung position when unstrung. There are also variations of recurved and straight bow designs.

HOW TO SELECT A BOW

The first advice given to any new archer is: don't "overbow." Generally, a 5-pound heavier bow than the one that can be easily drawn will work best. It's always better to start with a bow that's easier to pull and handle, then as accuracy and confidence are developed, move to a heavier bow. A heavier bow won't shoot straighter, it will just cast an arrow farther. The chart at the top of the page gives draw weight recommendations. Before buying a bow for hunting, check your state game laws for minimum draw weight regulations.

SHAKESPEARE COMPANY, KALAMAZOO, MICHIGAN

BOW WEIGHT RECOMMENDATION CHART

	20 lb. & under	20 lb.	25 lb.	30 lb.	35 lb.	40 lb.	40 lb. & over
Children 6-12	X	X					
Teen (Girl)		X	X				
Teen (Boy)		X	X	X			
Ladies			X	X	X		
Men-target				X	X	X	
Men-hunting							X

TYPES OF ARROWS

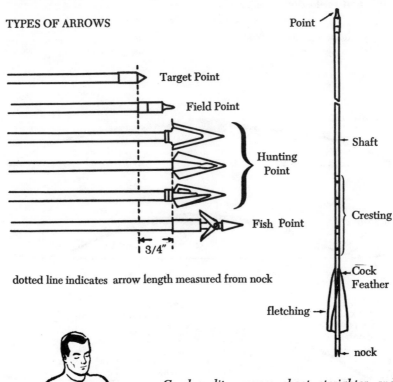

Point

Target Point

Field Point

Hunting Point

Fish Point

Shaft

Cresting

Cock Feather

fletching

nock

3/4"

dotted line indicates arrow length measured from nock

Good-quality arrows shoot straighter and last longer. When buying an arrow, you can gauge your requirements by seeing if the arrow will reach from your chest to your fingertips when held as illustrated. 28" is standard because the average adult arm-span is best suited to this draw size. SHAKE-SPEARE COMPANY, KALAMAZOO, MICHIGAN

right angles to the bowstring and straight on the arrow rest. A nocking mark can be helpful.

2. Proper stance is essential—feet are comfortably spaced and at right angles to the target, elbow high enough to keep forearm parallel.

3. Bow is held securely, not tight; fingers go to corner of archer's mouth (the anchor point) and sighting is over the tip of the arrow.

4. Be sure to have the proper length arrow for your natural draw. In the field, for high shots, be sure to bend at the waist and maintain position.

5. An archer should be able to shoot from a variety of positions.

6. Once the basic positions are mastered, the bowman is ready for the target range.

An autumn sun starts to spread its rays across a silent forest, flicking away the morning frost as you slip away from your bivouac camp. The first warmth brings an unmistakable thrill of excitement . . . this morning you are joining a special breed of sportsmen—you are a bow hunter! Even though you may be a veteran bowman, the thrill is always present: you know that you have to stalk your animal silently as the Indians did—more carefully than the rifleman, for your weapon is short-ranged. Your pulse pounds as a deer bounces away in front of you, or a bear crashes off through the woods! But be careful, Mr. Bowman, that in this exciting moment you do not get "buck fever." Take careful aim and send that arrow true!

Chapter 6

TIPS FOR THE SUCCESSFUL HUNTER

The Weatherwise Hunter Weather is something the hunter must take into consideration if he is to be comfortable on the trek or be successful in locating game.

Generally, game of all species water and feed twice a day, early in the morning and again toward evening. However, they all change their feeding program when a storm is in the offing, and will graze more or less continuously until satisfied, then hole up in sheltered hideouts and wait the storm out, or if the storm is prolonged, until hunger forces them to feed again.

Weather is a deciding factor whether you go or scratch the trip and thereby lose a weekend or more of hunting. If already in the field, a severe storm may cause you to abort the hunt or force you to stay over in camp unexpectedly for several days.

Waterfowlers are aware of this and prepare for good or foul weather by planning ahead: if the weather forecast is for wind and snow flurries, they know that ducks will be feeding from water and grain fields or from pond to pond to get their fill before a bad storm breaks.

If caught in a storm or if lost during inclement weather, the hunter must know what to do to protect himself. In camp he must know how to keep as warm and dry as possible. If caught out away from camp in a snowstorm he must know survival techniques.

To cite just one example: Over three thousand hunters became snowbound and marooned for a week one November several years ago while seeking elk in Arizona's Mogollon Rim country.

Six of the hunters died, and many more suffered frostbite and cold weather injuries and sickness. Most of these hunters were ill fitted for a situation of this sort, and lacked experience and proper equipment and knowledge of cold weather survival techniques. It is no wonder that many of them panicked when a blizzard moved in practically overnight.

Too many hunting trips end on a sour note because not enough of the right kind of food, warm clothing, raingear, and sleeping equipment was taken along. Another mistake is not having the right type of tent or shelter for cold weather hunting, and a small camp stove for warmth and to dry out equipment and gear.

To avoid running into foul weather (unless waterfowl hunting) on your hunting adventure, call up your local weather bureau or Coast Guard station and get a long-range weather forecast. Check with the Ranger or game warden before you leave the end of the road—local weather conditions can be radically different than those predicted for lowlands and large areas.

Weather Guides Here are a few weather guides that have worked fairly consistently for the hunter.

If smoke from your campfire rises high in a long thin spiral, the weather will remain good for at least 12 hours. If the smoke rises sluggishly for a short distance, then drifts off slowly and settles, have your raingear handy.

The Snowmobile is one of the newest hunter's aids. WISCONSIN CONSERVATION DEPARTMENT

If all the trees (particularly the maples) are showing the undersides of their leaves and the tops of the western hemlocks straighten up, rain is possible within 24 hours.

Heavy dew on the meadow grass or forest cover presages fair weather. Lack of it is likely to mean rain soon.

Clouds, in their various formations, often give advance notice on the weather. Look for the following:

The big white, puffy clouds called cumulus mean fair weather. Go ahead and make your plans. When they bunch up they form nimbus, or rain clouds. If they gather quickly you may expect no more than a shower. Hunting should be good! If it takes them a day or two to form in a mass, get plenty of dry wood in under cover. Be sure that you have a drain ditch around your tent and campsite.

Small cumulus clouds indicate fair weather. But watch the big ones that form like high mountains and hide nearly all the blue; they mean rain in the offing. Better not hunt too far from camp. If these clouds swell up and flatten out like an anvil, they are called "hammerheads" and you can expect lightning and thunder. Stay off high points and away from tall trees!

Cirrus clouds, or "mare's tails," those wispy affairs high up, are a bad sign. If they go scudding across the sky there is likely to be a storm within the next 24 hours. Better be prepared.

A denser variation of the cirrus clouds is known as a "mackerel sky." Look out for high wind. The woods will be noisy and stalking should be easy.

Clouds that move at different levels and in opposite directions are a warning of unpleasant weather ahead.

If the clouds float high about sundown and are tinged with red, prepare for high wind to follow. Tighten your tent guys!

Barometer-Wind Chart for Hunter Use

Wind Direction	Barometer Reduced to Sea Level	Character of Weather
SW to NW	30.10 to 30.20 and steady	Fair with slight temperature change for 1 or 2 days.
SW to NW	30.10 to 30.20 and rising rapidly	Fair followed within 2 days by rain.
SW to NW	30.20 and above and stationary	Continued fair with no decided temperature change.
SW to NW	30.20 and falling slowly	Slowly rising temperature and fair for 2 days.
S to SE	30.10 to 30.20 and falling slowly	Rain within 24 hours.
S to SE	30.10 to 30.20 and falling rapidly	Wind increasing in force, with rain within 12 to 24 hours.
SE to NE	30.10 to 30.20 and falling slowly	Rain in 12 to 18 hours.
SE to NE	30.10 to 30.20 and falling rapidly	Increasing wind and rain within 12 hours.
E to NE	30.10 to 30.20 and above and falling slowly	In summer, with light winds, rain may not fall for several days. In fall and winter, rain within 24 hours.

Look for a change in wind and probable bad weather to follow when distant objects which have been indistinct suddenly stand out clearly. Don't get too far out on large bodies of water!

Transportation Tips Pickups with four-speed shifts, Jeeps, and other four-wheel-drive vehicles will get you over rough terrain far better than the family car, but if you drive carefully and do not attempt washed-out logging roads any vehicle will do.

If you use the family car for the trip, a car-top rack will save space for passengers. The contents should be covered by a heavy-duty canvas that can be lashed down securely. A small two-wheeled utility trailer hauled behind the car can also be used to solve the space problem. One-wheel utility trailers are not too satisfactory for rough or high-crowned roads.

Instant Camp There seems to be a growing number of hunters who want to camp out, but still take the maximum number of home comforts along with them. If you haul a small travel trailer, tent trailer, or go into the woods with a pickup camper, you can go in style. Some even have inside plumbing of the chemical toilet type. Even some of the small compact cars can haul the smaller rigs with ease. You can rent one of these camper outfits from $7.50 per day

up. However, if you do camp-hunt with one of these rigs, it is best to make a dry run and scout the road ahead in the family jalopy, or you might run into difficulties attempting to negotiate back country roads while hauling a low-hung trailer. Travel trailers and pickup campers grow increasingly elaborate, and those over fifteen or sixteen feet long are difficult to maneuver off the road into a primitive camp-site.

Tote-Gote and Motor Scooters For the "go light" hunter, there are many models and makes of trail bikes. If you plan to use one of these back country two-wheel outfits, be sure to check in advance with the Forest Service; there are special rules and regulations regarding their operations on trails. Loaded down with a rider, camping gear, and, if you are lucky a deer or other game, they can be difficult to manage, and cause a lot of spills when crossing streams and water turnouts on the trail.

If You Don't Own a Car or Gun For the apartment or city dweller who doesn't own a car and wants to go hunting, but who can't wangle a ride with a friend, he can rent a pickup truck or other type of vehicle from $8 to $15 per day and 8 to 10 cents per mile depending on the make and type of vehicle. If he doesn't own a

Any vehicle can be used for hunting trips if you drive carefully and know your terrain. WISCONSIN CONSERVATION DEPARTMENT

rifle or shotgun, they usually can be rented from some sporting equipment stores for a nominal charge. So can the necessary camping equipment.

Instruments That Can Help the Hunter Some experienced and successful hunters take, besides a compass and large-scale map of the area, a barometer, a small thermometer, and a lightweight CB (Citizens Band) transceiver "walkie-talkie" radio weighing about a pound. It contains speaker, receiver, antenna, and transmitter in a single plastic case; also a few penlight batteries or a tiny 9-volt battery that will operate the set for about 50 hours, and often longer.

Their range fluctuates, depending on the terrain and weather conditions. Usually they can be used from 1 to 10 miles in range. They will operate more efficiently if you are up on some high point having no interfering ridge between you and the other set. The little CB radio is especially useful in keeping in contact with a hunting partner at camp, or if a member of the party becomes confused in the woods and turns around, or has downed game and needs assistance to haul his prize into camp. These little sets can be worth their weight in gold in times of emergency. However, a radio schedule should be worked out and decided upon so the receiver isn't in continuous service; otherwise the batteries may become weakened.

No license is required at present to operate CB radio. The prices range from $25 per instrument to over $100 per set of two.

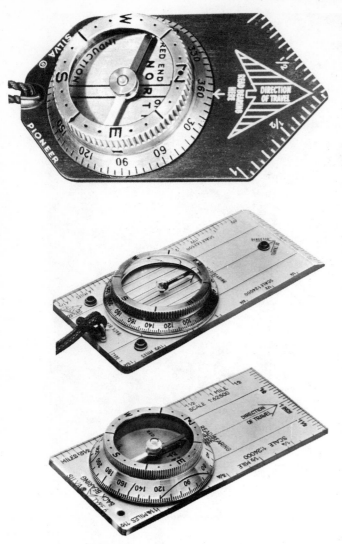

A compass can be improved upon, but it still remains an important part of a hunting trip. COURTESY OF THE AUTHOR

The Hunting Compass An excellent compass to have while hunting is the Silva Huntsman. It is liquid-filled to dampen the magnetic needle and keep it from fluctuating too rapidly. It has a pin-on fastener, sun-watch markings, and luminous points. The price is $5.95 from Silva, Inc., La Porte, Indiana 46350. Three other Silva compasses are shown above. The Leupold Sportsman is another fine medium-priced compass at $9.95 from Leupold & Stevens Instruments, Inc., 4445 N.E. Glisan Street, Portland, Oregon 97213. The U. S. Army type lensatic compass is another good buy for $3.95. The above compasses may also be

purchased from many sporting equipment stores. Some hunters throw a little gadget into their packs called a Kumbak. It is a little unit not longer than your index finger consisting of a matchcase with a whistle at one end and a small compass at the other. It is priced at $2.95 at Stoeger's or at the better sporting goods stores.

Inletted in the bottom of the pistol-grip of my personal rifle is a Gunner's Guide. It is a shockproof, compass-like instrument and is precision-jeweled for accuracy. This compass gadget is easily inletted into the stock of your rifle or shotgun, and is a helpful direction finder. I have it in case my regular compass becomes inoperative for some reason. The price is $4.95 and includes a special installation bit. Ordinarily you won't need a compass if you are observant and know the terrain, but you can easily become lost in unfamiliar country if visibility is poor due to rain or snow. If you do have a compass, be sure you understand how to use it. Some compasses have azimuth dials clockwise; some quadrant dials are counterclockwise and are read differently. Carefully read the directions with each instrument so you thoroughly understand how to use it; otherwise it will be of no use to you!

Why a Thermometer? It is optional. However, a small, inexpensive, minimum-maximum thermometer can be of considerable assistance when used with a barometer—especially when your hunting camp is at high elevation. The barometer and wind direction will let you know if there is going to be precipitation, and the thermometer will indicate a cold front and you will have time to gather plenty of dry wood for the old sheepherder stove in your tent.

Wind-Barometer Indications Sky conditions and sky changes should be carefully watched, since these are the best guides to short-term local forecasting by the hunter. The early definition of the state of the sky as clear, partly cloudy, or overcast is still descriptive and widely used by outdoorsmen.

Barometer readings fluctuate constantly—that is, there are regular rises and drops in daily pressure. A barometer that shows a rapid fall of .05 in. per hour indicates a storm building up —so you have time to prepare for it, or abort

The campfire is the hunter's good friend. But don't depend only on matches to start one. WISCONSIN CONSERVATION DEPARTMENT

the trip. Game are sensitive to barometric pressure and their movements and feeding habits are guided by these pressures.

Emergency Firemakers It is very important that the hunter-camper take along enough kitchen-size matches for his needs. Some pipe-smoking hunters seem to burn more matches than tobacco lighting up the old furnace. The result is that when they get caught out overnight or in an emergency situation, they have nothing left to start a warming or signal fire.

The matches should be kept in a waterproof case, plus some waterproofed matches scattered among various pockets and in the pack. Paper matches are apt to get damp from body condensation or rain and are then useless. They are not recommended in the field for the serious sportsman.

You might just as well forget the idea of starting a fire by the old Boy Scout friction method, because you just are not going to find the right kind of dry wood or material in the damp forest in the fall hunting season (unless you are lucky).

Most survival manuals suggest using the glass out of a binocular, eyeglasses, or a camera lens for starting a fire under emergency conditions. Use of a lens in starting a fire has been done under ideal conditions—but even then it can be a rough and time-consuming job. Try starting a fire by removing the bullet and most of the powder from a cartridge. Insert a small piece of cloth into the cartridge with the remaining powder and fire it into a bed of dry tinder. It takes lots of practice and expenditure of ammunition. And again, there is the old flint-and-steel method used by the pioneers. It will do the trick if you practice enough and have sufficient dry tinder—but you had better try these fire-making methods out at home before you attempt to do so under emergency conditions in the wilderness! There is a little gadget that I carry in my emergency kit that will throw more sparks than most methods. It is a little two-ounce aluminum gas torch-lighter that can be purchased for 50 cents at most automotive or hardware stores. If you pack a small magnifiying glass of about six-power you can get a fire started if the sun is out hot enough.

Best of all the fire-starting gadgets to back your matches up, is a good-grade leakproof cigarette lighter. It should be wrapped and sealed tightly with waterproof tape along with an extra wick and flints. If the flame isn't exposed too long each time it is used, it will give you approximately 600 to 800 lights.

Hunter Campfires.

What the Hunter Should Know about Fire
Fire has been man's friend since the beginning of time. It also has been his enemy when he has lost control of it through ignorance or carelessness! It has destroyed man and his possessions when he became thoughtless with this powerful and dangerous, but necessary instrument of nature used for his health and comfort.

Every small forest fire is potentially a *big* one if conditions are right. Forest and brush fires occur at an average rate of 500 per day! If a combination of dry weather and high winds occurs, a forest fire may spread with explosive violence, roaring through trees faster than a man can run, and generate waves of heat and gas that

Smokey means forest protection you can give. COURTESY OF THE AUTHOR

fan the flames to even greater fury. A really bad forest fire is a terrifying thing. It destroys everything in its path!

From August 27 through September 13, 1955, California was subjected to 436 wildfires burning over 480 square miles of prime timber, brush, and hunting grounds. To fight them, it took 18,400 firefighters, 519 bulldozers, 919 tank trucks, 57 planes, and 10 helicopters.

A shocking fact is that it isn't the inexperienced city dwellers who cause the large and difficult-to-get-at fires, but the so-called "woodsman"—the man who considers himself an expert in safe and practical woodsmanship! He thinks the city neophyte responsible for most forest fires. Actually, governmental agencies have ascertained that it is the local fisherman, the nearby resident debris burner, the experienced hunter or local people who have been responsible for most fires that get out of control. And, of course, we will always have the fellow with a grudge against his neighbor or the government who will set fires for spite.

There is no doubt that the inexperienced city traveler does toss his smokes into the litter along the forest roads and cause many fires. However, these fires generally are small and easy to control.

Forest fires can be averted if you make sure your campfire is always under control.
WISCONSIN CONSERVATION DEPARTMENT

What the Hunter Can Do about It The hunter or other recreationist who stumbles onto an uncontrolled fire should know what action to take. During the late fall hunting season, many of the fire lookout towers are closed for the season. Hunters and other outdoorsmen are key people in detecting lightning and other fires caused by someone's carelessness.

Generally, unless a fire can be quickly extinguished, fire-fighting agencies suggest that the hunter report it as quickly as possible to the nearest Ranger or fire station. Firemen will be dispatched to put it out.

If it is not practical to contact a fire warden or forest officer, and the discoverer sees he can accomplish effective control with safety to himself, he should stay and fight the fire. If it is beyond his control and of any appreciable size, he can be assured that help will soon be on its way. Forest patrolmen and game wardens are on continuous patrol during the fire and hunting season. Even though the hunter puts out the fire himself, HE SHOULD REPORT IT TO THE NEAREST RANGER STATION. It then can be checked for possible holdover or "sleeper" fire, and the Rangers can determine the cause and amount of damage from the fire.

Know How to Break the Fire Triangle For a fire to burn, three elements must be present. First, fuel, such as pine needles, leaves, grass, brush, logs, and trees. Second, heat is needed, usually between 600° and 800° F. to bring it to the ignition point. The third element in the fire

"Sleeper" fires that appear to be out are responsible for many destructive forest fires. Be sure yours is out. WISCONSIN CONSERVATION DEPARTMENT

triangle is oxygen, provided by air. Together, these equal fire. Remove one of these elements and the fire will go out.

If You Stay and Fight the Fire

If you decide that you can control a small fire by yourself or with the assistance of others:

Decide *what* is the most important work to be done first and *where* the most effective work can be done. After a quick size-up of the conditions within the fire, and in the surrounding country toward which the fire is spreading, choose the *point of first attack*—generally the head of a small fire. Go around the fire, or find a vantage point and inspect the entire edge.

Look for fuel burning adjacent to the fire's edge, particularly snags and logs, brush and thickets of reproduction. Look for fuels in the immediate path of the fire and natural barriers such as roads, streams, or barren ground to tie your fire line into. Watch for spot fires that might flank your fireline.

To use a relatively narrow line to speed control: Scrape a narrow line about a foot wide down through the pine needles through the duff to mineral soil, through stand of trees and reproduction seedlings to which fire will spread. Throw loose dirt or water on it to keep fire out of tree crowns immediately adjacent to your line. Why? To reduce intensity of burning and to minimize danger of spotting or crowning over your temporary line; in this manner you buy time until you can widen your fireline.

Use water or dirt for cooling down and extinguishing hot spots. Follow up temporary checking efforts by digging a permanent, clean fireline to mineral soil. Cut off from dangerous fuels as first effort, and

Water can be made palatable and safe by adding charcoal and letting it simmer.
WISCONSIN CONSERVATION DEPARTMENT

prevent the fire from becoming established in explosive-type fuels, such as thickets or heavy brush, and slash areas.

Try to confine fire to one area rather than let it develop into two heads. Locate and build lines and move rolling material so it cannot roll across the firelines. (Turn logs lying parallel with the slope to a vertical position with the slope if possible. If material is too heavy to move, cock it with rocks so it can't roll; dirt it down so it won't burn.)

To insure control you may have to sacrifice an area to make line construction and a line that you can hold. Use all existing barriers to full extent to shorten lines. If you cannot control the fire, work on the flanks to slow it down until help arrives!

Although a shovel and ax are not mandatory in public camp grounds, campers and hunters should have these tools. Always remember, a safe fire is a fire prevented!

Wilderness Drinking Water

Brackish or flat-tasting water can also be made more palatable by adding several pieces of charcoal from the campfire and letting the water simmer for about twenty minutes. Skim away the foreign material or just let it settle to the bottom of the container. It can also be strained through a clean cloth.

Water can readily be purified by the following chemical means: Place two Halazone tablets in each quart of water and let it stand for half an hour. Be sure to rinse the cork or canteen cover with the solution or the cap can contaminate the rest of the water.

In semi-tropical hunting regions such as Florida and some southern states, iodine water-purifying tablets containing tetraglycine hydroperiodide can do a more thorough job than the chlorine-type tablets. Generally, one tablet will purify one quart of water.

If the water appears discolored or full of decaying vegetation, use a minimum of two tablets per quart. Be sure to sterilize the cap and neck of the container with some of the solution.

Using three drops of 2 percent iodine from your first aid kit will also do the trick.

I personally carry a small vial or bottle of household Purex or Clorox bleach in my kit for purifying water in the field. Use ten drops per gallon of water in this case.

It is usually safe to obtain drinking water from a spring flowing from rock or clean gravel or sand in back country away from any contaminating influences.

In some regions and especially in the desert hunting areas, a few water holes may be poisoned from minerals or be so heavily alkalized that they are unsafe to drink from. If dead animals or their bones are lying about or all plant life is bare—DO NOT DRINK THE WATER FOR ANY REASON! IT MAY BE DEADLY!

What to Wear The clothing and footwear you select for hunting should be designed to do three things for you: (a) be strong and light to wear, and allow you to move about freely; (b) protect you from heat and cold and from snags, dirt, insects, etc.; and (c) protect you from being mistaken for game and shot!

Because weather, terrain, and tastes differ from region to region, it is almost impossible to select clothing for all types of hunting to suit everyone. Here are a few tips in selecting yours: White, yellow, and scarlet, either ordinary or the new fluorescent colors, are the most easily identified ones, but check your local game regulations. Heavy stiff canvas, corduroy, and some other harsh cloths may be water-repellent and used in waterfowl hunting, but the material is too noisy when stalking big game.

A billed cap serves some hunters better than a hat, since it can be covered with a poncho or parka hood in inclement weather. It should shade you and protect you from rain, wind, or snow. There are several excellent ones on the market which are reversible for waterfowl and big-game hunting—red on one side and brown on the other—and with ear flaps. If still-hunting in damp terrain, water-repellent pants and parka will make your wait in concealment more comfortable.

For your feet, the Barker or Sno-Pac (rubber bottoms with leather tops) six to eight inches high are a good bet for wet country. You can use them on snowshoes too without damaging the webs. For upland game, the lightweight "bird shooter" model is an excellent buy. Hobnailed boots, once popular, are noisy and slippery over rocks, although some hunters consider them necessary in mountainous terrain. Insulated leather boots are good for cold weather, but if the climate is warm they will cause your feet to sweat. For all-around hiking and climbing, I find that eight-inch leather boots with composition lugged soles work best for me. They are quiet and non-skid. On prairies, felt shoes under four-buckle overshoes are much used and are a recommended combination for warm, dry feet. However, they are cumbersome to hike in. For duck hunting, I use my lightweight insulated fishing hip-boots over knee-length wool socks because they are warm and comfortable for wading or cross-country walking.

Wool socks and underwear will keep you warm even when wet if you move around a little. Net or thermal-type underwear is fine when dry. However, it won't keep you warm like wool when wet. For foot comfort, I use cotton or white wool lightweight inner socks, with heavy wool socks over them for boot socks. The other socks should be ½ size larger. One hundred percent wool underwear is too scratchy for me, but I find 60 to 80 percent wool comfortable.

Minimum Gear Each Hunter Should Carry Take at least a sharp skinning knife and small whetstone, belt ax or small folding camp saw, 30 feet of ¼-inch nylon rope, some twine, several pieces of cheesecloth for wiping the inside of a carcass dry, red or orange flagging, and four muslin game sacks, each large enough to hold a quarter of an animal. If you want to save the hide and head for mounting, take a pound of salt along to preserve them, and a can of black pepper to keep flies off the carcass. You will need a knapsack to carry this and any emergency gear you take along.

Hunter Survival Gear It is a wise hunter who goes prepared in case he has to spend a night or two in the woods due to a severe storm or be-

Clothing must be strong and light, provide freedom of movement, and protect you from heat, cold, and other hunters. U. S. FOREST SERVICE

cause he became turned around. You might someday be one of the several hundred thousand hunters who become lost or get into some type of outdoor trouble each year—so it is well to be prepared.

This Is the Gear Contour map of area to be hunted; huntsman compass; waterproof matchcase and matches; small 6-power magnifying glass to back up your matches; cigarette lighter and small can of lighter fluid. The cigarette lighter will give you 600 to 800 lights if you do not expose the flame too long each time used. The lighter fluid will assist in getting damp wood started when you need a fire for warmth, cooking, or signaling. Three feet of heavy aluminum foil to use as a campfire reflector or for foil cooking; ½-gallon can for making coffee or for cooking; dehydrated rations for 24 hours; 10 extra cartridges or shotgun slugs; 8×10 feet of plastic sheeting for a shelter tarpaulin, and a warm jacket. A poncho can be used to cover you and your pack in case of rain. What will this gear weigh? With a lightweight knapsack and a 7½-pound rifle, the total will be only 15 pounds!

Finding Your Way Fear-gripping and agonizing "lost-in-the-woods" experiences, common outdoor injuries, and hunter-caused fires can be avoided by going into wilderness hunting areas properly prepared. Even the professional hunter has been unable to find his camp several times over the years when fog, rain, snow, or darkness has cut visibility to zero. However, it is possible to make a comfortable bivouac camp until weather conditions moderate. Why? Because one can go prepared, by carrying a lightweight knapsack with sufficient equipment to care for any game killed plus items for comfort if forced to camp out for a day or more. You will have to judge what items suit your personal needs best. With your map and compass you should be able to find your way back to camp or car under most conditions. If you are hopelessly lost, make a comfortable bivouac camp and await rescue.

Hunter's Winter Apparel Checklist The greatest difference when hunting in cold weather is the importance of maintaining body warmth. Warm clothing, shelter, good food, an eiderdown sleeping bag if you can afford one (if not, blankets added to a summer sleeping bag will serve), some type of stove to keep the tent and occupants warm, good boots to keep your feet in shape, and of course snowshoes if the job calls for them are a few of the items necessary for winter travel and hunting. Here are some helpful tips:

Keep clothing as clean and dry as possible to maintain maximum insulation properties.

Snow should be brushed from boots and clothing before entering any shelter.

Carry extra dry socks, gloves, and glove liners. To dry your wet socks, liners, or mittens, put them inside your jacket or parka or dry on a line in your tent. Be sure not to get them too close to the stove. Drying boots should be kept well away from campfire or stove.

Keep clothing items loose and free from binding, particularly on the feet. Your clothing, particularly woolens, should be large enough to allow for shrinkage from washing or dampness.

This is very important in freezing weather: When more than one pair of socks is worn from inner to outer layers, the socks must increase progressively in width as well as length to prevent constriction or pressure on the feet—watch out for wrinkles! Any

Winter hunting can be a great experience if the hunter is properly clothed. BEAR ARCHERY COMPANY

sock-boot combination must allow free movement of the toes. Constant toe and foot exercising when feet begin to numb will prevent a freezing injury.

In extremely cold regions, always control your comfort through intermediate layers of clothing rather than by dispensing with the outside layer. If some garments are removed to keep cool, be sure they are safely stowed in your knapsack. Keep gloves or mittens tied together by a lanyard so they cannot become lost—otherwise a hand or fingers may become frozen.

Don't sweat; keep comfortably cool at all times. Underdress rather than overdress. You may spend much time changing clothing layers, but the effort pays off in helping you keep dry.

If you get too hot, take the following steps until comfortably cool: Take your gloves or mittens off; loosen or remove belt or parka waist-tie; open shirt or parka throat; remove hat or cap or throw parka hood back; shed sweater, shirt, or parka; when through hiking or stopping to rest, put on spare clothing before you start to chill. Be sure that knapsack straps are securely fastened so that no clothing or other articles can become lost!

You will sleep more warmly if you place your sleeping bag on a ground cloth or pad on the tent floor than if you try to sleep up off the tent floor on a cot.

Wear a stocking or knit watch cap at night, and by adding a hot water bag at your feet you should be comfortably warm in freezing temperatures. In a pinch, you can wrap hot rocks from the campfire in whatever cloth you can spare and place at the foot of your sleeping bag.

To keep warm at night in sub-freezing weather, I sleep in a suit of wool long-john underwear with wool socks on my feet, or at times I have found a hooded sweatsuit works very well. Don't ever try to sleep in wet or damp clothing—it just won't work; you'll be cold all night.

Safety First Always make that your motto!

The first requirement in using a hunting weapon is to know how to operate it safely.

Don't go hunting until you have obtained, read, and understand the game laws in the area or state where you plan to hunt.

Comply with all regulations—remember, the fish and game laws are for the benefit of all, not just a few!

Your hunting license doesn't give you authority to enter on or trespass or travel over private land without the permission of the owner.

Don't walk on or across seeded ground or growing crops or you will see more and more "No Shooting"

or "No Trespassing" signs on private property. Don't blame the farmer or rancher if he tries to protect his property from careless hunters or vandals who destroy it.

Close all gates after you. If gates are found open—leave them that way!

A reward will be paid by the Cattle Growers' Association for information leading to a conviction of anyone stealing or shooting cattle. (It happens every hunting season.)

Report anyone who damages any farm, ranch property, buildings, signs, etc. not belonging to him.

Don't approach too near range cattle on foot. They may charge you.

Do not camp too near a water hole. Your camp and activities may frighten away stock that want to drink.

Never attempt to climb over or through a fence with a loaded gun! Hand your weapon to a companion on the other side. If alone, slide it muzzle first through the fence, then crawl under or through it.

Don't be a litterbug by leaving lunch debris, bottles or open cans lying anywhere—the bottles and cans can be dangerous to humans and animals. Leave a clean campsite and your fire OUT!

Always carry your firearm so you can control the direction of the muzzle should you fall. Always keep the safety on until ready to shoot. COURTESY OF THE AUTHOR

Never enter a boat, car, or building with a loaded gun. Unload your weapon before entering camp!

Never discharge a firearm into or across a body of water; bullets tend to ricochet for a great distance on water.

It is not safe to shoot at birds in trees or along a skyline with a rifle. Always be sure to have a safe backstop. A bullet can travel from 1 to 3 miles when shot up at an angle and may kill or wound someone at a distance unknown to you. Use a shotgun for bird shooting; it's safer.

It's against the law to discharge a firearm from a vehicle or from or across a highway!

Unattended firearms should be left unloaded, and in a safe place. Always store guns out of reach of children. It is safer to have them locked up securely so accidents just can't occur.

Do not drink liquor if you are hunting, and don't hunt if you have been drinking! This can be as dangerous as driving a vehicle under the influence of liquor. Wait until you are back at camp or at the hunting lodge where you can enjoy your drink in comfort and safety.

Always carry your firearm so you can control the direction of the muzzle even if you stumble and fall; keep the safety on until you are ready to shoot.

Don't forget that some hawks, owls, eagles, and other birds are protected by law!

Be sure of your target before you squeeze the trigger. Don't shoot unless you can clearly see and are sure of what you are shooting!

REMEMBER that you will be prosecuted if you kill a person while hunting—so don't mistake your father-in-law or someone else for a moose! If you kill or wound another person, it can be costly and you may have to serve time in jail plus paying a fine and heavy damages. Lawsuits can be costly!

Teach your youngsters to be good sportsmen and -women. Teach them safe hunting practices. Teach them conservation, and set good examples.

> "It is the duty of every man to protect himself and those associated with him from accident which may result in injury or death."
>
> ABRAHAM LINCOLN

Tips on Care of Game It is a shame that approximately half of the game shot is mishandled after going to the expense and trouble of getting it out of the woods.

Some "green" hunters hike six to eight or more miles into rough country and kill an elk or moose with no more equipment than a rifle and a hunting knife. After killing one of these animals far in the woods, they haven't the faintest idea how to field dress or get the carcass back to camp or to a road where it can be removed to a freezer. A few will carry a packboard and are able to bring out a quarter of meat at a time. Others are fortunate in being able to reach their kill with a pack animal and remove it before the meat sours. On the Olympic Peninsula and other North Pacific areas, it rains off and on all through elk season and the meat spoils rapidly if it is not properly handled and cared for.

Actually it is not imperative to stick or cut the throat of big game as most hunters do. A modern high-velocity bullet will so disrupt the chest and abdominal cavities that sticking is unnecessary. The cavities fill with blood almost immediately, and very little blood will leak out if the animal's throat is cut.

Don't hunt in rough country unless you're sure you can get the carcass back to camp or a road.
MAINE DEPARTMENT OF ECONOMIC DEVELOPMENT

Put your license tag on the carcass according to your state law as soon as the animal is killed. MAINE DEPARTMENT OF ECONOMIC DEVELOPMENT

Most expert outdoorsmen who wish to preserve good game flavor will dress their kill as soon as it is shot. Birds and fish and all other game should be field dressed as quickly as possible.

Helpful Hints These steps will help you care for wild meat:

Take the following equipment: hunting knife, whestone, belt ax or folding saw, 30 feet of ¼-inch nylon rope, some twine, several pieces of clean cheesecloth (to be used to wipe the inside of the carcass dry), and four muslin sacks, each large enough to hold a quarter of the animal.

Put your license tag on the carcass according to your state law as soon as the animal is killed. In dressing out the animal be sure to retain evidence of sex if bull or buck law applies or according to any specific law of the state in which the animal is killed.

As soon as the animal is felled insert the knife at the point of the brisket with the back of the blade against the breastbone; point the knife toward the backbone at the top of the shoulders just under the windpipe, and cut toward the head. Turn the animal with its head downhill so it will bleed well and quickly. Remove the male sex organs.

After the animal is well bled and drained, open the carcass from vent to throat. Use the hand ax to break the pelvic bone and breastbone. Be careful not to puncture the intestines, paunch, or bladder, or you will taint the meat. Tie these off with twine so that they do not leak fluids.

Turn the carcass with head uphill. Slip your knife forward between the ribs and the paunch and cut the diaphragm loose. Next, cut the windpipe and gullet free at the throat. Take the windpipe and

The practice in some sections of the country is to "hog dress" the animal in the field and bring in the carcass with head and feet intact. U. S. FOREST SERVICE, SOUTHWESTERN REGION

gullet in the left hand and pull backward, at the same time cutting free from the carcass that portion which tends to hold.

CAUTION! Be careful not to cut or nick your hand or fingers while cutting in the confined space of the throat. If you do cut yourself, wash your hands carefully as soon as you finish dressing out the carcass and apply an antiseptic to the cuts to prevent any animal bacteria from causing an infection!

Remove the head (if permissible by local state law) and the remainder of the windpipe and gullet. Remove the legs at the knees. This will remove the metatarsal or musk glands, which are located below the knees.

The customary practice in some sections of the country is to just "hog dress" the animal in the field and bring in the carcass with head and feet intact.

Place the carcass in position to drain. Wipe the inside of the carcass dry with a clean cloth. Do not wash with water. Trim away all bloodshot areas and any parts affected by gunshot or faulty butchering.

In case the carcass cannot be hung or is not to be quartered immediately, place it with the opening down and propped wide open on logs or rocks so that air can circulate underneath. Air will cause the inside to dry and form a protecting glaze on the meat.

To keep flies and insects off until dark, apply black pepper to exposed meat to discourage them.

If the carcass is skinned in camp, hang it with head down, using a gambrel stick between the hind legs. Hang with head up if it is to be transported hog dressed. Spread the carcass open with a short spreader stick across the chest to cool as rapidly as possible to prevent the meat from spoiling. Special precautions are necessary with some carcasses, such as large deer, elk, and moose.

According to local custom and methods of transportation, hog dress or quarter the carcass on its back and with hand ax or saw, split the brisket and down through the center of the backbone from end to end. In order to make the quarters balance, cut the side in two so that the floating ribs remain with the hind quarters. Hang the quarters up high in a cool, dry place overnight to cool and drain.

After the meat has been allowed to cool overnight, place in clean muslin bags.

Packing the meat should be done after the animal heat is gone. Pack the meat in clean canvas with the hair side toward the horse if you are using pack stock. Unpack the meat each night, remove the sack, and hang high up in a cool, dry place out of reach of bears. Of course, this will not be necessary if you can get the carcass into town after it has been field dressed where a butcher can take care of the rest of the butchering, packaging, and freezing.

With automobile transportation, game is often spoiled by hauling carcasses long distances on the fenders next to the hot motor. Travel during the cool of night in hot weather. In many hunting areas there are cold storage plants that will freeze or store meat until the hunter is ready to leave for home.

Don't make a target of yourself by carrying an exposed hide or antlers! If you pack out a game animal by yourself, put plenty of flagging on both you and the animal.

Game meat may be canned, smoked, salted down, and cured the same as beef or pork. Or you can make deer- and elkburgers from scrap meat. Jerky is very tasty, too! (The state game laws should be consulted as to game in possession during closed seasons.)

If it is desired to save the head and scalp for mounting, do not stick the animal in the throat. Just drain well and hog dress. Open the skin squarely on the side of each shoulder, skin down to the leg on one side and cut across to the other leg, preserving the brisket skin intact. Roll the animal over and skin down from the shoulders in the same manner until the cuts in the hide meet. Then starting on the top of the animal and between the shoulders, open the skin up the back of the neck almost to the horns. Pull the skin free from the neck and shoulders and up to the head. Then, and not until then, open the animal's throat and bleed in the usual manner. Blood will ordinarily flow free and drain for at least 30 minutes, and the skin may easily be pulled free.

The reason for skinning the animal so far back is that it is impossible for the most skilled taxidermist to make a decent-looking mount without the entire cape. A neck skin cut where the usual inexperienced hunter thinks is proper will be 8 to 12 inches too short for good mounting.

If you do not care to keep the hide, turn it in to a local Boy Scout troop and they will make good use of it.

Liver, tongue, and kidneys should be placed in a bloodproof or plastic bag. This meat can be eaten at any time. The rest of the meat must cool and hang for a week or more. Green or uncured meat can cause diarrhea unless it is aged properly.

Your Host, the Game Warden Your host in the hunting area is your local game warden. He and the forest officers are there not only to enforce the game laws, but to help you. They will be the first to assist you if you get into any difficulties or become lost.

The smart hunter gets acquainted with his local game warden in town or in the field. The game warden can tell you where your chances are best for securing game and where to pitch your hunting camp to advantage.

Some clubs and lodges have the warden speak before them, and he can obtain many interesting wildlife and hunting slides and movies of interest to the sportsman. Generally, he teaches safe gun handling and marksmanship to the tyro and youngsters under the National Rifle Association program.

Forest Ranger   Park Ranger

Your Forest Ranger and Park Ranger are as anxious as you for a safe, successful hunt. COURTESY OF THE AUTHOR

Chapter 7

THE HUNTING TROUBLESHOOTER

How to Stalk and Still Hunt—the Right Way
The knowledge of how to stalk and hunt is a must if you are going to be successful. Stalking is the ability to travel through the woods unseen and unheard. Can you? If you can your chances of filling your license will be greatly increased.

There is adventure to stalking. It is also a wonderful physical fitness conditioner for the armchair or fireside nimrod who hunts only once a year. However, the conditioning should take place well in advance of opening day; otherwise, as in some other unaccustomed sports, some deskbound characters might be working toward a coronary.

Stalking takes plenty of muscle control, in walking silently and keeping your body in perfect balance at all times; otherwise you might slip, trip, and fall. And to do the job right, it takes strength to move forward in the unaccustomed positions that stalking calls for, using muscles you don't ordinarily realize you have.

Successful stalking is difficult and requires great patience, physical endurance, and experience. If you do not have these traits, you will be more apt to meet with success if you take a stand or shoot from a blind.

Stalking is best done by a lone hunter moving as quietly as possible along ridges, game trails, and areas showing signs of fresh tracks and droppings until game is sighted.

Why Game Spooks Many times while on game patrol during hunting season, I have watched one or more hunters at a distance through my binoculars, stalking deer. In one instance the hunter was moving along a deer trail quietly enough, but I could see light reflecting from his eyeglasses and the stock of his shiny new rifle. Some 50 yards ahead of him was a nice fat three-point buck moving ahead that no doubt had been alerted by these reflecting mirrors. Finally, the deer sneaked behind a stump in some brush a few yards off the game trail and

Successful stalking is difficult and requires patience, endurance, and experience. U. S. FOREST SERVICE, SOUTHWESTERN REGION

the hunter continued right on by, unaware of the deer's presence. A moment later a hunter who had been hiding nearby shot the buck.

Other times I have heard hunters talking or calling to each other as they moved through the forest, and again I have noticed a silent one that was perched high on a rocky point where he could observe the canyon below; but he spoiled his chances by standing up and moving around every few minutes.

I have had hunters walk right past me while I was eating lunch just off a game trail near a little spring. The two were whispering loudly enough to be heard 25 yards away. Both were smoking, and since the fire season was still on, I called for them to stop, and requested that they smoke only at places of habitation. My voice must have been harsh, for it startled them. One dropped his rifle and the other swung around with his gun pointing at my belt buckle. Guess he must of thought I was a bear! Others drag their feet through dry forest litter and loose rocks and spook every deer into the next county.

To get back to the gentleman with the reflecting glasses and shiny rifle stock. About the only

When stalking, be overcautious, move slowly and as silently as possible against or crosswise to the wind. COURTESY OF THE AUTHOR

way to reduce light reflection in this situation would be to attach nonreflecting plastic clip-on lenses and to sand off the highly polished gun stock and forearm and apply a dull, hand-rubbed oil finish.

When stalking, be overcautious, move slowly and as silently as possible against or crosswise to the wind. Watch where you put your feet and look ahead so you don't step on noise-making forest litter. Stop every few yards and look all around you—and listen. Unsuspicious animals sometimes make noise—listen for crackling brush, moving gravel, and rolling rocks; watch for betraying movements . . . the flicking of an ear or tail in the brush. Try and see your game before it sees you. In tracking game, stay on a game trail and look for fresh spoor. On topping a ridge, crawl up the last few yards and peek out through a bush or other forest cover and carefully scan or glass the area beyond. Keep close to the ground while observing the surrounding terrain so you have an advantage over game that might be grazing nearby or at a distance. Never silhouette yourself against the skyline. If game has sighted you but hasn't fled, stop and freeze for a short time. If the animal drops its head to continue grazing, back up slowly out of sight and go around or tack back and forth across your line of approach, always remembering to keep above and to the windward even if you have to go a considerable distance around.

Watch Air Currents In mountain country, a knowledge of the local air currents at different times of the day on each particular slope is helpful. Warm air tends to rise faster on the sunny slopes. Updraft in the daytime and downdraft after the sun drops over the ridge toward evening. The windward and shady sides of the slope cool off quickly. Wet your finger and hold it up or toss a handful of dust or dirt to test the wind direction.

Remember that most wildlife have a keen sense of smell and sight and that you are matching your wits against an adversary that has to be smart to fight enemies and live with nature and the elements. And by all means, don't use after-shave lotion if you shave in the morning. Don't smoke while hiding or while trailing. Air currents carry and waft enough man scent as it is without alerting game to strange smells.

You will be matching your wits against an adversary used to living with natural enemies and the elements. MAINE DEPARTMENT OF ECONOMIC DEVELOPMENT

If there isn't any snow or wet ground for tracking, sneak around the edges of mountain meadows, bluffs, and passes bordering favorite feeding spots. You will recognize the spot—there will be trails, droppings, and other signs.

If you decide to take a stand, sit up against a bluff, rock, or stump. Have at least some brush in the background to break your silhouette. Remain absolutely still. If you have to move your head, do so very slowly, first holding still and observing by turning your eyes right or left. Sitting in "bear clover" or some other pungent plant will help keep man scent to a minimum. If you have to answer a "call of nature" don't leave your rifle standing against a tree out of reach. You might get caught with your pants at half-mast if a startled deer should bounce out from some nearby brush. When finished, emulate the cat by burying it!

Drive Hunting More whitetail deer are taken in the eastern part of the country on deer drives than by any other method, although some sportsmen are successful when using a combination of stalking and driving while others are fortunate by shooting from concealment.

There are two ways of driving. The first is the "area drive," in which watchers locate themselves along game trails, and a number of hunters beat the woods driving game ahead toward the waiting watchers. (However, some smart old bucks will outflank the drivers by sneaking off to the side and backtracking.) This method is best accomplished by stalking quietly so game will move ahead of you. Both stalkers and the men on station will get a chance to shoot, but *extreme caution* must be exercised as the stalkers advance toward the men on watch so that no one is endangered or in line of fire of the other hunters. This method is only used by experienced men who have hunted together for several seasons, and who can rely on each other.

Another technique of drive hunting is the organized still hunt. Two or three hunters accustomed to hunting together and who know the country will hunt different sections of a district, timing it so they converge at approximately the same time at a point where game running ahead of one or another of the hunters cross from one strip of woods to the next. In this type of hunting, game may be moving in more than one direction, and chances are good for each of the gunners to get in a shot. Great care must be used when hunting in this manner because you cannot know exactly where each companion is moving.

In all cases where watchers are left on stand, it is important that each has an unobstructed view for no less than 100 yards to both sides of him so that time is allowed to see game distinctly. It is the responsibility of each hunter to know where the watchers are placed so that he will not shoot in that direction. This can be accomplished by placing each watcher in a prominent spot—near a large rock, big snag, pond, etc., that can be observed by the stalkers as they move along. Each watcher should find a rock, bush, or tree to stand or sit against to break his outline and make himself less visible. The watcher must not move about on stand or leave his allotted post. Never leave your stand and head for camp

Whatever method chosen for driving game, extreme caution must be exercised as stalkers advance. CANADIAN GOVERNMENT TRAVEL BUREAU

because you are cold or tired or haven't the patience, or you will never be asked to hunt with the same companions again. First of all, they do not know what happened to you, and again you may walk into someone's line of fire or frighten game near other watchers.

In the West, the most successful hunters after the big mule deer are the gunners who stalk the wide-open places and those who range far on horseback. Due to having my left hip smashed by a soft-nosed bullet in my earlier ranger days, I don't roam over the hills as easily as I used to. Now I ride horseback to a good spot, turn my horse loose to graze, and shoot from a blind or a place of concealment.

The Advantage of Shooting from a Blind Many successful rifle- and bowmen prefer to shoot from a blind set up near a game crossing where they wait patiently for game to pass by as they leave their bedding grounds early in the morning

Many successful rifle- and bowmen prefer to shoot from a blind set up near a game crossing. BEAR ARCHERY COMPANY

heading for water and feed. If the gunner doesn't see a deer to his liking, he can wait a few hours and hope that these and other deer may return to the same bedding area.

Deer are creatures of habit, and roam around in one general area and watershed until they migrate to their winter range. They also tend to use the same deer runs, so the blind shooter usually has four chances, as the mule deer parade passes his blind twice a day—from bed to water and feeding area and back again in the morning, and again toward late afternoon. And there is always the chance of a bonus shot if other hunters prowling through the woods spook a deer past your hidden blind. Remember —deer head where it is quiet!

Five Types of Blinds Generally, there are five types of blinds: the elevated tree blind, ground, tower, pit, and portable. The elevated blind seems to give most success. Deer haven't many weaknesses, but one of them is the fact that they seldom look up unless some noise, reflection, or movement draws their attention above

them. They constantly scan the landscape and test the air currents about them, but since danger and enemies virtually never come from overhead (mountain lion or cougar excepted), they rarely check above them. Perhaps another point in favor of an elevated blind is the factor of scent. We know that warm air tends to rise upward, and the body scent of the hunter perched in a tree or on the roof of an abandoned cabin or tower-blind may never drift downward to alarm an approaching animal. Air currents tend to rise uphill shortly after sunrise and downhill toward evening as the land cools. However, at times, in some hilly and mountain sections, the wind is apt to become variable.

The Blind Site No blind is any better than the location and the site upon which it is erected. That calls for a reconnaissance of the area before the hunting season opens. Look over the lay of the land for game, and signs to insure that game is present. Look for areas that deer are using: forest openings, meadows, edges of swamps, springs, busy runways and deer crossings, old abandoned orchards—then locate and build a blind so that you have natural woods cover in the background, generally above the game trail. On which side of the trail you build your blind will depend on the local prevailing wind direction. You will want the wind toward you or at least quartering.

An elevated blind can be any kind of a structure which will not be too conspicuous and will place the hunter above the "scene of action." Once I killed a deer while perched quietly on top of a large stump. The buck walked right by me about ten feet away, looked around, seemed a little suspicious, snorted, and started to trot off stiff-legged—when I dropped him. The stump was approximately eight feet tall. The deer never looked up!

Blind Construction A blind should do at least three things: blend with the surroundings or at least look natural if in the open; provide freedom of movement and for shooting; and conceal the hunter.

I generally have good results using lightweight camouflage netting that comes in a roll 38 inches wide and 15 yards long; and only costs me $3

The right way to construct a blind is to use material that blends well with the background. BEAR ARCHERY COMPANY

The dark evergreen limbs in this blind are out of place among the light poplar trees.
BEAR ARCHERY COMPANY

and lasts for several seasons. I tack it to the railing around my tree blind platform, then add several sections of natural brush cover to break the even outline of the railing and netting.

Naturally, the bow hunter will have to build his blind closer to a deer run than that of the rifleman—about 25 to 30 yards is about right for me. The rifleman can stand his off about 50 to 100 yards or so, just as long as he has a clear line of fire and knows the midrange of his rifle and has it sighted in for 100 yards.

Camouflage Outfits It is sometimes wise to cover a ground blind with inexpensive camouflage netting. If snow is on the ground, I use old white sheets plus netting for cover. Added to this is a white parka with hood, or white coveralls, white cotton gloves, and a white painter's cap. During warm weather I cut a headhole through the center of a piece of camouflage netting the size of a single bedsheet and wear it as a serape, and find it cooler than a full camouflage suit. During cold weather I wear the works—camouflage suit, cap, facemask, and gloves. If I happen to be hunting with a bow, I use a camouflage bow sock or boot. To cut light reflection on my pet rifle, I have had the barrel parkerized, and have sanded the glossy finish from the stock and forearm and added a hand-rubbed oil finish. However, my wife wouldn't let me touch her personal firearms—she likes the beautiful shiny finish.

Digging a pit for the feet and legs puts the hunter lower to the ground and he can thus use less material for the blind construction. BEAR ARCHERY COMPANY

If you are using a pit blind, only the upper half of your body needs to be camouflaged. If the weather is inclement, I sometimes use a camouflage poncho. However, I find that the material makes a swishy noise, and that isn't good.

If you decide to build a ground blind from natural material nearby, it should be more or less circular in shape—about 6 feet in size will do, and it should be high enough to cover all but your head. Place it against a background of bushes or trees to hide your silhouette.

You may have to wait all day in your hideout to ambush the animal you want to put in your home food locker, and to do a good job of watching a gunner must be able to sit down, stretch, and change positions without causing too much of a disturbance. Otherwise, after a long, silent wait, you may become too cramped to aim and shoot accurately. The ground inside should be cleared of all leaves, twigs, and other noise-making debris so that any necessary movement inside can be made silently.

Don't forget, a hunter who waits in ambush for game to pass by his blind or place of concealment has a big advantage over the stalking nimrod attempting to "pussyfoot" over dry, crackling forest cover. Movement in the woods is as conspicuous to animal and bird life as a three-alarm fire is to us in the city, and I have yet to see the sportsman who can move through the woods unseen, unheard, or unscented! The average hunter sneaking along usually moves too fast, doesn't stop enough to listen for woods and animal sound, and isn't too careful where he steps. Man is a stranger in the woods, and this stirs up all the little woods "tattletales"—jays, magpies, and crows start squawking the alarm, and squirrels start their scolding—all signaling their "deer" friends of the presence of intruders.

If you are hunting with a bow when game approaches your blind, let the animal come broadside to you if possible. Otherwise, if you release your arrow while it is coming toward you, you may hit it in the face or spook it. A frontal shot is difficult to make and usually just badly wounds the animal. The rifleman can shoot from many angles with his longer ranged weapon, and therefore has a little more edge over the bowman.

The River Hunt   Silent float hunting in a canoe, or drifting down a stream in a rubber raft or portable car-top boat can be a wonderful experience if you plan ahead for this little-known method of hunting. Check with your local game warden and ascertain the rivers and streams that are near and safe enough for a weekend float jaunt, and if the game conditions along the route are good. Be sure that there are no rapids that might force you to portage, or at least "line" your craft around them. Usually by this method (floating) you can reach regions that the average hunter never gets near. Because you float downstream silently, your chances of spotting game are greatly enhanced. Why not try this method sometime and see if you are not more successful in bagging game? It also saves the strenuous hiking and climbing that the foot stalker is forced to make. It has worked for many others, and it should for you! You can drive your car-top craft or trailer your boat to the nearest launching site, and take off. A small outboard motor can be used for the return trip upstream to your car, or arrangements can be made to have someone pick up your gear at a designated spot downstream Sunday evening. You can use the checklist on the following page for ideas on what to take. Take as little or as much as you deem necessary to fit your own personal needs. You can best determine this after a few trial jaunts.

Storage of Gear   Gather all your gear a few days ahead of the trip and store it in a mouse-proof, safe place. To save time, pack all your gear and equipment in your car the night before so that no time is wasted getting an early start in the morning. This is basic for any hunting trek!

Packing Your Craft   The load should be packed in waterproof duffel bags. Put heavy loads on the bottom for ballast and balance. The load should be securely lashed down with the tent on top and a canvas tarpaulin over all to keep the contents dry. If the craft should capsize for any reason, you will be able to salvage the craft and its contents on some sandbar or in the shallows downstream. All personnel should wear life preservers!

The river hunt can be a wonderful experience if well planned. Usually by this method you can reach regions the average hunter never gets near. JOHNSON MOTORS NEWS BUREAU

Canoe, Raft, Boat, Float Hunt Checklist—Two Hunters

	Lbs.	Ozs.
2 Air mattresses	4	0
1 Aluminum fire grate	1	0
1 Aluminum griddle	3	0
1 Ax, single-bit	3	0
1 Bottle water-purifying tablets (50)	0	1
1 Bucket, plastic	0	8
1 Bug bomb or insect repellent	0	8
1 Camp kitchen kit	2	0
2 Candles	0	4
1 Canteen, gal. filled	8	0
1 Compass w/sight line	0	4
1 Cook kit, nesting type	6	0
4 Duffel bags, canvas	3	0
1 Fire permit if required	0	0
1 First aid kit	1	0

	Lbs.	Ozs.
2 Flashlights	1	0
1 Folding saw	1	6
2 Knives, BSA or marine	0	6
1 Map, large-scale	0	2
2 Match safes	0	2
1 Matches, 1 box, waterproofed	0	2
1 Notebook and pencil	0	4
2 Ponchos	2	8
1 Reflector oven	2	0
2 Rifles or shotguns	14	8
2 Sets of moccasins for camp use	2	4
1 Shovel, "O" size	3	2
2 Sleeping bags	8	0
2 Pr. sunglasses	0	4
1 Tarpaulin, optional	6	0
1 Tent, optional	6	0
2 Toilet kits	2	0
1 Rope, ¾-inch nylon, 100 feet	1	8

Good planning can make a many-vehicle hunting trip a pleasure. U. S. FOREST SERVICE,
SOUTHWESTERN REGION

Add two pounds of dehydrated food per day per person. Don't forget ammunition, gun-cleaning gear, or your licenses. Wear life preservers if the water is rough. An extra paddle is warranted. Take mosquito netting if appropriate. Plan on which side of the craft each of you will shoot from. Camp above high water mark for safety from any possible flash flood!

Checklist for the Automobile Camper—Two Hunters If you, like most other hunters, are limited to the car trunk and possibly a car-top carrier or small two-wheel utility trailer for storage, you'll want to think about packing the most comfort in the least space. Otherwise you may cramp a hunting partner forced to sit in the back seat with most of the gear. Don't forget that the last things to come out of the vehicle should be the first to go in. And don't pile gear on top of the spare tire, tools, jack, shovel, ax, or skid chains. Pack them so they are handy for emergencies. Some thought should be given to providing storage space for game on the return trip; few hunters give this the consideration it deserves. One or two deer or a bear plus hunting, camping gear, and passengers can load the car down dangerously low on the springs, making it difficult to steer. It's hard on tires too! You are cautioned to drive carefully on steep curves, especially with a top-heavy camper.

The following list is made up for two hunters. If there are more in the party, perhaps another vehicle is indicated. Additional sleeping bags, tableware, and camp chairs if you use them—and extra grub! Your summer vacation sleeping bags will do for fall hunting if you add a couple of blankets inside them, unless you want to go to the expense of buying a feather bag.

Air pump (1), optional; can use car pump or mouth to blow up sleeping bags

Aluminum griddle (1), optional

Aluminum or canvas folding chairs (2), optional

Ax, with 2¼-lb. head and 28-inch handle w/ sheath, (1)

Ball hitch for trailer (1), optional

Broom (small child's size) (1), for sweeping out floor of tent

Buckets (2), one folding canvas and one plastic

Bug bomb (1), insect repellent, small bottle per person

Camera, film, filters, flashbulbs, optional

Camp stove, folding grill type (1), optional

Camp stove, gasoline or canned gas type, two-burner (1)

Camp stove, wood, cook and heater (1), optional

Canteen (1), gallon size; water bag (1)

Canvas windbreak or tarpaulin for sun and rain, 10×12 ft., optional

Chain, tow chain for car, or steel cable, hook at each end—15 ft.

Charcoal briquettes for grill, optional

Cleaning material, detergents, sponges, soap, steel wool, etc.

Coffeepot if one in nested cook kit isn't large enough (1), optional

Compass with sighting line and adjustable for declination, (1) each

Cook outfit, 4-man aluminum nesting type, add kitchen and tableware, knives, forks, spoons, can opener, spatula, salt and pepper shakers, butcher and bread knives, extra plastic bowls and dishes, washpan, etc.

Fire permit if needed in certain areas of the Southwest, etc.

Fire extinguisher, Du Gas or CO_2 (carbon tet. not used any more), (1)

Firearms, gun-cleaning gear, ammunition, hunting license, binoculars

First aid kit, add prescriptions needed, laxative, roll of two-inch tape, wire splints (2), etc. Ask your doctor to help make up a list for your personal needs. Add a snake bite kit (suction type; if you are hunting much in desert country or southern states, snakes stay out late, add an antivenin syringe type, metal wound clamps (6), water-purification tablets (50), codeine, sulfa, sleeping tablets

Flashlights (2), with extra batteries and bulbs

Funnel with strainer for filling gas stove and lantern (1)

Icebox, insulated type (1)

Jack, bumper type (1); hydraulic type (1)

Jacket and extra clothing for each member, rain-gear for all

Kits, toilet, kit bags, duffel bags for protection of sleeping gear and tent

Lanterns, electric, gasoline, or canned gas, (1), extra gas mantles, generators, wrenches, etc.

Maps, road type and Geological Survey contour, large-scale of area

Matches, large kitchen size box (1)

Mattress or cot ticks (2), optional

Mirror, steel type for shaving and toilet (1)

Night clothes, warm flannel type, blankets, cots (2), optional

Oven, camp stove type, reflector oven, optional

Pick, small Army type (1)

Pillows (2), optional

Plastic washbowl, juicer, and Jeep water can, (1) each, optional

Portable folding camp toilet or old-fashioned "highboy," optional

Pressure cooker (1), optional but strongly recommended

Saw, folding camp type (1), optional

Shovel, "O" or Forester type (1)

Checklist for the Small Travel Trailer or Self-Contained Pickup Camper In Addition to above:

Flags, red road signal type (3)

Flares (3), red glass road reflectors or kerosene bomb type (3)

Flashlight, electric, with flashing red light and white spotlight, (1)

Funnel for filling water tank (1)

Funnel with strainer for filling gas tank (1)

Hose, sewer hose, carry in 4-in. hose carrier under trailer (1)

Hose, short piece for draining into "gopher hole" near trailer (1)

Hose, sink hose, largest size that will fit standard fittings (1)

Hose, (2), 25-ft. high-pressure type for filling water tank from hydrant

Jacks (2), screw type for under trailer axle while parked

Light cord, electric heavy-duty type for plugging in trailer lights, minimum of 50 feet

Stepup, Pullman type (1)

Deer hunters bring this fine 8-point buck into camp on a pole over their shoulders.
U. S. FOREST SERVICE

Tires, spare for car and spare for trailer, tool kit, four-way lug wrench, extra valves, butane or propane tank connectors and washers, rubber tape, extra fuses for car and trailer; and be sure that your car and trailer insurance is still in force!

Pointers on How to Increase Your Hunting Skill
It doesn't matter whether you walk, sit, or stand, the secret of the successful hunter of any of the deer species is SILENCE, and *knowledge* of deer habits and of the terrain. Next to shooting from a blind, sitting in concealment is the most effective method of bagging deer, especially whitetail bucks. Particularly when the woods are bone dry, noisy, or full of hunters, the sitter must choose the proper place to sit. His "sit" or ambush should be off to one side of a deer run as was outlined earlier in shooting from a blind. The sitter's best spot should be in fairly

dense cover, since deer move from swamp to oak or beech ridge in the East to lower country, and through deerbrush, bitterroot and chaparral in the West; from bed point to abandoned orchard or meadow edge, by protected routes rather than through open meadows or saddle passes.

If the hunter can get above the likely route or deer crossing, so much the better, since the visibility is better and deer seem less conscious of danger from above. Furthermore, no matter how gentle the breeze may be, the prevailing wind must be taken into consideration. The thermal draft is gradually uphill as the sun warms the earth, and downward as the sun sets and the woods cool. Deer take advantage of this and bed down on the windward or warmer side of ridges during the night, then move to the cooler section during the day. During cold weather you will notice more of these bedding grounds on the warm side. Droppings, tracks, and other signs will be more plentiful. Hunt out these small "bedding grounds" and you will have better luck. In heavily hunted areas, deer will feed during moonlit nights, and hide out and bed down during the day—usually just over the top of a ridge in dense brush or in a thicket of trees. In this case, they have to be kicked out with dogs (if this is legal in your state), or by the hunter. This is difficult to do since the deer move out ahead of the hunter searching the bedding ground. It is best to post a hunting pal or other hunters around the sides and other end. In that manner someone will probably get a shot at a deer sneaking out. If you try this stunt, be sure it is a deer you are shooting at and not one of the other hunters. It has happened!

During heavy rain, snow, and stormy weather, deer and other game seek shelter the same as people do, and it is practically useless to hunt during these periods; and there is always a possibility that you may become turned around or lost in strange terrain due to poor visibility. If the storm lasts several days, as the deer become more hungry they will come out and feed during a lull and then "hole up" again until the storm breaks.

Deer tend to gather near salt blocks that cattlemen have placed in mountain meadows. Shooting deer at these salt licks is comparable to shooting quail on the ground or sitting ducks on the water. Most sportsmen won't do it.

What Caliber Rifle or Shotgun Gauge for Deer and Bear? If you want to get a good argument started, just say that the so-and-so gun is the best all-around deer musket. The type of firearm you use should be tailored to the terrain (long or short shooting distance) in which you are going to hunt and kind of hunting you are going to do—plus state regulations. So before starting out, be sure to check state game laws and type of arms allowed. As a matter of fact,

Remington 870 Wingmaster pump action shotgun, 12-gauge, 5-shot. REMINGTON ARMS

.22-caliber Autoloader, Nylon 66. MOHAWK BROWN

Remington 552 BDL deluxe .22-caliber automatic rifle. REMINGTON ARMS

before you purchase a deer rifle you'd better find out if the state will permit a rifle at all!

Where to Aim to Get a Killing Shot When you sight your animal, try and judge the range as accurately as possible. In short-range shooting from a blind, you will have to remember the range your rifle is sighted in for, and remember the midrange trajectory or you will overshoot the animal. The same applies to longer range shooting—remember your point-blank range! The best area to aim on game is the heart-lungs region, just behind the foreshoulder and just below midway of the animal.

Snap shooting is necessary only when the gunner is in cover where game in flight is visible for just a few seconds. This may be when the animal flushed from cover is forced to cross a short opening in the woods. The point now is to concentrate your aim on one tiny vital spot—never shoot at the whole animal or you may "gut shoot" it and spoil a lot of meat if your bullet connects, or you may just wound the animal and lose it entirely. *Squeeze off the shot* —don't get excited and pull the trigger as you would with a fowling piece, or you will miss your mark. Any shot through the ribs close to the shoulder will hit the heart or lungs.

Look for Evidence of a Hit When the animal is hit, check its line of flight if it isn't killed instantly and takes off. Then remain quietly where you are for 20 to 30 minutes. The animal will shortly lie down and stiffen up in the first available cover until death occurs (that is, if you wounded it fatally). Usually wounded game will head downhill or along the lines of least resistance. If you push game too closely after a hit, it may travel a considerable distance and make tracking difficult.

Never leave the area after having fired at game without checking and following up the tracks for signs of blood or hair that indicate a hit. If the animal flinches, drops its tail, or hunches up, it likely has been hit. Try and find the spot where he was when you fired. If you "tagged" him at all, there usually will be a spray of hair cut by the bullet on the side opposite his tracks from where you shot. Look for blood or pieces of shattered bone which may indicate the nature of the wound. But remember, lack of blood or other sign doesn't always mean that you have missed. When you finally locate the animal and it is still alive, you should do your utmost to make your next shot count—otherwise, once frightened out of its bed he may lead you a long chase or escape, and a lot of good meat will have been wasted.

Tracking Game It takes good woodsmanship trailing and tracking wild game, and it cannot be overemphasized. Any sportsman worth his salt should learn to track game, especially if he has wounded a critter. Tracking game or human beings is one of the world's oldest skills. In snow, in mud, sand, dust, and moist soil, tracks can be easily observed. You have to get out into the woods, visit the beaches and mountains, hit the trails and old logging roads, firebreaks and motorways and follow and reason them out to become an expert hunter and tracker.

Taking Care of Your Firearms Rifles and shotguns are built to last a lifetime with proper care and maintenance. New guns should be gone over carefully and all grease or spray preservatives in which they may be packed when shipped should be removed. Firing a weapon with heavy gun grease in the barrel can result in a serious accident not only to the gun, but to the shooter. If you accidentally drop your gun in dirt or snow, be sure none of it has gotten into the barrel—wipe the gun off and *don't fire it* until you are sure the bore is clear. If you are hunting in extremely cold weather, oil and grease can stiffen and slow down the action of the firing pin to the point where it does not strike the cartridge primer with sufficient force to fire it. Use a gun solvent and remove all oil.

When hunting in the foggy and wet coastal areas near salt water, the firearm should be wiped off now and then during the day with an oily cloth to prevent rusting. When through with the day's hunt, it pays to run dry cleaning patches through the bore. When the patches come out clean, repeat the process, now using a good solvent on the patches. When these come through clean, dry the bore and run through a patch soaked with a light grade of gun oil. Use a soft oily cloth to wipe out the action and all outside metal parts so that all moisture and perspiration from your hands are removed.

Storing Arms If you store your gun(s) for several months they should be thoroughly cleaned and oiled. If stored for longer periods, they should be given a light coat of gun grease, or a preservative should be sprayed on them. Never plug up the barrel or leave an oily rag or cord in it. Beware of some sheep-lined gun boots and cases. Sometimes the material contains tanning chemicals or dye that will cause rust and ruin the gun finish.

Free Gun-Cleaning Guide Send for your free gun-cleaning guide to Frank A. Hoppe, Inc., 2321 N. 8th Street, Philadelphia, Pennsylvania 19133.

Chapter 8

THE SPORT AND TECHNIQUE OF UPLAND BIRD HUNTING

Men and women who hunt love upland bird hunting for a multitude of reasons. There is something about the adventure of bringing down a fast-flying bird on the wing that challenges one's coordination and reflexes. The wily pheasant, the unpredictable woodcock, the rocketing quail, and the crafty grouse are among the nation's most elusive game birds, worthy of matching wits with the cleverest hunter and retriever. Many a startled gunner has stood and watched a bird zoom away without even raising his weapon. It takes quick reflexes, alertness, and skill born of experience to make a real upland bird hunter. But when the birds fly thick and fast, and when you and your hunting dog work together in perfect coordination, you can't beat upland game hunting for real sport.

While tramping the woods and fields with smoothbore and dog, one senses a feeling of freedom and relaxation from the cares of urban life. When out hunting, you breathe fresh air, smell woodsy odors, feel the good earth underfoot, and get the exercise most of us need today. Ahead of you stretches a whole day of adventure.

Quail There are perhaps more hunters out for the several species of quail than any other upland bird. More than forty states have quail of one or more species. Quail season, too, is the longest of all game birds.

The bob-white ranges from central New England down into the deep South and from the Atlantic coast throughout the midwestern states.

When birds fly thick and fast, and when you and your dog work together in perfect coordination, you can't beat upland game hunting for real sport.
MAINE DEPARTMENT OF ECONOMIC DEVELOPMENT

The scaled and desert Gambel are found throughout the southwestern states, and valley and mountain quail from the state of Washington south into Mexico.

Valley quail is not only the most popular game bird of its genus, but a worthy competitor of the celebrated bob-white. This quail will lie well to a dog, and some old quail gunners say the valley birds are more alert and make sportier shooting.

Mountain quail, sometimes called mountain partridge, are the largest of the quail group, weighing from one-half to three-quarters of a pound, and measuring twelve inches in length compared to the average nine inches of the bob-white.

The primary difference among the three types of mountain quail is in minor variation of coloration, for they all range between eleven and twelve inches in length, and are similar in habits.

Although this bird is an inhabitant of the mountain slopes, it is found in widely diversified range along the Pacific coast, and lives from humid valleys of the California coast to the plains of Oregon, from chaparral brush thickets to the banks of rushing streams.

The northern bird is found on the Cascade and Sierra Nevada Ranges from Oregon south to Nevada and west to California. The central bird inhabits the high coastal mountains as well as the semi-arid sections of Oregon south to California. The southern mountain quail is distributed along the mountains of Southern California into the mountainous sections of Baja California.

The scaled quail is a bird of the arid southwestern regions of the United States and northwestern Mexico. The behavior pattern of this desert bird and that of the bob-white is similar, since the quail is characteristically a bird of habit. When undisturbed, it is given to repeating its feeding time and place and roosting hours in the same routine manner each day.

It feeds on the seeds of mesquite, cactus, sage, and weeds and, near agricultural areas, grain such as wheat, corn, oats, etc. The most important fruits are from orchards and wild desert berries from juniper, desert hackberry, mistletoe, barrel cactus, and other desert plants. Its animal food consists mostly of insects such as grasshoppers.

The Gambel or desert quail is one of several species of western upland quail. It is a handsome and good-eating bird, and has its own following of sportsmen. These birds of the desert are talkative when feeding. Their most common call is a shrill "chu-chaaa, chu-chaaa" uttered by the cock and audible at a considerable distance. Both male and female birds use the scatter call,

"quirrt, quirrt." Like the bob-white, valley quail signal with the familiar "cha-qua-qua." Mountain quail have more of a shrill call than the smaller birds.

How to Hunt Them   When hunting any species of quail, the gunner must look for areas where their natural food is abundant. All quail food consists of wild fruits, berries, weed seeds, field grain, and insects—and of course they will move in on the farmer's orchards and berry patches occasionally.

If you hunt in a new or unfamiliar area, contact the local game warden for the best hunting section for coveys of quail. If you cannot contact the warden, ask a few ranchers where to shoot. If they have quail on their property, ask for permission to hunt if the land is not posted.

In most regions, dogs are used to advantage to point and retrieve quail. However, unless the dog is well trained, it can spoil your hunt by ranging too far in advance and flushing game out of range. Desert quail would rather run than fly, and even some good bird dogs will flush them before the gunner can get in a shot. Bird dogs are a necessity in dense cover, otherwise too many crippled and downed birds would be lost.

In the Southwest, Jeeps and other four-wheel, four-speed-drive vehicles are used for cross-country hunting so that vast sections of desert can be searched for birds. The dogs ride until a covey is encountered. Some hunters outfit their dogs with soft leather bootees to keep them from becoming sore-footed in cactus areas. Saddle horses are also used, with the dogs foraging ahead or trailing the riders.

When hunting in Arizona and along the Mexican border, I often carry a few shells loaded with buckshot or slugs in case I run into a herd of peccary (wild pig). Some hunters are fortunate and obtain a mixed bag of quail, rabbit, and peccary.

If you are an experienced quail shooter, you will recall that at one time or another the quail has shown his full bag of evasive tricks. If you are a novice, you conclude that they just can't be hit. But there is something about quail shooting that is a challenge; so you keep on trying until you learn how to drop him, and there is the thrill even if you miss him.

Some scattergunners will admit that more

times than they want to recall, they have had jangled nerves when Mr. Quail rocketed off unannounced practically under their feet. With a whirr, those short wings beat a tattoo on the thin air and startle and thrill you all in an instant—and he disappears like magic if you are not prepared for this.

Why are they difficult to hit? The answer is because quail are temperamental. They just refuse to obey or conform to a fixed pattern when it comes to survival. Quail will get up practically under your feet and fly straight at you; behind you; and sail straight away from you, suddenly climb, or quickly dive. But *he can be hit*, with a little practice.

First of all, you must train yourself to remain calm. (But how can you when a ball of feathered dynamite explodes in front of your face and cannonballs off brush-high and out of sight?) At least you can be prepared by expecting a bird or covey to flush any moment when you have located birds and have your shotgun at the ready. Many easy shots have been missed simply because the shooter was not expecting a bird at the moment and was not ready to swing, lead, and fire. And again, the tyro makes the mistake of shooting at the whole covey instead of picking out a single bird and staying with it. I personally have better results picking out one of the lead birds and working back. In this manner I have at times been able to collect doubles before the birds were out of range.

Generally quail are shot at close range. This, together with their explosive flight, calls for a lightweight, short-barreled, open-bore shotgun using Nos. 6, 7½, or 8 shot. For thick brush areas most hunters find that No. 8 or No. 9 give a more dense pattern. For the species of quail that gets up and away, No. 6 shot is the answer.

What Gun? Just as in any other type of hunting, the gun one shoots best will be the most practical for quail, but the 12-gauge is the most widely used. The 16- and 20-gauge are also excellent choices. The gun should have a fairly open bore, for a closed-choke barrel gives too tight a pattern at close range resulting in too many mangled birds. If a double-barreled weapon is your choice, a left barrel of modified choke and a right barrel of improved cylinder

is best. For the gunners who prefer the pump gun, the autoloader, or the single-barrel, without the addition of a choking device, a modified choke would be most practical.

To balance out on both short- and long-range shots, I use No. 8 shotshells for the first two shots in my lightweight autoloader with a charge of No. 6 to back them up if I am lucky enough to get a third shot, which naturally would be at longer range. On my particular shootin' iron, I have set my choke device at improved cylinder for best results. The pump-gun man can do the same with whatever choke device he has. For the double-barrel shooter, a load of Nos. 7½ or 8 shot can be used in the more open barrel, and No. 6s in the tighter barrel to cover both short- and long-range shots. Each hunter will have to pattern his particular shotgun to find out the load and shot patterns it gives to best advantage.

Chukar The chukar partridge is one of the newest upland game birds that have been imported into this country from Asia. It is catching on fine and is increasing in most areas where planted—and it is excellent eating, too! Chukars have been established with considerable success west of the Mississippi, but do poorly east of it. They do best in arid and semi-arid regions of our western states. While they are creatures of the more brushy country of their homeland, they have become well adapted to prairie terrain here in the States. Grouse-size, they are easily distinguished by their red legs, gray coat, and scalloped wings. They are identified by a peculiar chu-a-chuk, chuk-a-chuk calling, and can be heard on a still morning over a mile distant. The chukar with practically all white meat is one of the tastiest of upland birds.

Unlike other partridge, the chukar keeps to dry bluff edges where foliage leaves off and dirt slides begin, arroyos, and on ridges having sparse mahogany, chamise, cedar, and sagebrush-like foliage. Chukars feed similarly to quail and other partridge. Like many game birds, the "redlegs" is more omnivorous and is able to live off the land in semi-arid areas with little difficulty.

In hunting "chuks" the first thing is to learn in what regions they have been planted. You will be more successful hunting this wily bird if you use a good bird dog. Any dog that will work quail will do. It will also save a lot of leg-work running down cripples or birds that have been dropped across an arroyo by having a dog retrieve for you.

Chukar, like quail, travel in coveys and if pinned down by a dog before they start running will flush like quail; it will be a spine-tingling experience. A hunter coming upon a covey unexpectedly can have his nervous system so shocked by these birds flushing close in that he may fail to raise his gun in time to shoot. Hunting singles after a covey breaks cover is more difficult than with other birds, since they scatter over a longer distance.

The chukar is a fast flier, and an amateur at the game might do well to use a 12-gauge shotgun using Nos. 6, 7½, or 8 with their considerably greater shots per shell than a 16- or 20-gauge gun. However, that is a matter of opinion among sportsmen.

It would be wise to carry at least a belt canteen, for water is not only scarce in chukar country, it may be alkaline or otherwise undrinkable. And don't forget that your dog(s) will need to drink too!

Presently, the following states have open seasons on chukar partridge: California, Colorado, Idaho, Montana, Nevada, Oregon, Utah, Washington, and Wyoming.

Grouse Grouse are fairly numerous in species, and range the North American continent. The ruffed grouse is one of the larger of the upland game birds, and is about the size of a small chicken. An adult male measures an average of 19 inches long and weighs from 24 to 30 ounces. Mr. Drummer is the most popular of the grouse family, due to his widespread distribution, which includes the entire eastern part of Canada and states south to the northern tier of the southern states. The Oregon ruffed grouse is a subspecies found in northern California, Oregon, Washington, and British Columbia and as far north as Alaska. This bird has much more reddish plumage than the ordinary ruffed grouse. The gray ruffed grouse, another subspecies, is very similar to the Canadian ruffed grouse, but is generally lighter in color. It is found chiefly in the Rocky Mountain regions of the States, and as far north as Alaska and east to Manitoba.

The Canadian or spruce grouse lives in northern New England, New York, Michigan, and Minnesota, westward to Alaska and Canada and along the northern border of the States. The Franklin, blue, dusky, and sooty grouse inhabit conifer country of the West among pines and firs of that region. The sharptail is largely confined to the Northwest, but is beginning to edge in with the prairie grouse of the plains country. The prairie "chicken" or pinnated grouse, unlike most of the other species, likes open plains and inhabits the prairies of Canada and scattered spots of the Midwest grasslands. The sage grouse is the granddaddy of them all and is the largest of the grouse family. It is found in most of the sage areas of the West and Middle West.

Hungarian Partridge The Hun or gray, as it is sometimes called, is a tough bird that can stand drought and severe winters better than most upland game birds. Hun partridges are gregarious at least part of the year, and travel in coveys like quail and chukar. Such coveys are generally led by an old cock that has survived several years. Like quail, they roost on the ground and in a circle with their heads pointing outward. When flushed, they rise as a group like the white-winged dove, then scatter to the four winds, frequently uttering squeaks, and their wingbeats whirr as loudly as those of the grouse.

They prefer wide-open terrain and are seldom found in wooded areas. Their diet consists of both grain and insects, about the same as that of the other grouse.

The Hungarian partridge does not migrate, but remains fairly constant over its entire range. These tasty birds are widely distributed throughout the wheat belts of Canada and the United States, and are found throughout small areas in some of the eastern states to a lesser degree.

The Hun flies like a quail, but seemingly faster, runs like pheasant with a tailwind, and is smart enough to outwit some bird dogs. The pheasant usually takes off running in a more or less straight line down a corn row, fence, or ditch, but Mr. Hun doubles and twists and circles until a keen-nosed bird dog cannot unravel the scent and escape route.

Grouse and Partridge Staples Grouse, like

other wildlife, lives close to its food supply, which includes the wild berries, grapes, the bright fruit of black alder and dogwood (including the poison sumac which do grouse no injury), grain dropped in stubble of harvested fields, the foliage of many plants, and leaf buds of numerous shrubs and trees. In northern forests where berries are prevalent, grouse are plentiful. Clover is also a favorite food for grouse. Other dainties preferred include crickets, grasshoppers, bugs, the larvae of caterpillars, and the wild nuts of beech and chestnut. This varied menu high in protein is responsible for the bird's luscious, tender flesh and its roving disposition.

How to Locate Them First find out from your local game warden or forest officer where they are located, then enter the territory ahead of the hunting season and reconnoiter so that you may become familiar with the terrain. Grouse will be where their food is plentiful. Look for bird tracks, droppings, and dust baths along old logging and fire roads. Listen for drumming grouse!

The male to attract the female during courtship will drum its wings, while sitting on a log or stump. This drumming is so rapid that it sounds similar to a chainsaw starting up. Grouse are never far from water. The experienced grouse hunter will follow up the small creeks rather than the ridges, especially in the pine- and fir-belt area. Grouse like man-made trails and roads where they can get gravel to digest the food in their crop, take dust baths, and strut about. Grouse is one upland bird that can be hunted without the service of a dog. If flushed, it will run too far ahead of a hunter as some covey birds are apt to do at times. Invariably, a flushed grouse will dodge between trees, leaving brush and timber between it and the gunner.

When hunting grouse in low-level cover, move slowly, for they will often lie close to the ground and allow the hunter to come within a few feet before taking off like a jet. The grouse is one of the most alert of upland game birds and will stick pretty close to dense cover in most regions. The action is swift, sudden, and startling, catching many hunters flatfooted and off base with the sudden roar of whirring wings. In flight the grouse is erratic, and swiftly speeds away—dipping and dodging to put all possible natural cover between itself and its pursurer. The

birds must be hunted slowly and easily and you must be prepared for their erratic flight. Sometimes a bird will thunder from practically under your feet and startle you so that you may miss your target. Other times he will flush silently as a ghost! This calls for snap shooting, so it is imperative that the gunner be alert and ready to shoot instantly!

If wounded, grouse will not run far. Downed birds may be located from the sound of the rapid fluttering of their wings, a trait of dying grouse. If you miss, don't give up. Unhit birds seldom fly far and will generally sit tight until flushed again. Try and mark where the bird was dropped, and hunt in a more or less straight line and then in increasing concentric circles until you locate your quarry.

Where to Go for Prairie Chicken Nebraska, South Dakota, and Idaho offer simultaneous hunting for both sharptails and greater prairie chickens. Both these prize prairie grouse are similar in appearance, habits, and habitat. Adult cocks of both species weigh between 2 and 3 pounds, and adult hens weigh almost 2 pounds. Going away, both birds are predominantly gray-brownish and hen-pheasant-like in general appearance. However, the sharptail is easily distinguished from the prairie chicken, even in flight, by its sharply pointed tail and white underparts. The tail of the prairie chicken, however, is short and rounded, and the underparts are heavily barred with black and white feathers.

These States Have Them These states usually offer sharptail gunning: Alaska, Colorado, Idaho, Michigan, Minnesota, Montana, Oregon, North Dakota, Washington, Wisconsin, and Wyoming. And three other states usually hold prairie chicken seasons: Kansas, New Mexico, and Oklahoma. By writing to the Fish and Game Department of any of the prairie-grouse states listed above for upland bird hunting dates, the nonresident can generally return home with a productive mixed bag containing prairie grouse and other game birds.

How to Hunt Them You won't have much luck stalking blindly and without a plan across the endless grassy sandhills hoping to find birds.

For successful gunning, you first have to identify those isolated spots most likely to contain birds, then concentrate hunting efforts there.

Areas most likely to have birds are usually in the rolling prairie sandhills covered by lush native grasses, surrounding green short-grass meadows and mowed grass crops. The high native grasses provide the basic food and cover required by prairie grouse during the summer and early fall months. This cover provides nesting for the rearing of the young chicks and essential summer and fall diets of tender green leaves, buds, fruits, and insects. They are especially fond of wild rose hips. These are brown and stand out like road flares against the gray grasslands.

In September most prairie birds are still scattered in their summer habitat in the grassy hills. However, by October most birds will be found in or very near the lowland meadows or hayfields. Keeping these migratory shifts in mind can be a big help in locating these grouse.

During the early part of September, experienced gunners hunt throughout the day in the grassy sandhills, staying within three-quarters to a mile or two of the green lowlands. During this period, the birds are pretty well scattered in family groups of 5 to 10 or more.

Prairie grouse can be killed without dogs, but the hunter will have to cover a lot of territory and wear out a lot of boot leather. If you do not have a dog, be on the lookout for droppings, tracks, dusting areas, and other spoor in the sand, then circle such areas until you flush some birds.

October and November hunts should be concentrated in short-grass meadows or cut hayfields in the early morning and late afternoon hours. Fields or meadows with thick stands of clover or alfalfa are especially productive. Flocks of birds are easily spotted in short grass if they are unaware of the hunter or his dog. A general practice is to drive near the edge of big fields and meadows, then get out and glass the area with your binoculars. Sometimes a sentinel bird on top of a rock, haystack, or bale of hay is a dead giveaway that a covey is present.

Careful stalking is required. During the stalk, the hunter should take every advantage of any available cover—weed-choked fences, brush, ditches, or haystacks. Generally, when the birds see a hunter approaching they will crouch or squat down flat against the ground, and sometimes the whole flock will wait until the hunter is within gun range before flushing. Even when it appears that the whole flock has taken off, the gunner should continue over the area, for often a bird or two will still be holding there. When birds are sighted feeding in a short-grass meadow or field and you are using dogs, it is best to leave them in the car or tied up before beginning the stalk unless they are well trained and will heel. Otherwise they may forge ahead too far and flush the birds before you are in shotgun range.

Weather and Grouse On warm rainy days, grouse and prairie chickens gather around in open spots or doze in whatever cover they can find. Snow, sleet, or heavy rain will drive them to dense cover. If you are forced to hunt them on windy days, you will find them in protected slashings, windfalls, or prairie brier patches.

What Weapon for These Birds? You will need a close-shooting smoothbore with loads that will deliver a wallop such as high-base shells loaded with No. 6s. A good double-barreled shotgun for this "blue-gray streak" would be one with the right barrel modified and the left barrel full-choked. Pumps and autoloaders with a variable choking device can be used with modified or full choke. Another good bet is to have the first shell No. 8 and the second ones No. 6s, for both grouse and prairie chicken can stand lots of lead before folding in flight.

Pheasant The ring-necked pheasant, like the chukar, is an import from Asia and a game bird that provides the sportsman with good hunting and delicious meat. The pheasant has no fear of the farmer or rancher. Give it rural farm fields to feed and hide in, and it will furnish shooting to the very edge of urban traffic. The pheasant has a wide range, having been introduced in every corner of the land. How-

Dogs are a real asset in hunting pheasant, for flushing and retrieving. MAINE DEPARTMENT OF ECONOMIC DEVELOPMENT

ever, they became better established in the northern half of the United States and southern Canada, and westward to the Pacific coast. They are found in greater abundance in agricultural areas, especially in South Dakota, which produces more pheasants than any other state at this writing.

Pheasant love the stubble of harvested land in the Wheat and Corn Belts, and the grape of California and the feed they can find in farm areas. This is perhaps the reason pheasant are so tasty.

Basic Hunting Method The basic technique used in upland bird hunting can be applied more or less to pheasant. Dogs are a tremendous asset in hunting the ringneck, both for flushing and retrieving. A lone hunter has to work harder for birds than a small party, no matter what the cover, and a well-trained dog can solve many of his problems.

One method that has proved successful while hunting pheasant in grape or corn rows is to move along cautiously on a zigzag course in as erratic a pattern as possible, then stop for several seconds. This pause makes the average bird so nervous that it becomes jittery, and it will

Fields or meadows with thick stands of clover or alfalfa are especially productive for grouse. MAINE DEPARTMENT OF ECONOMIC DEVELOPMENT

often fly out of concealment instead of running for cover as many will do.

If enough hunters are together, several should be posted about 80 yards apart at the far end of the field. The others form a line and comb the field, driving the fliers or runners toward the gunners at the lower end.

When moving along, check for signs of half-picked corncobs or saucer-shaped depressions of dusting bath spots. In snow, the tracks will show up clearly. When the birds flush at the end of the field, the hunter(s) may get a fast going-away shot. If no one is at the end of the field, the fast-running birds may not flush.

Dense thicket and brushy woodlands are good spots, as are the edges of hedgerows. Some of the finest pheasant hunting I have encountered in the Pacific Northwest has been in wetlands, in swamps and marshes, where cover is heavier than in surrounding upland terrain, thereby providing better protection for this hard-hunted bird. In this case, the upland bird hunting boot is exchanged for knee or hipboots for cross-country hunting.

A good time to look for ringnecks is at sunup, when they come in from the open meadows and grain stubbles where they have roosted overnight, to assemble along the roadsides to replenish gravel for their crops and gizzards. In states where sunrise shooting is legal, country roads and lanes are good places to find pheasant.

Shortly after daylight, the birds slip into grain fields where they fill their craws and then head for hedgerows, brushy ditches, and other cover to rest during the heat of the day. Their midday dusting and resting period over, they head again for the grain or other fields. Once their crops are filled toward sunset, they again head for roadside gravel and then to roost far out in the stubble fields.

A Gun for Pheasant One source of failure in pheasant gunning is that far too often the beginner is poorly advised in regard to his gun and ammunition. We still hear it said that one needs a full-choke gun for ringneck, and that they are so tough that nothing but big shot will kill them. From years of observation in the field, there is nothing so conducive to misses on the part of the average upland hunter (unless he is an expert) as using a full-choke smoothbore. An improved cylinder barrel in a properly loaded 12- or 16-gauge, if pointed right, will account for every bird that flies within 40 yards. For myself, my old 6¼-pound Savage 12-gauge autoloader works best on pheasant when the Poly Choke is turned to improved cylinder, and using No. 8 shot. You will probably have more success with the action, bore, and load that has worked best for you in the past, too!

Mourning Dove The mourning dove is the smallest of our upland game birds, and is the least man-shy of all. It is distinctive among game birds in that it breeds in every state except Hawaii and Alaska and in all Canadian provinces. Like most other birds, the mourning dove lives in a moderate climate and migrates back and forth. Like the pigeon, the dove needs grit to grind its food. Dove food is similar to that of the quail and pigeon. When located, they will be found in singles to a dozen or more. Being migratory in nature, they move with the seasons, and are hunted in a wide variety of foliage and terrain. Regardless of the area, they will be near the source of their food supply and will be seen early in the morning and evening flying to springs or other watering places. An excellent place to locate them is near and in outlying grain fields, stubble, along roads, brush, and tree borders, cedar patches and, in the desert regions of the Southwest, along irrigation ditches and reservoirs. Dove are often perched along fences and telephone and power lines in rural districts.

Methods of Hunting Them One method of hunting them is to drive along through the countryside and glass the terrain with binoculars. When birds are located, stop the car and take off afoot.

White-Winged Dove The white-winged dove is found along the southern part of North America. It is divided into eastern and western subspecies. The bird of the West is better known, because it is more numerous and is common to the irrigated desert and valleys of the southwestern United States and Baja California.

In the desert, while hunting the larger white-winged dove, the best areas are available creek beds. Simply work the foliage along the water course and look for dove along the willows or brushtops. When flushed, the white-wing rise as one bird, not in ones, twos, or threes as do the mourning doves. Shoot them as they rise. Like quail, dove are fast and erratic in flight. Both mourning and white-wing dove give excellent sport and will try the nerves of all comers. The gunner is called on to shoot from so many positions that no set rule for shooting form can be laid down. Over a point with a bird lying well, the shooter advances slowly in the orthodox way common to all forms of upland bird hunting. The point is, be prepared at any moment to go into action.

Water Hole Shooting Shooting at a water hole or roost is easier than walking up the birds in stubble fields or old fireburns, for dove come in more slowly, and generally arrive in a straight flight. Dove shooting is fun and sporty whether by a boy in his teens or by a veteran of many seasons.

The Gun It doesn't take a cannon to kill dove, but an openbore or improved, modified 12-gauge using low-base shells containing Nos. 7½, 8, or 9 shot will throw a larger and more dense pattern. Women and teen-agers seem to do better with a light 16- or 20-gauge scattergun.

Band-Tail Pigeon These big, fast-flying pigeons offer great sport, and the west coast sportsmen have it all to themselves. Since it is a migratory bird, check your game regulations before attempting to hunt them.

The band-tail, or white-collared pigeon as it is sometimes called, is distributed over the western states and from British Columbia to Mexico, and south to Central America. Like quail, it is a seed and fruit eater, and inhabits chiefly those hill regions where acorns, its favorite food, can be secured. During the summer and fall it feeds mainly on seeds of dogwood, salal berries, elderberries, blueberries, salmonberries, and wild nuts. It prefers the western slopes of the coast ranges and natural forests and higher elevations of the West. It is common for a flock to fly down a mountainside to lower foothills or valley bottoms, feed, and return to roost in high forest in the evening. The pigeon, like other birds, needs gravel to grind its food.

Check with local people and ranchers for information regarding their flight line, since they head for water and feeding grounds between 7:30 and 8 A.M., feed their fill, roost during the rest of the day, then feed again in late afternoon until nearly dark when they head back to roost in timber.

Stalking Them   Once a flyway is located, it is important to find a ridge the birds have been flying over, then find a place of concealment, since the birds have keen sight. The incoming pigeons select a low spot or pass between the hills and dive through in flocks varying from a few to many—sometimes 100 or more. This is "pass" shooting at its best!

The Best Gun   Sorry to say, there is no "best" gun for pigeons. However, a good combination would be a 12-gauge double-barrel shotgun with a modified right barrel and a full-choke left barrel loaded with No. 6 shot. Since there isn't time to change a choke device, the single-barreled pumps and autoloaders should stick with full choke for best results.

Turkey   The wild turkey has made a fantastic comeback throughout the country. In fact, wild turkey have been introduced in states that never had turkeys before. Most of the wild turkey's original range has been restocked, and the birds are on the increase in these areas. Eighteen states have reported successful plants, and

Successful turkey hunt in the Gila National Forest. U. S. FOREST SERVICE, SOUTH-WESTERN REGION

twenty-six states now have open season for one or more subspecies. Only five states—Alaska, Delaware, Maine, New Hampshire, and Rhode Island—report no turkeys. The small flock in Vermont is reported on the increase—so may have an open season later. Today's best turkey shooting in the East is confined to the Appalachian area, in parts of Pennsylvania, Maryland, and West Virginia, in the heavily forested lowlands of the South, and west to Texas and Mexico.

Their favorite foods during open season are the white oak acorns and other wild nuts, wild grapes, crabgrass, tubers, berries, and various insects. The average well-fed Tom will weigh in up to 15 pounds, with hens somewhat smaller.

This largest of our game birds has excellent vision and keenness of hearing, along with an uncanny instinct for knowing when it is being stalked, making it one of the most difficult to bag of our upland birds.

In the lowlands, the birds are stalked in lush river-bottom swamps where Spanish moss mantles the cypress trees, black gums, and oaks. Here is food, and rank undergrowth provides protection and cover. In most of the mountain country, where birds feed through thin stands of hardwoods, they are found along slopes between 3000 and 4000 feet elevation.

Turkeys are creatures of habit. In the fall they tend to form in flocks of a dozen or more and move into areas of several thousand acres. They roost in trees in some part of their general range each night, and make a wide circle and feed back toward their roost in late afternoon.

No other bird leaves so much "spoor," and on clear ground the tracks are unmistakable. They have a habit of scratching up the forest ground cover, throwing leaves and pine needles in whole piles. It is a noisy bird, and turkey "talk" can be heard for some distance.

How to Bag Him A method that has proved successful in bagging Mr. Gobbler is by scouting carefully through turkey range. Look for tracks, droppings, scratch patches, and dust baths. Find the feeding areas and determine the route the birds follow from one to the other. Then, by watching the feeding spot from a distance, it is possible to ascertain the approximate time the flock will appear every day. When glassing

the birds use extreme caution that the sun doesn't reflect from your binoculars or other equipment or that they are not disturbed by undue movement or noise. Once their habits are learned, all the hunter has to do is find a good spot for ambush, then settle down quietly in concealment in forest cover and wait. However, turkey do have a habit at times, even when food is abundant, to take off for no apparent reason, to regions at some distance. Best results may be obtained when the hunter wears a camouflage suit, gloves, and cap to break his outline, and remains absolutely quiet until ready to shoot. Try to get positioned so that the wind is in your favor. Some hunters have success when shooting from a blind made from forest cover, and by using a turkey call. When talking "turkey," it must be done *exactly right!* Otherwise leave the "call" alone! Best advice is to hunt with an experienced caller.

Rifles are more practical when hunting them in the mountains. Some riflemen prefer the little over-and-under .22 magnum 20-gauge combination with good results, using No. 4 shot for the first shot and the .22 magnum barrel for the second shot. Others prefer using rifles such as the .22 Hornet, .222, or a 12-gauge shotgun. (Be sure to check your local game regulations as to whether or not hens may be taken. Some states only allow Tom shooting.)

Marsh and Shorebird Shooting Marsh and shorebird shooting can be found along the coastlines or near large bodies of water where there are mud-bottom marshes: Wilson's snipe, clapper rail, sora rail, coot, and the woodcock, which is a shorebird only in name are still on the game list; the sandpiper and plover are still on the protected list.

The best locations at present are the southeastern states, both Atlantic and Gulf coasts, with Louisiana best for the wily woodcock.

Practically all marsh and shorebirds are good eating, and bag limits are generous. However, this is one of the most neglected types of shooting, and hunters should take advantage of this fine sport. Rail shooting provides excellent training for the quail and dove hunter and sharpens his eye for waterfowl shooting. Seasons on marsh and shorebirds as a rule open well

A good day's hunt. COURTESY OF THE AUTHOR

ahead of those for other birds. Marsh and shorebirds are migratory, so they come under the Migratory Bird Act. Be sure to check these regulations before hunting them to prevent game law violations.

One method of hunting "rails" is to wait until high tide pushed by a strong inshore wind floods the marshes; it is then that the birds can be flushed from the marsh grass. It is here that the sharp-bow sneakboat is poled through the partly submerged marsh grass, forcing the birds to flush. If you hunt rails from the shore, hip boots or chest-high waders are a must.

Woodcock, though classed with marsh and shorebirds, has been called the "upland snipe," but the long-billed woodcock is primarily a bird of the bogs and swamps, as is the Wilson's snipe.

Woodcock hunting, like dove hunting, can be exciting or frustrating, depending upon the nervous reaction of the individual shooter. When alarmed, the woodcock will freeze and his drab foliage coloration makes him difficult to detect in his natural habitat except to the well-trained eye. As the gunner approaches, he will flare almost straight up. When this happens, hold your fire; he will probably level off at the treetops and zoom away, giving the gunner a fast, high, and easy shot. It is better to take a retriever along, because woodcock or rail once dropped and not marked is difficult to find.

Dropping Them Many shorebirds are easy to bring down, but due to their erratic flight pattern call for a modified choke and low-base shells containing Nos. 8, 9, or 10 shot for average shooting. The exception to this would be coot (sometimes called whitebill or mud hen). In this case use No. 6 shot.

Chapter 9

HUNTING WATERFOWL SUCCESSFULLY-DUCKS AND GEESE

The heritage of waterfowling is, to many of us, one of the greatest legacies we have. Wind-driven snow, sleet, and rain, and cold, miserable weather do not discourage the died-in-the-wool waterfowler. The sport can be simple and inexpensive, but generally isn't if you belong to a duck club. Generally, duck and goose shooting demands a great deal in the way of planning, equipment, and know-how.

The best hunting is usually during stormy weather when the armchair hunter hugs the fireplace; but the real sportsman enjoys inclement weather, for he knows that ducks and geese will be coming in from the north, and other spartan-like characters like himself will be heading out for the best shooting spots. This great sport attracts many men and women from all walks of life. The magic of ducks quacking and geese honking their "eaur-awk, eaur-awk" way across the sky pull these red-blooded nimrods to the rivers and bays, ponds and stubble fields like magnets. How else can you explain the spectacle of thousands of people leaving their warm beds hours before dawn and braving the arctic-like weather, traveling miles by car, boat, and on foot through subfreezing cold, to sit perhaps for hours in a blind or boat just to collect a scanty limit of waterfowl?

The newcomer to this enjoyable field of sport needs to know the fundamentals of the game.

The veteran hunter already knows these, but may pick up a few pointers here and there. Each area has its own way of hunting waterfowl that works better there than some other method. Unless one shoots from a duck club or lodge, it is more or less a day-at-a-time proposition—leaving early from town, arriving at a hunting area blind, trying for a limit, and returning home or to a motel or wherever you may be staying.

The Flyways Almost all ducks and geese breed north of the Canadian border—many in Alaska and the Northwest Territories. There are four great waterfowl flyways: the Pacific, Central, Mississippi, and Atlantic. When the breeding season is over and the young ducks and geese have attained their flying feathers, they raft up and head down these main flightways in the fall and head south for the winter. It is one of nature's greatest spectacles for both bird watcher and hunter to observe these flights. It is along these ways that the waterfowlers gather for the shoot.

Know Your Ducks and Geese Before you ever enter the field to hunt, you had better spend some time visiting a nearby waterfowl refuge or pond in your city park so you will know what the various species of ducks and geese look like and how each species sounds and acts. This will be a good time to invest in a good duck or goose call. Listen to their visiting and feeding chatter and try to imitate it very carefully. In time you will be able to call them properly to your hunting blind when you go afield. It might pay to purchase a waterfowl record so you can practice at home (if the little woman will let you). Olt's game-calling records for ducks, geese, squirrel, fox, and other game sell for $2 each and are well worth the money. It is also advisable to have the little booklet *Ducks at a Distance,* a waterfowl identification guide published by the U. S. Fish and Wildlife Service, Department of the Interior. Write to the U. S. Government Printing Office, Washington, D.C. 20402.

With over 60 species of waterfowl, it is no wonder sportsmen become confused at times. It is *important* to recognize the various species, as some are protected and some hardly edible. Learn to recognize the birds on the wing, to avoid taking birds you don't want. Otherwise you may shoot an illegal bird and have to spend an expensive visit to the courtroom. After you have followed the above instructions go out with an experienced waterfowl hunter.

Watch the maneuvers of a flock in the air; this will help indicate the species. Mallards, pintails, and widgeons form loose groups; teals and shovelers flash by in small bunches; mergansers often appear in single file; canvasbacks shift from waving lines to temporary "V"s; redheads "boil up" in short flights from one end of a lake to the other. In closer view, individual silhouettes can show large heads or small, broad bills or narrow, fat bodies or slender, long tails or short ones. Experienced observers also identify ducks from their wingbeats; they may be fast or slow, short rapid flutters or long strokes. Depending on light conditions as they close the range, color areas can be positive. In early morning and toward evening before the sky lights up they may not appear in their true colors, but their size and location will help identify them. The sound of wings can be as important as that of the voice. The pinions of goldeneyes whistle in flight; the swish of wood ducks is different from the steady rush of canvasbacks. Not all ducks quack; many whistle, squeal, or grunt. Knowing the species of ducks

and geese can be a rewarding experience for the scattergunner, and when extra birds of a certain species are permitted in the bag, sportsmen who know their waterfowl come out ahead of the game with a more abundant bag limit. If you shoot birds you cannot identify, you may meet up with a game warden, and spend a day in court! *Remember,* habitat, action, color, shape, and voice all help distinguish one species from another! It is also well to recognize the brighter plumage of the male bird.

Two Groups of Ducks Ducks are more or less split up into two groups; puddle ducks and diving ducks or deep water ducks that are found around coastal bays and inlets—some which are not edible due to their extremely fishy flavor. Their diet of fish, shellfish, mollusks, and aquatic plants is the cause of this. Canvasbacks and redheads that fatten on ell grass and wild celery are the exceptions. However, the coastal ducks can be made edible by soaking in vinegar overnight and by cooking them with herbs. Some cooks prefer to parboil them before roasting. Each person has his own manner of dealing with this problem.

Puddle ducks are typically birds of fresh water, shallow marshes, and rivers rather than large lakes and bays. They are good divers, but usually feed by dappling or tipping up rather than by submerging. There are various ways of distinguishing to which group a duck belongs. For example, puddle ducks leap straight up into the air when taking off, while divers skim along the surface. Another difference is the hind toe of these two groups. The diving duck has a broad lobe which acts as a rudder; the puddle duck's is smaller. All birds and waterfowl will attempt to take off into the wind.

The speculum or color patch is generally iridescent and bright, and often a tell-tale field mark.

Any ducks feeding in croplands will likely be puddle ducks, for most of this group are sure-footed, and can walk and run well on land. Their food is mostly vegetable, and there is nothing finer than grain-fed mallards, pintails, or corn-fattened wood ducks. The puddlers ride higher in the water than the divers, and launch themselves directly upward when rising, whether on land or water.

Types of Shooting Generally there are three types of waterfowl shooting for either ducks or geese: jump shooting, pass shooting, and decoy shooting. Let's take them in order:

Jump Shooting Jump shooting is popular across Canada and the United States, especially in pothole or prairie country. Jump shooting, practiced mostly by natives of the area, involves stalking quietly through marsh cover and creeping up on small ponds, sloughs, and creeks where single ducks or small flocks are hiding and flushing ahead of the gun. When they rise above the rushes and tules, the shooting takes place. The trick is to approach with the wind, since the birds will head into the wind and fly straight up and away. When jump shooting from a scullboat or other craft, the reverse is often best. The sneakboat can get closer to the sitting or rafted ducks, so the gunner usually approaches upwind, taking ducks as they fly straight away from the boater.

Another form of jump shooting is from a canoe or sneakboat when the ducks are sitting tight in the bulrushes. One hunter rows or paddles quietly among the rushes while the other shoots from the bow. If the birds are sitting real tight, the paddler can bang a paddle against the side of the boat occasionally to stir the ducks to flight.

Pass Shooting In pass shooting you locate a spot where birds pass over early in the morning and where they return in late afternoon to raft up in protective waters for the night. The birds will travel this route daily as they trade back and forth from one body of water to another or from one grain field to another.

Once the pass route is located, the hunter conceals himself in whatever cover is available and waits until birds come over. This, however, is shooting at maximum ranges, and substantial leads with magnum loads of Nos. 4, 5, or 6 shot with choke device set at full choke is in order.

In other instances, shooting is done over water or from a point of land projecting out into a bay or river. A boat or a retriever is needed to recover birds that have been shot and fallen into the water, especially so if there is any current or wind drift. Too many birds are shot over water with no means to recover them.

To save hauling a boat back and forth from their homes, and to save time, some waterfowlers cache or hide a boat in advance of the season near the area they plan to hunt. If you do "cache" or moor a boat, be sure to take some means to secure it from theft. Other hunters make arrangements well in advance to rent a boat from the nearest town marina. Sometimes a boat can be secured from a rancher who lives near the water that you want to hunt over.

Decoy Shooting Decoy shooting is by far the most popular form of waterfowl hunting, and generally is the most successful. The hunter first builds his blind well in advance of opening day. When the season opens, he arrives ahead of shooting time so that his decoy stool is "set" in the water before waterfowl start to take wing for their feeding ground.

The type of blind you build depends on the area and terrain. Often the hunter will improvise on the spot and take advantage of nearby material. Another consideration is the species of waterfowl being hunted. For example, black ducks require carefully constructed blinds that are well camouflaged and do not loom up on the landscape, while other puddle ducks and divers will usually come into decoys in front of a blind not so carefully designed.

The best waterfowl blinds are those that stay in the same place year after year and become part of the natural landscape. New blinds often startle the birds. Permanent blinds are usually found on private property and at waterfowl clubs, and are used for such shallow-water species as blacks, mallards, widgeon, teal, etc., because the areas these birds "work" can be more easily determined than those of the divers. To build a permanent blind in a good location, the hunter must find where the birds will pass close enough to a point of land, a curve in the river bank, or the edge of a lake.

Temporary blinds, like permanent ones, range widely in size, shape, and comfort. Sometimes it is possible to improvise a blind by utilizing nearby natural cover, such as thick patches of reeds, brush, rocks, corn shocks, or wind-thrown trees. If the ground is soft, a two-foot pit can be dug and pieces of chicken fence wire three feet wide can be used around the upper edge laced with reeds. Inexpensive camouflage netting can be used to cover the wire. The arrangement of the blind should be so that the waiting hunter(s) has his back to the wind if possible. This allows him to face waterfowl coming in naturally against the wind.

One of the greatest handicaps to the blind shooter is the character who has to walk around outside the blind to keep warm, and can't keep his head down inside and his face concealed from approaching birds.

If it is necessary during a quiet period to pick up downed birds, take your scattergun with you. If you get caught out in the open and ducks are approaching—freeze, and they may still come within range.

Perhaps you are wondering how to get all your gear from your car to the blind. One way is to pack all your gear in a large packsack similar to that used in the North Woods by canoe guides in portaging to the next water. Another method is to pack everything in a large gunnysack or a canvas duffel bag and fasten to a packboard. With your gun in one hand, the other is free to open gates, etc.

Stubble Shooting with Decoys   Stubble shooting is practiced on the prairie, mainly in western Canada and parts of the Middle West in the States where mallards and pintails feed in harvested stubble grain fields. From some high point, try to observe the line of flight as the birds trade back and forth from water to field and drive or go until you locate this feeding ground. Once located do not disturb, but allow them to leave by themselves. If it is on private land, and it very likely is, contact the owner for hunting privileges. If granted, the hunter can take advantage of the natural cover or dig a well-concealed pit blind. If the breeze is coming from your left, the decoys should be placed in scattered feeding positions upwind of the blind, with the right-hand edge of the spread opposite the pit and about 20 to 30 feet off. A dozen or so blocks should be about right. (When shooting on small marsh ponds, half a dozen decoys is sufficient for puddle ducks.) Get comfortable and wait until the next feeding period when birds are coming in or passing over. Don't open fire on them until they are 25 to 35 yards

off. Ducks generally feed twice: right after daybreak and again from late afternoon until they raft up in the middle of open water or hide out in the tules and marsh rushes for protection from their enemies. In late season and during stormy weather, the birds feed continuously, flying back and forth between field and protective water.

Types of Decoys and How to Use Them   Gone are the days of using live decoys and baiting ducks. It is legally taboo—so now we use various types of artificial decoys. Duck and goose decoys come in many sizes, species, materials, and prices. Wooden, molded, cork, and plastic decoys are bulky and weigh heavily when the shooter has to make a big stool layout for diving ducks on large bodies of water. The waterfowler has enough gear to pack to a blind—gun, shells, decoys, lunch, Thermos bottle, etc., without wearing himself out lugging bulky or heavy blocks. Much as I prefer wooden decoys, I have found out by trial and error that Deeks (trade name) work best for me. By the use of one or more dozen of Deek's seven varieties, you can decoy any species of duck if they will come to decoys at all. Made of latex rubber, they weigh less than 6 ounces apiece. By holding the Deek 6 or 8 inches above the water, it will inflate the instant you drop it on the water and deflate instantly when you lift it off. When deflated for carrying or storage, the anchor is dropped inside and is tucked in the head. Gone forever are tangled anchor lines. Deeks don't glare, gloss, or shine which is another thing waterfowlers have to take into consideration. Even the slightest breeze or marsh current puts them into action. They weathervane naturally in the wind and ride high or deep as you desire, with perfect action in most all weather conditions. A ring in the stem and ballast prevents unnatural side-rolling or whipping back and forth found in some types of decoys.

Another popular decoy is the folding cardboard silhouette. These are lifelike and designed for field use, and can be obtained with adjustable heads, upright and in feeding positions.

The most expensive, of course, is the taxidermy decoy, duck and goose skins stuffed and mounted in a variety of positions. However, these are bulky and weigh up.

Setting the Stool Duck hunting is always at its best when the weather is at its worst, and if there is any wind to speak of, ducks will invariably land upwind, which means at the head or upwind end of the stool. If the wind is blowing from the right of your blind, for instance, set the decoys somewhat to the left of center so the landing area will not be too far to the right. Reverse the setup if the wind is opposite.

The question arises, how many decoys should be used in a stool? For large bodies of water, the more the better. However, there are two schools of thought on this subject. The same applies for how far from the blind the decoys should be set.

A dozen decoys suffice for puddle ducks, but the amateur seldom realizes how many are needed for real success with open-water ducks (divers and skimmers). Experienced gunners may place as many as 100 to 200 decoys in a "set." To ease the burden and expense of so many decoys, many hunters pool their "birds," and shoot together.

Some stool setters declare that ducks are less suspicious if the stool is pretty far out—40 to 50 yards. In my opinion this no doubt accounts for more cripples and misses, because generally, ducks seldom light between the decoys and the shore.

A knowledge of how, when, and where to set decoys is essential, and can be learned from the experience of old-timers. There are, however, a few fundamentals that apply in all waterfowl areas. The decoys should be set so their formations look real and placed so the birds can get to them easily as they cruise along upwind ready to glide down to the lure of the decoys.

Puddle ducks and divers decoy in different ways. The divers usually pass over decoys before landing, while puddle ducks either pitch right into the middle or land outside the stool and swim in.

All these things have to be taken into consideration when setting the stool. If it's divers you are after on bays and inlets, remember that they overshoot, so set your decoys slightly downwind from your hideout. For puddle ducks, set your "Deeks" so that they have landing room right in front of your blind—15 to 25 yards

out. Often a half dozen decoys is sufficient for a small pothole lake, and a dozen or more for larger lakes and river sandbar shooting. That is the way the puddlers work each spot.

There are many ways to make a set. Watch how the expert waterfowler does it. Two methods that have proved successful are the "V" and "J" patterns. Wind is vitally important in planning a big water layout. Where puddle ducks can get in and out of a tight landing area, even on a crosswind approach, the faster divers will always make their landing approach upwind and usually well out, and need a larger area to skid down into. When using these time-tested sets, place the "V" with the opening downwind and the point in front of the blind for puddlers, and the "hook" of the "J" which is suitable for large sets for divers.

This method is of no interest to the gunner of the prairies who is shooting in grain fields, or "stubble shooting," as it is called. Here the decoys are spread out as though feeding, and the ducks are shot as they pass over or come in to land.

Tips to Remember Don't mix diver and puddle duck decoys in a set! A few "Deeks" placed in the reeds adds realism and helps quell suspicion, and they are attractive to incoming birds. Six to 18 blocks are sufficient for puddle ducks as mentioned earlier, and don't crowd them. Divers will come into large close spreads of 3 or 4 dozen or more decoys if conditions appear normal. Black ducks are the most wary, but sometimes a few goose decoys will allay their fears, and they might draw in a stray goose or two to add to your bag. Set the goose decoys upwind from your spread and not too close. Don't set your duck decoys closer to your blind than 20 yards, because if a duck skims too close in and you blast him, there may not be enough meat left to cook, or it will be so loaded with pellets that you may break a tooth when you do eat it.

Estimating Range An odd decoy set out in front of your blind at 40 yards will give you a marker for range estimating. I go a little farther and place a stake 40 yards away on either side of my blind and hardly ever shoot beyond these markers. If you shoot with a companion, in the case of a right-handed shooter, he will naturally shoot only from the center front of the blind and to his right, and the left-hander from center to his left for safety reasons. Try to visualize how ducks will look to the shooter at various ranges.

Leading Waterfowl When hunting waterfowl, or any other species of bird, one of the most important things is to *remember* to lead the first bird picked as a target and stay with it until you drop it. Don't just haphazardly shoot into a flock of birds hoping to make a hit. You will probably just blast a hole in the sky or wound a bird or two that will fly away and die.

In most areas, the first waterfowl to arrive are small ducks which decoy easily. These are bagged with light loads if the shooter leads the bird properly. As the season advances, the big puddlers and divers come in on the north wind, and heavier or magnum loads are indicated. For these, it is suggested you use Nos. 4, 5, or 6 shot. Here again, an adjustable choke device will give good results and versatility.

What Kills Ducks What kills waterfowl, and upland game birds too, is a combination of pattern density and penetration of shot into vital areas. Since most waterfowl will be shot within 30 to 40 yards, beyond which range positive identification is difficult for the average hunter, there is little need for a heavy, long-barreled shotgun. The smart waterfowler will wait until ducks are within upland game bird range before pouring on the lead. Under these circumstances, they can be taken with light-weight, short-barreled upland guns with modified choke with the above-mentioned shot size. When shooting over decoys or when jumpshooting along creeks and potholes, the long-barreled, heavy duck gun becomes a handicap to many shooters. That is why there are more and more lightweight upland game 12-gauge guns used today in duck blinds. In turn, many more water-fowlers are becoming better marksmen, since they have to concentrate on identifying ducks and geese. That means that the gunner must allow the birds to approach, or to attract them into closer range. Naturally, you will have to be more careful with camouflage, with blind building, and even with calling.

During the early part of the season, I personally have better luck with close-in blind shooting by using No. 8 shot with my choke device turned to modified choke. Later in the season, after the birds have been gunned considerably, I find that I can do better with No. 6s for my particular cannon.

Recommended Reading *Prairie Ducks*, $4.75; *Hunting Ducks and Geese*, $5.95; *High Tide and an East Wind*, $4.50; *Golden Retriever*, $3.95; *Ducks, Geese and Swans*, $6.50. The Stackpole Company, publishers, Kelker and Cameron streets, Harrisburg, Pennsylvania 17105.

Chapter 10

WHAT YOU SHOULD KNOW ABOUT GEESE

Geese To simplify the classification of geese, waterfowlers generally divide the geese of this continent into three groups: the gray, the white, and the blue. Under the gray classification come the Canadas and their subdivisions, such as cackling, Hutchins, lesser Canada, and western Canada. The white geese comprise the greater snow goose, which is confined to the east coast, and the lesser snow, sometimes called wavey, which occurs throughout most of our western states and Mexico. The Ross's goose is another "whitey," and the smallest of the North American geese, and spends most of his winters in the Sacramento Valley rice field areas of California. The blue goose is medium-size and is almost always associated with lesser snow geese on land and water, on breeding grounds, on migration, and on the wintering grounds. The blues probably are the most plentiful of all geese. These birds favor the Mississippi flyway and head from their Hudson Bay summer range almost directly to the Louisiana marshes. Added to these are the Brant from the cold Arctic regions. This coastal salt-water goose, about the size of a cackling goose, uses both the Pacific and Atlantic flyways.

The Largest Goose The largest and most important goose is the Canadian, often referred to as the Canadian honker, that ranges from Alaska to Mexico. This bird is the prize of all waterfowlers and flies in large "V" formations or long "strings" and back into "V" formation again. One can hear their cry, "eaur-awk, eaur-awk"

North American geese are generally divided into three categories: the gray or Canadian; the white, found on the east coast; and the blue, the most plentiful of all. SAVAGE ARMS PHOTO

for nearly a mile or more. These large birds mate for life. When one is shot down, the mate will generally hang around until it too is killed.

How to Hunt Geese In goose hunting, as in any other gunning, a knowledge of the bird's habits is vital to success. Besides stalking, pass, and jump shooting, the methods in hunting geese of all species include the use of all sorts of blinds and goose decoys. Sneakboats are used to hunt geese at times, and to tend offshore blinds. Boats are used to recover crippled and dead birds.

When geese arrive from the north, they tend to settle down upon coastal marshes and inland prairies from Maine to California and from Washington to Florida to spend the winter months. They rest at night on protective waters and fly out at the crack of dawn to feed in grain fields and tidal marshes.

In the early part of the season, geese are content to graze lightly on waste grain of winter rye or wheat and ell grass in the tidal flats. Later they tend to feed on harvested leavings of corn, milo, cane, barley, and wheat. At such times they settle down in certain fields and feed there twice daily, just before sunup and again in late afternoon.

In hunting this wily bird, you must first locate its feeding ground. They will fly from 20 to 40 miles to stubble grain fields time and again until they are spooked out by heavy hunting, or until they pass on to another field where feed is more abundant.

Stubble Fields Reconnoiter the stubble grain fields and look for goose tracks, droppings, and feathers. Usually they will be found in the low spots in fields where moisture has gathered. A pair of binoculars will be helpful when watching where geese light. Once a feeding ground is located, wait until the birds have fed and left the area before you decide where you want to build your pit blind. Geese are creatures of habit and will come back to feed where they left off.

Since the grain fields will be on private property, you will have to seek permission from the owner to dig goose pits and use the property. To keep up good public relations with a rancher, you will have to respect his property, fences, gates, stock, and unharvested crops. All too often, a few thoughtless hunters will leave litter such as empty shells, bottles, and lunch papers. Sometimes they forget to fill in the goose pits, making extra work for the rancher. You cannot blame some wheat ranchers for posting their land against hunting! If permission is granted, perhaps the owner would appreciate a goose for his dinner, too! Find out when you quit for the day, perhaps he will invite you and your party back again.

Geese are smart and watchful. Unless forced by strong winds, they will not fly near thick brush patches or shocked corn or other obstructions that might conceal an enemy. If they do head or fly over obstructions, it will generally be high and wide and possibly out of shotgun range before they land in a field. They like open fields where they can watch from all directions. Here is where a well-concealed pit blind is a *must*.

The Goose Blind The wind has much to do with where you place your blind and goose decoys. Geese never jam up in a tight bunch when they put up for the night, but when ready to take off, they go in a tight bunch until they form in a long string and then go into a more or less "V" formation. They tend to bunch up in the same manner when frightened off a field.

Some hunters never dig a pit blind, just a shallow depression where they place an air mattress or pad on a piece of old gray canvas or a weathered piece of burlap 8 or 9 feet long and 3 or 4 feet wide. They then cover themselves with a somewhat larger piece of camouflage netting or other dull-colored material. This in turn is covered irregularly with field straw and chaff collected nearby. The straw should be picked so that you do not leave bare spots that the cagey birds will notice. All footprints should be erased leading to the blind. This can be accomplished by brushing the tracks out with a handful of straw. When doing this, avoid leaving tell-tale straight streaks in the snow or on the bare ground. Do the job irregularly or the sharp-eyed birds will edge off. Hide all fresh dirt signs the same way by scattering them and covering them with field litter. Pit blinds should be dug deep enough for concealment when sitting, but with sufficient room for shooting. When using the depression type of blind, place it where geese left off feeding the day before.

If you dig a pit blind, dig a small sump at one end of the pit so that any rainwater or melting snow will drain out of the main blind bottom; then use a box or dig out a shelf in the back of the blind to sit on. Again, scatter all fresh dirt and cover with straw. To keep warm in a cold blind some smoothbore gunners select a strong wooden box large enough to sit on, and one shaped so it will hold a kerosene lantern underneath. Bore holes about an inch in diameter on all sides. When ready to use, light the lantern and put it inside. This is called a "hotbox" by some old-time goose hunters, and it really works. (It will work in a duck blind, too.) There are some commercially made "Heat-Pal" type stoves that are good too. Hand warmers, hot water bags, and chemically treated heating pads will help ward off the chill while waiting for birds.

Another thing to keep in mind is the glint of bright-colored shells carelessly ejected around your hideout; even more obvious, the staring white faces of the ambushers will spook geese from half a mile away.

Don't Be a Johnny Jump-up Don't spoil your friend's hunt or that of nearby gunners by being a Johnny Jump-up for any reason—whether to reload, gawk at a departing flight while another is boring in unseen, or start shooting before the birds are in range. And if stationed in the left side of the blind, don't blast off at birds flaring to the right—that is your partner's side. I am still hard of hearing on the left side since a "character" let go with a muzzle blast practically in my ear and in addition adding a few more gray hairs to the sparse crop I own.

A Word about Goose Decoys Wind has much to do with the proper placing of decoys. The honkers tend to alight short of feeding geese or goose stools. Thus the spread should be scattered loosely within 15 to 25 yards of the pit blind on calm mornings; right between the hunters when the wind is 8 to 16 miles per hour, and as much as 40 to 50 yards upwind on really rough windy days. If you have some decoys that have adjustable heads, it is a good idea to have several decoys with their heads down as though feeding, and at least one with its neck straight up, simulating the sentinel bird which always remains watchfully on guard while

its companions eat. On water, you will need a minimum of 20 to 30 or more decoys. You can get by on land with more or less the same number.

Stalking Geese The Canadian honker and other geese are hunted in a variety of ways, depending on the locality. In Canada and our midwestern grain states, they are hunted from wheat stalks and goose pits, and along the Mississippi and other flyways from pits dug in sandbars. On the great sand barrier reefs of our coastal states, they are hunted from pits, brush piles, and floating blinds.

Geese are exceptionally difficult to stalk in ponds and potholes. They are usually situated so they can observe all directions, and are generally out of shotgun range. However, they are more easily stalked from the curving bank of a river. The idea is to spot them as they light on the water, and then allow some 40 minutes or more to elapse, then creep and crawl through the brush or thicket the last 100 yards or so. Be especially careful not to make any noise or cause the brush to sway if there isn't any wind to make the movement look unnatural.

A full-grown Canadian honker is a big bird, and looks enormous even to waterfowlers who have shot only ducks, cacklers, or blues. He appears to be coming in slowly but is actually cutting the air much faster than the less-experienced hunter thinks. Deceptively, geese really move faster in normal flight despite their slow wingbeat than do puddle ducks.

My advice is to take him while the selected bird is incoming just as he comes in range. This first incoming shot leaves time for a second shot (if you are on the ball) with the flight just overhead; the whole underside is then exposed to the shot pattern. *Don't* shoot at a retreating bird or you will likely get him in the "pants," and the gut-shot bird may sail beyond recovery and be wasted.

Brant and Other Coastal Geese In order to shoot these restless birds you have to get near them, and that isn't always easy unless you are a good hand with blind construction and are subtle in setting brant stools.

Tides are important in taking brant in coastal areas. When the tide is high, all the ell grass, the brant's favorite food, is covered. Then the birds sit it out in the middle of a large bay until the tide recedes and the first areas of ell grass begin to show above the surface of the falling water. Between flights, the decoys, silhouettes, and floaters have to be moved out farther in the shallow water. One thing brant gunners don't do often enough is move the decoys out to keep up with the falling tide. Brant won't come to decoys that are left high and dry on muddy tidal flats.

When any species of bird is hunted over deep water like this, you need a boat or a well-trained retriever. With a falling tide or an off-shore wind it doesn't take long for a downed bird to drift out of wader reach.

Dry Off Your Retriever Many times while I have been a guest at a goose shoot, I have observed retrievers returning wet and cold to the blind with a bird from the icy waters of a bay. It makes me colder than I really am just watching these helpmates shiver. When my Llewellyn spaniel, Penny Royal, brings in a bird, I dry her off with an old terry towel and give her a piece of jerky that she appreciates very much. Afterward she sits quietly on an old blanket and scans the sky for the next flight of birds. When working the saltwater marshes I carry a half-gallon canteen full of fresh water for both man and beast. A dog gets thirsty, too, and cannot drink salt water.

Goose Fever Whether the quarry is Canadian honkers in California or Baja California, or snow geese in Louisiana marshes, a big flock of honkers working over your decoys brings a malady the old-timers term goose fever. It occurs each year and isn't cured until you are in a blind with your favorite retriever.

Waterfowl Boats It is possible to hunt ducks and geese without using a boat. Nevertheless, boats of one sort or another play a prominent role in waterfowl hunting. Hunting boats come in various sizes, shapes, weights, and seaworthiness. They may be lightweight car-toppers, canoes, blunt-nosed scows, jonboats, dories,

skiffs, or decked-over scull- or sneakboats. For big waters, where wind, wave, and current are strong, a more seaworthy craft like the dory is safer. In this case, the boat should be equipped with an outboard motor if you are unable to row against a strong outgoing tide or strong off-shore wind. The motor is to be used only in case of emergency, since waterfowl may not be hunted from a powerboat. The motor should be stopped and tilted up on arriving at the shooting area, and not used until you head for shore.

What Shotgun for Geese? Some waterfowl gunners seem to favor heavy, long-barreled, full-choked 10- or 12-gauge shotguns using Nos. 2 or 4 size shot. These long-barreled outfits may shoot a yard or two farther and have a slightly longer pointing sight, but they are not so easy to swing and will not do much better than the standard 12-gauges with shorter barrels—26 and not over 28 inches including a choke device. The weapons handle nicely and, equipped with a good recoil pad, a compensator, and using magnum loads, will do as good a job as their big brothers with more shooting comfort. They are more versatile in that they can also be used for upland bird hunting without lugging heavy artillery around all day. The biggest fault of the "big ones" is that so many hunters scrape the sky at birds 100 yards or more distant, thereby spoiling the shooting for nearby gunners. Of course, the 16-gauge is used, but it and the little 20-gauge should be used only by veteran water-fowlers shooting over decoys from a blind. Geese take a lot of shot lead to make a clean kill—for the average hunter a 12-gauge shotgun will serve better.

Migratory Wildfowl Regulations Regulations concerning the open season, bag limits, etc., for migratory birds, as established by the U. S. Department of the Interior, may be obtained by writing the Director, Bureau of Sports Fisheries and Wildlife Service, Washington, D.C. 20240, or find them at your local sporting equipment store.

Chapter 11

SMALL-GAME HUNTING

Due to our present restrictive game laws pertaining to ducks and geese and the short hunting seasons, more and more hunters are turning to weekend small-game hunting to keep in shooting trim and to put tasty meat on the table.

Cottontail Rabbits The cottontail is North America's foremost small-game animal. No other variety of small game is gunned for by as many hunters, and hunting cottontails with a good dog is still a thrilling form of gunning, whether you are 12 years old or 12 plus 60.

Rabbits have moved in on farmland in droves. Each year they do thousands of dollars' worth of damage to crops. Hardly ever will a farmer turn away rabbit hunters so long as they do not shoot near his buildings and livestock or damage his fences and seeded crops. Many farmers will permit rabbit hunting on their property when they will not permit bird hunting of any kind.

Old Molly Cottontail, however, is not a dumb bunny, and finds refuge in swamp and marsh thicket, in brush along streams, in shocked grain stacks, near irrigation ditches and culverts, and close to brush piles.

When to Hunt Them The cottontail hunter need not get up at the crack of dawn to hunt this tasty rabbit. Br'er rabbit isn't going anywhere until kicked out of his hiding place, unless jumped by predators, dogs, or gunners. This cagey little animal holes up during stormy weather, and it is useless to look for him with any success during these periods.

Cottontails are hunted near their favorite haunts and along country roads in the evening

The weekend hunter turns most frequently to small game to keep his eye sharp and rabbit stew on the table. COURTESY OF THE AUTHOR

by stalking them or by using rabbit dogs such as the beagle or basset hound. There is nothing complicated about cottontail hunting if you use rabbit dog(s). Simply take the little "crooners" to good rabbit terrain, turn them loose, and wait for them to ferret one out of some brushy gully or thicket. Once the rabbit is flushed, the zigzag race is on. Usually the rabbit will circle, and the hunter tries to pot him as the dogs run it past him.

What Gun for Rabbits? Just about everything that shoots has been aimed at this little target. The scattergun probably wins out as the favorite rabbit-getter, and is a must if you use dogs. However, the .22 Long Rifle using hollow points or a .22 magnum rifle, and various handguns are also used to advantage. The average hunter has better luck using a 12-gauge scattergun with a modified choke shooting No. 6s. This combination will do a better all-around job, and there will be fewer cripples and more rabbits in the stew pot.

Mountain Cottontails Usually this rabbit is hunted after the main hunting season is over in the Rocky Mountain and Sierra Nevada ranges.

The mountain rabbit behaves differently from his lowland relatives. On top of deep snow he likes to sit and watch instead of hopping around or away through the willows and aspens.

Late afternoon is generally the best time to hunt. However, after a fresh snow, the morning is also an excellent time, for rabbits like to come out and sunbathe—soaking up the warm morning sun. Stormy weather is hardly ever productive, for Ole Cottontail stays below in his den.

You will perhaps need snowshoes if snow is deep, especially after a fresh fall. Snowshoes will help keep you up on top of the snow, and the going won't be so tough. Most rabbits will sit tight on snow until approached too closely. If they do take off, they will generally stop once, offering an excellent standing shot.

Dogs are seldom used when gunning for mountain cottontails. The snow normally is too soft and deep for good use of rabbit hounds, and when crusty will cut their paws to pieces. So don't cripple or tire your dogs when these conditions prevail—leave them at home!

The Snowshoe Rabbit The snowshoe rabbit is slightly larger than the cottontail bunny, but smaller than the "jack." The snowshoe or varying hare is found in many of our cold-weather states and has many of the characteristics of the cottontail. He will run a pound or two heavier than his cousin, the cottontail, has a brown coat in summer, and gradually changes to white in the winter.

He is hunted in northern swamps, cedar and pine plantations. The thicker the cover the better he likes it. This species will not hole up when chased, as the cottontail does, but will run and jump in great bounds and most always circles back to where you flushed him. Generally, when startled, he will hop a short distance, then invariably sit up and look back at his pursuer; this is the time to pour on the lead.

You can stalk, walk them up or, best of all, turn your rabbit hounds loose. Almost any dog with a little hunting experience will make a fair rabbit dog. You will probably need webs to track Mr. Snowshoe. In deep snow beagles and basset hounds are too short-legged to be of much help. If you do use dogs, don't let them depend on snow for moisture. Carry a canteen of water and a bowl for the dogs, and put a few dog biscuits in your pack, unless you plan on sharing your noonday lunch with them.

An autoloader 12-gauge shotgun is the most popular snowshoe weapon when used with low-base No. 6 shot.

The Swamp Rabbit The swamp bunny is the biggest and most elusive of the edible rabbits, and is found mostly in the southern states. He will weigh up to six pounds, and can run like his smaller cousins, swim like an otter, and climb up on sloping trees like a raccoon. Although taken with a rifle or handgun, the "swamper" most often is bagged by a 12-gauge smoothbore.

Jackrabbit The jackrabbit is widely distributed in the United States and Canada. However, Mr. Big Ears is found in greater numbers on the Great Plains and west to Washington, Oregon, California, and the southwestern states. Those of the Midwest are heavy-bodied and often fat, frequently weighing 12 to 15 pounds, while those gunned in the arid Southwest and in desert terrain are stringy and tough. About the only way the latter can be eaten is to parboil and then roast with vegetables or by making a rabbit stew out of the meat. To the farmer these hare are a pest. In some towns they will denude your lawn if control measures are not taken.

The burrows the "jacks" live in are another reason they are unpopular with agriculturists. They are a large crater and can be dangerous to horseback riders and cattle as well as damaging to crops. Jacks fatten on alfalfa and other crops, so the farmer and rancher welcome the rifleman as long as he keeps gates closed and is careful with his shooting.

Because "Big Ears" is hard to get close to, but will often freeze when he senses danger, he is hunted with a scoped rifle or handgun more often than with a shotgun. A good combination is a .22 W.R.F. or .22 magnum autoloader, pump or lever action rifle using a 40-grain hollow-point bullet, equipped with a 4X scope and sighted in for 100 yards.

Rabbit Fever After bagging any species of rabbit, field dress as soon as possible and the meat will remain fresher than if carried all day in your game bag. This is true of any game.

Some rabbits (deer, elk, moose, and bear, too) are infected with tularemia or "rabbit fever," so wear a pair of rubber gloves when cleaning them. Gloves will help prevent infection through cuts and any scratches you may have on your hands in case you do down an infected animal. As long as game is well cooked, even if it happens to be infected, no harm will come through eating the meat. Another point, never let your dog(s) eat rabbit entrails or uncooked rabbit flesh.

Tree Squirrels Bright-eyed and bushy-tailed, squirrels are found throughout Canada and the United States. For the small-game hunter they are like the jay at times to the deer stalker because their incessant chatter announces the presence of an intruder. The red, also called the pine squirrel, is a scolder like his cousins, the gray, fox, and tassel-eared squirrel. All make excellent pot meat.

The tracks and other spoor are similar. The eastern gray is found in the eastern half of the continent, and the gray inhabits Washington, Oregon, and California along with the pine squirrel. The eastern fox, so much like the gray in size and appearance, extends just a little farther west.

Good squirrel habitat can be located by a few preseason scouting jaunts into the woods. Fresh spoor signs such as hulls from pine cones, the shells from hickory nuts, walnuts, acorns, pecans, etc., found on old stump tops and logs are signs of squirrel activities. Grain fields in the vicinity of woodlands are also attractive to old bushytail.

There are a number of ways to hunt this toothsome animal, but still-hunting usually proves the most effective for some gunners. Look for den trees and the clawmarks on the bark and well-worn cavity entrances.

To be successful, you must get up early in the morning—this means before daylight. From then on it is a waiting game, which usually pays off because squirrels are curious creatures. If a hunter can find a ripe mulberry tree, he is in luck. Squirrels are extremely fond of mulberries. They are also attracted to elm buds in the spring.

Raccoons The raccoon can be found in nearly all wooded areas of North America. This two- to three-foot animal prefers living in trees or hollow stumps, generally near water for easy feeding and washing. They like rough terrain, with thick briars, brushy thickets, creeks, marshes, and sandy beaches.

When cornered, a raccoon will fight anything, including man and dog. Woe to the dog that meets a big male 'coon in the water. He will climb on the dog's back, dig in his claws, and stick like a burr until the dog drowns.

The 'coon is a nocturnal animal, and is usually hunted in late evening on through the night until early morning. You usually hunt following hounds until the quarry is treed; then you knock the 'coon down at short range with a handgun or arm of your choice. Here again, the .22 is tops!

Opossum The opposum is traditionally an inhabitant of the southeastern part of the country, but has spread as far west as California, Oregon, Washington, and north to Michigan.

This slow-moving, ratlike creature, like the raccoon, is not particular about what he eats.

Small mammals, frogs, birds' eggs, insects, fruit, or whatever it can scrounge make up its diet. It inhabits about the same type of terrain as the 'coon. Usually found in wooded areas, swamps, and along streams or lake shores, it seeks shelter in old dens of other animals. Its trail pattern is very similar to that of the raccoon. However, in snow, the ratlike tail will leave a more or less zigzag trail between the foot tracks.

Since his habits are nocturnal, you won't have an easy time finding one if you wait too long after sunup. Early in the morning, however, you will stand a good chance of success—especially in the southern states. A .22 rifle will be adequate if you only try a still shot. Like a squirrel, he can scamper around a tree surprisingly fast. Many 'possum hunters stick to the 12-gauge shotgun and No. 6 shot.

Varmint Hunting a Year-Around Sport For the sportsman who wants to keep in good shooting form, there are all kinds of varmints: woodchuck, ground squirrel, badger, prairie dog, weasel, fox, coyote, bobcat, lynx, cougar, skunk, porcupine, wild house cats, and marauding calf- and sheep-killing dogs in some areas nearby. Jackrabbits and many other pests fill out the varmint bill-of-fare. Crow and magpies eat or destroy game bird eggs and nests, damage crops, and are a year-around varminter's target. These also provide fine wing-shooting practice.

Your local game warden can advise you where, when, and how to hunt varmints in your county and state.

The .22 L.R. and .22 magnum will take care of the smaller varmints. However, for long-range chuck shooting, a .222-, .243-, or .244-caliber bullet will be about right. So will most of the wildcat calibers!

Much varmint hunting is done by reloaders using "wildcat" cartridges—which is simply a cartridge which is not a regular factory production job. They usually are made from existing cartridge cases that have been necked down to take a regular production bullet. Some of these loads are hot stuff and flat shooting!

For general varmint shooting, use the .222 and calibers listed above sighted in at about 225 yards, and if possible with a variable-power scope mounted on it—or at least one of the 6X makes an excellent varmint shooting iron. It is light to carry, tremendously accurate, and of such light recoil one can shoot it all day and it won't mess up your shoulder as a bigbore rifle would.

Chapter 12

NORTH AMERICAN BIG-GAME HUNTING

The Trophy Hunter With the exception of the sportsman fortunate enough to live in the Far North, hunting in Alaska or the Yukon for big-game such as Alaska brown, grizzly, and black bear, moose, caribou, Dall or Stone sheep entails time and money. Generally it costs the out-of-state hunter $100 to $150 per day plus license to hire an outfitter and guide to take him into the interior by saddle and pack train, or to have a "bush pilot" fly him and his equipment into remote back country. It costs about $2000 per trip to hunt polar bear, which is done mostly via aircraft flying 100 miles or more over the northern ice floe to secure the great white bear.

Game for Everyone Some species of big game can be found for every hunter in the United States, Canada, and Mexico. Though hunting pressure is heavy along highways, big game is underhunted in many of the best places not accessible by road. Some sections can still be reached off main highways and by following old logging roads and fire motorways. Still more remote regions are reached by rail, boat, aircraft, or by pack outfit.

Hunting lodges, motels, and free primitive forest campsites are available and will suit most local or nonresident hunters who may be on modest budgets.

The three main species of deer—whitetail, blacktail, and mule deer—are the most popular, widely distributed, and the most hunted big-game animals on this continent.

The Whitetail Deer The whitetail is the smallest of the three, and ranges the entire United States with the exception of a thin belt of country through the central states, and a wide strip along the Pacific coast. This species is easily identified by antlers that have all points branching out from the main beam, and by the large broad whitetail or "flag." The whitetail is largely a brush country deer and spends most of its life in thick foliage, marshy country, and brush-bordered open meadows, and around farm fields, orchards, and heavily timbered areas. Unlike the mule deer, the whitetail doesn't migrate from summer range to winter range, but lives within an area of a few square miles. Whereas the mule deer is not much of a brush country animal, it will tend to move into high, rough, mountainous or wooded terrain to escape heat, flies, and natural enemies in summer.

Although the whitetail is the smallest of the three species, exceptional bucks have weighed in at 300 pounds. Mule deer, on the other hand, average heavier than whitetail or Columbia blacktail. All overlap each other's range to a degree.

The Blacktail Deer The blacktail is a Pacific coast inhabitant and a subspecies of the mule deer, with many of its characteristics. It has the same antler type, even the same stiff-legged bouncing gait, but has a flat tail shaped like that of the whitetail deer.

Blacktail roam from the Sierra Nevada and Cascade ranges to the coasts in California, Ore-

The mountain sheep is one of the great hunting trophies available in America. OREGON
GAME COMMISSION

gon, and Washington and northward along the coast of British Columbia into the southern part of Alaska, where they provide excellent hunting.

In the West, a popular method of hunting blacktail is to hunt with a partner. One hunter works along a ridgetop of a canyon or valley; the other, slightly behind, works up from the bottom. In this manner one is apt to push spooked deer to within shooting sight of the other.

Mule Deer Mule deer range over the greater part of the western United States and Canada, and south into the upper part of Mexico and Baja California.

The muley has several distinguishing characteristics, and derives its name from its mule-

like ears. The blacktails and mule have lighter faces with a dark horseshoe mark on their foreheads. The mule have a light patch similar to that of the elk, and a thin white tail with a black tip. The whitetail has the largest tail of the three species, pure white underneath and darker than the body color on the outside. The summer coat of these deer is red or yellowish red or light brown. The fall or "blue" coat of all three is deep gray brown or olive brown, blending into yellow brown on legs and flanks, white inside legs, under tail, and underbelly.

The following drawings will illustrate the characteristics of antlers, tails, and size and location of the metatarsal or musk glands on the legs.

Deer are grazers as well as browsers—i.e.,

Whitetail deer is generally considered the smallest of the three North American species. WISCONSIN CONSERVATION DEPARTMENT

they tend to live on grass and small plants in the spring and summer, feeding on brush and acorns in the fall, and as snow grows deeper, subsist on tips of brush and the branches and twigs of various trees as well as bark and moss.

If a hunter will locate a deer crossing or trail and keep it under observation for several hours (or even a full day) and has the patience to sit perfectly still without smoking or shuffling about, he is fairly sure to see game.

Squirrels and jays may announce your pres-

ence with their chattering, but if you remain still, they will soon quiet down. Also they will signal you when game approaches. Deer, bear, or other game make noise too as they meander along, such as the snap of a twig underfoot, the soft crunch of snow, or the shuffle of leaves and other forest litter. This should put you on guard!

While most mule deer are hunted by stalking, I have had excellent results on the western slopes of the Sierra Nevada Range in California

If you're the kind of deer hunter who would rather wait for the deer instead of stalking, dress properly for it, and bring an inflatable cushion. SAVAGE ARMS PHOTO

by sitting in semi-concealment in hard-hunted areas on opening day—letting other hunters push game by my hideout.

To keep comfortable in the cold, frosty mountain air waiting for the right buck to come along, I dress warmly. On extra-cold mornings I drag out an old olive-drab blanket from my "stampede" hunting pack. It has a hole cut out of the center and I slip it over my head and wear it like a Mexican serape. However, I suppose some day I'll be mistaken for a deer. To stall this off, I carry a shrill referee's whistle that I use when another hunter comes close or aims his scope at my noggin. Another item of comfort is an air pillow that I blow up and seat my old saddle-toughened seat on. Guess this old Ranger likes his comfort—why not?

Scattergun or Rifle for Deer? The rifle has long been a favorite weapon of the deer hunter. Today, however, the shotgun is gaining increasingly wide acceptance in certain sections of the country, and several factors are involved in this.

One is the simple fact of regulations. In the heavily populated industrial East, for example, hunting with rifles is considered too dangerous, and as a result in Massachusetts, Rhode Island, Delaware, New Jersey, part of New York, and some of the other eastern and southern states, shotguns are the only firearms that can legally be used to hunt deer. There is another reason for the shotgun's growing popularity in the East (and in brushy thickets in the West and Southwest). A great number of hunters have discovered that in the thick, brushy terrain in which most eastern deer hunting is done, the smoothbore is often superior to the rifle. Most shots are snap shots taken through brush at distances from 20 to 100 yards. Within this range, buckshot and rifled slugs are highly effective. However, I believe that slugs do a better job than buckshot. Buckshot scatters over too large an area and is apt to gut-shoot an animal as a result, leaving it badly crippled to slip off, suffer, and die. With a slug shell, a hunter can place his shot in a vital spot. Deer and bear rifle calibers are listed on page 46. Shotgun slugs and buckshot gauges follow these.

Elk Our western elk is a regal and huge animal compared to other species of deer. The Roosevelt elk of the Olympic Peninsula is the largest elk in the world, and roams from northern California on up into northwestern Canada. The Tule elk is much smaller and makes its home on the eastern slope and valleys of the Sierra Nevada Range. The American elk habitat lies coincident with the Rockies in a large strip of land from eastern British Columbia and Alberta, Canada, southward into Arizona and New Mexico to a short distance over the Mexican border. States having the largest bands are Oregon, Washington, Idaho, Montana, and Wyoming, and in northern California. The largest herds are in Yellowstone and Grand Teton National Parks. Winter snows drive the huge park herds from higher elevations to their winter range outside the parks where the elk do enormous damage to ranch crops and fences and compete for forage so that control measures are necessary to keep cattle and domestic animals from starving to death.

Elk Signs The hunter will do well to look for elk signs. The droppings are larger and rounder than that of the mule deer and somewhat larger than that of moose. Since elk share the same range with cattle, there may be some difficulty distinguishing the tracks, for they are similar. There are other signs to look for. In winter you will find pits dug into the snow where elk have been pawing through for feed, or you may find beds in snow patches in the summer at the higher elevations where they lie to cool off or flattened places in the grass where they have bedded down. During the hunting season you will note elk "trees" where bulls have scraped the velvet from their antlers or where a bull in anger has pawed and scraped the bark from trees and tramped brush down to the ground. If you are in high mountain elk country and come on a shallow alpine lake or pond, look for tracks at the muddy border. If the water is roily it denotes that elk have been there to bathe, drink, and graze nearby. Still another sign—you will find the bark of certain trees scored with toothmarks, where the elk have fed on the bark.

How Elk Are Hunted On the Pacific coast and the Olympic Peninsula, elk are mostly stalked on foot, since horses cannot always negotiate

North America has many big-game trophies waiting for the intrepid hunter. Fred Bear bagged this moose with a single shot. BEAR ARCHERY COMPANY

the steep slopes and through the heavy timber. Most of the weekend hunters from Seattle, Olympia, Grays Harbor, and nearby towns drive the access roads off U.S. 101 that circle the peninsula for 326 miles. They travel the back country roads and fire motorways, park their vehicles, set up camp near one of the elk crossings, and stalk them on foot. The elk tend to use old elk trails or "runs," so the best bet is to lie in concealment and wait for them to come along. Snow drives the elk out of the higher elevations of Olympic National Park onto their winter range outside the park, usually in late November when the large bands break up into smaller groups and scatter. Many gunners are lucky and collect their elk the first day and head home with a winter's supply of steaks, roasts, and elkburgers.

Canada requires the hunter after big game to hire a guide. In the United States, having a guide is not mandatory. However, in the Rocky Mountain regions of the West, most hunters, unless they own their own stock and know the country, hire a guide and pack train to take them into elk country. A base camp is set up and the hunters work out from there. Saddle horses are used to get into a likely "elk park." The stock is left in a protected timber area and the hunters stalk on foot. Many hunters, not wanting the heavy expense of retaining a guide and pack train for the duration of their hunt, have their camp outfit and gear packed in, and the packer returns to his station, coming back for the hunters at a predetermined date to pick up the hunting outfit and any game killed.

The Spoilage Law Every year I have been on game patrol, I have encountered a hunter who has stalked many miles into rough terrain, downed his quarry, dressed it out, and then wondered how he was going to get an animal the size of a horse to his camp. Several times I have found a large mule deer or elk carcass in the back country with a hindquarter missing and the rest of the meat left to rot. In many states there is a waste or spoilage law requiring a hunter to bring out all usable meat. In Washington the elk hunter must bring out the head with the carcass.

Horses Needed The hunter unable to hire a horse to pack his kill from where he shot it can sometimes, by offering to divide the meat, get another hunter or two to assist him in removing the elk quarters to his camp or car. By using packboards, this may require one or two trips from the quartered animal to camp—depending on the amount of help involved. The best bet is to use a horse or mule to do the packing. The prospective elk hunter should, before arranging for an elk hunt, assure himself that horses are available. This means making arrangements months in advance with a rancher or packer, for once the hunting season starts, most pack stock is booked for the season.

What Power Rifle for Elk? An elk is a big animal and requires a bullet weight of at least 180 to 220 grains. You are referred to the ammunition chart in Chapter 4.

Moose The moose is North America's largest game animal and the largest of the deer family. Of the three North American moose, Canadian, Alaska, and Shiras, or Wyoming moose, the Shiras is the smallest. Some Alaska moose have weighed in at from 1200 to 1800 pounds. Along the Alaska Railway, train crews have had to stop the train to get moose off the track—and in turn have been charged by an angered bull.

Today the moose is found northward into Alaska, and its over-all range includes all the wooded country of Canada and Alaska and extends southward inside the borders of the northern states, and along the Continental Divide in parts of Idaho, Montana, and Wyoming. Unlike mule deer and elk, which migrate to lower elevation for winter forage, moose remain within the same general area the year around.

Concentration of willows in meadows is excellent moose food and these are known as "moose pastures" or "moose parks." Moose food is varied. In summer they may be seen feeding on aquatic vegetation growing in ponds, lakes, and stream beds, or at the edges of such water. In the winter, when succulent plants are no longer available, moose diet consists of leaves, twigs, bark and branch tips, but they favor willow and quaking aspen. In some wooded areas moose will graze the limbs from trees as high as they can reach—even standing on their hind legs to do so.

The moose track is nearest to that of the elk in size and shape, though it is larger and more pointed. When running in mud or snow, the dewclaws will show. Other signs for the hunter are the droppings. In winter they are distinctive. Because of the dry browse diet they appear like compressed sawdust, and may be round or elongated, and usually smooth. Like other deer, if they are fresh they will glisten and even steam for a short period. In summer, when feeding on green forage, the dung is much like that of cattle.

Generally, getting into moose country requires time and effort, a hunting camp and partners, and for the nonresident, the use of guides and outfitters. However, moose can be hunted with success even by the weekend hunter in parts of Ontario and in other provinces by aircraft, canoe, boat, train, and car. Hunting pressure is heavy along some highways, yet moose are underhunted in other less accessible places. They are hunted by stalking and by calling with a moose horn made from birch bark.

Moose are also hunted successfully by canoe in vast back country lake regions of Canada—chiefly in Ontario, Manitoba, Nova Scotia, and Newfoundland.

The Moose Gun Use the same large-caliber, high-velocity bullet that is recommended in the ammunition chart (see Chapter 4).

Caribou The caribou is most numerous of all the big-game animals in the state of Alaska. This magnificent member of the deer tribe is primarily a northern animal, and ranges in much of Canada and throughout most of Alaska. Though he has advanced far into the bleak and cold Arctic, a region too cold for other members of the deer family, he once ranged through the northern states. Now there are only token herds that occasionally range into the northern tips of Idaho and Montana. Generally, they live on a wide and changing range primarily in Alaska and the Arctic tundra of Canada.

Caribou are migratory animals. Of all the caribou, the barren ground caribou moves about the most, when herds of many thousands travel from one range to another in search of food. The mountain caribou are less migratory because

their range is limited, and confine their feeding to the mountain meadows near the timberline, leaving only to seek shelter at the lower elevations during the more severe winter weather. The mountain caribou do not travel in large herds, and in summer will run alone.

Caribou Fodder In winter caribou feed mostly on lichen, sometimes called reindeer moss, dead grass, and the bark of Arctic willows. In summer they graze on green grasses, plants, and shrubs. On occasion they will chew on shed antlers for the calcium they contain to balance their diet. Rodents and other animals also gnaw on the antlers of the deer family for the same reason.

Hunting Technique The majority of hunters select a hunting area which offers an opportunity to hunt bear, big-horn sheep, mountain goats, elk, or moose in addition to one of the three species of caribou. However, a few hunters will make it their purpose to hunt only caribou, chiefly for a trophy head. The caribou is stalked similar to elk, and the hunter must be very careful in his approach with the wind in his favor or the beast will head over into the next range of mountains.

What Gun? The most flat-shooting deer rifles will be adequate for caribou. However, most gunners use a high-velocity, heavy bullet to take brown bear or other game on the same hunt. Check calibers and bullets on the ammo chart.

Antelope The antelope is a western plains animal, ranging from southern Saskatchewan south into northern Mexico. It is found in Montana, the western sections of North and South Dakota, western Nebraska, Wyoming, Idaho, Utah, Nevada, Colorado, eastern Oregon, and parts of California, Arizona, New Mexico, western Texas, and Oklahoma. In some states antelope is hunted by permit only—so check the game laws for the state in which you plan to hunt.

This graceful animal is fleet-footed, and its running gait is smooth and level, with hardly any rise in the air at each bound. However, it can bounce along and leap 8 to 10 feet at a jump, and has been clocked at over 40 miles per hour. When running, the pronghorn will run with its

This outfitter packs elk out of fog-shrouded Montana wilderness area. U. S. FOREST SERVICE

mouth open, gulping huge breaths of air to speed it on.

Antelope Tracks Antelope tracks are much like those of deer, but the hind foot is usually broader. In some areas mule deer share the same range as the antelope, and their tracks may be confused. In many respects the scat (droppings) resemble those of deer and mountain sheep. When looking for antelope spoor or tracks you will find that they have a habit of scraping the ground with a hoof, then depositing droppings or urine on the bare spot. This is just the reverse of the wildcat's habit of scratching the earth, then covering its mess with dirt and debris. Thus, types of scratch signs can be distinguished by the hunter.

When frightened or worried, the antelope produces a loud whistling sound similar to that made by deer. When annoyed or curious, the animal will stamp a foot as deer often do.

Hunting Methods On arriving on antelope range, the hunter parks his car and seeks out an elevation with reasonably good cover, and glasses the area for game. For this job, good 7×50 or 8-power binoculars are excellent. Many riflemen carry a 20-power spotting scope to insure the quality of a trophy head before beginning the stalk. Others seek out an elevation with good cover and wait for other, more active hunters to move herds or individual pronghorns within fair rifle range.

Bow and Arrows for Antelope If you are a good stalker, antelope can and have been taken with the bow and arrow. However, shooting them Indian style is no easy way to hunt them.

Some Browning high-power rifles. The Safari with 4X scope; the Magnum; the Medallion; the Olympian. BROWNING ARMS COMPANY

The black bear outnumbers the Kodiak, Alaska brown, and grizzly bear. He's still one of the hunter's toughest opponents. BEAR ARCHERY COMPANY

The stalker must take advantage of every bit of cover (the rifleman, too!), for the pronghorn, though he depends little on his nose, has seemingly telescopic vision, and can spot movement at unbelievable distances.

The Best Rifle Most antelope shooting is done with a longe-range, "flat-shooting," telescoped rifle at ranges from 150 to 500 plus yards. Long shots are the rule rather than the exception. The rifleman unfamiliar with the trajectory of his weapon at any distance within these extremes is unlikely to eat pronghorn steak or -burgers.

Many hunters are still using the .30-06 with a .150-grain bullet or the .270 Winchester, using the .130-grain soft-point bullet. However, the more recent calibers are moving ahead of these old-timers, such as the .243, .244, .264, .280, .284, and .308 caliber ultraflat shooters.

The Bear Facts The four bear, the Kodiak, Alaska brown, the grizzly, and the American black have many similarities and are hunted to a greater extent than the polar bear that trek the icefloes and islands of the Arctic Ocean. All members of the bear clan are inclined to be solitary in their habits, except during the breeding season, and only unusual circumstances bring them together in groups of two or more. The black bruin outnumbers the other species by the thousands, and exists nearly everywhere on the North American continent. Mr. Blackie may appear in several colorings—black, brown, cinnamon, and variations of these colors.

Bear Paths Bear have well-established trails, and the hunter should take these into consideration while stalking bear. Blackie prefers to utilize game trails, old logging roads, and fire motorways. He enjoys grazing along telephone and power line right-of-ways to feed on the tender shoots of grass and young plants. In bear country, you will find man-made forest trails used more than any other terrain without paths.

Bear, like other animals, like to move about in the earlier hours of the morning and toward dusk in the evening. While most game species will work the edge of mountain meadows, bear prefer to stay closer to brush and wood patches or to foliage that will conceal their movements.

Bear Stables The hunter may run across a resting or bedding nest scooped out in the vegetation among willows, alders, and wild cherry thickets. Sometimes beds will be found where moss or pine needles have been scraped together in piles, some 10 to 12 feet in diameter with large piles of bear dung in evidence. These are called "bear stables" by some old-timers. In wooded terrain it will be noticed that bear trails will go under obstructions that deer and other game have to go around. It is the wise hunter who avoids following under these tight quarters that might lead into a bear stable. Due caution must be used, for there may be a number of bear nearby, or a sow and her cubs may be resting at one of these points. And don't sell the black bear short, even if he is sometimes called the "clown of the woods," for he can turn vicious when wounded or cornered.

The Bear Signposts Bear wallows, mud baths, and "bear trees" are other signs that bear have been around. The observant hunter will notice "size trees" where a large bear has placed claw scratches as high as he can reach, which is a means of showing the height of the bear as a challenge to rivals. Next is the "rubbing tree," where bear sit or rear up against the tree and scratch their backs or sides, causing hair to be rubbed off or stuck into bark crevices. These sign trees are similar to the scentpost of the dog tribe. A third tree is the "candy tree." Bear will bite and pull off large strips of bark from pine and other coniferous trees, in many cases gir-

dling the tree. Having pulled away the bark, they scrape the sweet juicy cambium layer away between the outer bark and wood with their incisior teeth, leaving vertical toothmarks on the trunk. In some states black bear are placed on the predator list. In western Washington, black bear do so much damage to young conifers that they are hunted the year around.

Bear Menus Like deer, black bear like to feed in old abandoned orchards and berry patches, and are bagged while the hunter is primarily after deer or other game. So look for Blackie around these spots where fruit trees have returned to the wild. He also enjoys manzanita and huckleberries at higher elevations. When feeding on berries, bear droppings will be well spliced with berry seeds. Bear will eat meat whenever they can, killing faun and crippled or sick animals. They will even dig out ground squirrels or marmots on occasion. A meat-hungry bear will attack sheep at times practically in the rancher's yard. When feeding on furred animals, the dung will contain large amounts of hair. The smell of carrion will draw jays, crows, and buzzards, and in turn attracts a bear if one is in the territory. Although the bear is pretty much a vegetarian, he will fish whenever he can do so easily. Occasionally you will come across a bear "cache" where a bear has covered part of a carcass of some animal to ripen.

For dessert, bear like slash and windfall areas where wild berries are apt to be found—and he is a *bear* for sweets. Bee or honey trees are other bruin delicacies the *pièces de résistance* of most bear.

Don't overlook garbage dumps near resort areas in the mountains that have been closed for the season; they can be bonanzas at times. Other spots are abandoned sawmills and old camps where bear like to nose around. However, if bear spoor isn't fresh and plentiful it is best to look elsewhere.

Stalking Blackie There are certain conditions under which the hunter may forget the food angle, and hunt along a bear trail. Generally, such trails are made by old bruin moving from a bedding spot to a place he can pick up odds and ends. He sleeps wherever night overtakes him within his territory of approximately six

*Bear baiting, leaving entrails for bruin to clean up, is illegal in some states. Wild
berries and honey trees are other delicacies that will give you a shot within 12 to
36 hours.* MAINE DEPARTMENT OF ECONOMIC DEVELOPMENT

square miles. If a sign isn't fresh, don't give up if you don't connect on the first day, for bear will travel this route every few days. Hunting a bear trail, once you have located one, is simply a matter of taking a stand where the terminal breeze will not give you away, and quietly waiting and watching for his appearance.

Bear Baiting Some hunters attract bear by baiting with a large can of offal secured from a slaughterhouse. The ingredients are placed in a burlap sack or "croaker sack" and hung on a tree limb to ripen. If there is a bear passing within a mile or so of the bait tree, he will come and investigate the goodies. The only drawback is that you have to be on the windward side and he may get your scent too. Check the game laws in the area you plan to bait to find if baiting is legal. If it is not, I doubt if you could be prosecuted if you watch over the entrails of any game you or another hunter has gutted in case a bear comes by to clean them up. The odds are that every pile of deer or other big-game entrails will be visited by at least one bear within 12 to 36 hours after the kill is made.

The Bear Gun Many hunters want to know what is the best weapon for black bear. To this I might add that archers have hunted and killed everything from polar to black bear—so you can see bear are shot at more or less short range. Your deer rifle or slug-loaded shotgun are sufficient to drop black bear.

Old Silver Tip There are about fifteen subspecies of old *Ursus horribilis*, with about half living in western Canada. Alaska has the largest number in the States. South of the Canadian border the grizzly is a threatened species. Most of the stateside grizzlies are located in the high rough mountain wilderness areas of our western national forests, chiefly in Wyoming, Montana, Idaho, and Colorado, with a few scattered in northern Washington. The largest number, however, are concentrated in and around Glacier, Yellowstone, and Rocky Mountain National Parks.

The grizzly's coloration varies from creamy yellow to dark brown or almost black with silver-tipped guard hairs along the spine. The black bear does not have the broad head, high hump at the withers, and the dished-in face of the grizzly or brown bear, nor the silver guard hairs that characterize the silver tip.

Old Humpback's range is normally in the most remote and inaccessible mountainous back country. Here he stakes out a huge domain which he protects against a contant challenge by other bear and scavengers. Each spring he renews his "claim" on trees bordering his range by rearing to his full height and scratching his mark as high as he can reach. Then he rubs his itching skin, which aids in the removal of his winter coat.

Grizzly Fare Upon emerging from his winter quarters after his long fast, the grizzly generally shuns heavy cover and drops down to the foothills where he grazes on green grass, rock chucks, gophers and insects, or whatever else he can manage to find. He is a great feeder on salmon that have spawned and died, and will flip the floaters out of the shallow waters onto the bank where they are consumed. With the arrival of warm weather he retires to the shade and coolness of the mountain forests, where his diet is made up of roots, nuts, and berries. To top it off, he isn't above helping himself to the kill of other animals. One of his enemies, the black bear, finds his only safety from his larger cousin by climbing a tree. A grizzly can climb a tree during his cub days. However, when he grows toward maturity he is unable to climb because of his tremendous weight and extra-large claws, plus the stiffening of his wrist joints.

Methods of Hunting Hunters after sheep, goat, elk, moose, and mule deer are most likely to get a shot at a silver tip if they will watch from concealment, the spot where they have dressed out game. Generally, they will pack into a known grizzly range on a grizzly safari, establish a base camp, and then climb to some vantage point that offers a wide view of the surrounding terrain. Here carefully glass the vicinity with a spotting scope or pair of powerful binoculars to locate the quarry. Once spotted, the stalk must be planned. A hurried stalk too often proves unsuccessful.

One method used is tracking. However, this requires a thorough knowledge of woodsmanship, grizzly habits, and considerable endurance. Another method is by baiting, as outlined earlier for black bear.

The Grizzly Gun This bruin is heavier and larger than the black and can stand more *lead;* therefore, it calls for a more powerful weapon than used for deer and black bear. See ammunition and caliber chart.

The Big Bear The great Alaska brown bear is the largest on the North American continent. Like the grizzly, the brownie varies in size and weight in different regions, with the average weighing in the vicinity of 800 pounds. A few of these record giant bear have weighed in at up to 1600 pounds!

Brownie Diet This bear also has the typical characteristics of other species of the bear family, that of unpredictable behavior. Like other bear he is omnivorous. He will generally try to avoid trouble, but will fight off man or beast when he is feeding on a kill he has made, or while feasting on the remains of a winter-killed animal. Like the grizzly, when he leaves his den in the spring he moves down the mountain to the valleys, where he browses on grass and green plants. During the summer he spends his time along the coastal and other streams, where he lives on salmon that are trapped in shallows while spawning, or have died and floated along until they have beached on a sandbar. He also likes berries for dessert.

His Range The brown bear is found over a wide area on the Alaska mainland; he also inhabits a number of Alaska islands—Kodiak, Baranof, Admiralty, and others.

Hunting Methods The hunter after Alaska brownies is required by law to employ a guide, and this bear is hunted similar to the grizzly. Your guide will advise you where and how to take this monstrous animal.

The Weapon to Down Him First, it is inadvisable to use a deer or black bear weapon on this huge animal! Every experienced guide and hunter has emphasized the need for a big-bore rifle using a heavy, high-velocity bullet to down this enormous chunk of meat. Warning: Watch out for him when wounded or running into him when he has a toothache! Refer to page with caliber and ammunition chart for brownie ammunition size.

The Great White Bear The polar bear, because of the remoteness of his habitat, is not usually hunted by the average hunter. However, its coarse, furred pelt is sought by a few sportsmen who have the time and don't mind spending a few thousand dollars for an Arctic safari of this magnitude. This king-size bear of the northland ice pack is one of the largest of the surviving members of the big bear family. It ranks in size with that of the largest Alaska brown bear, often weighing between 1200 and 1600 pounds dripping wet.

Its hunting is strictly regulated and enforced by the Alaska Fish and Game Department and federal law, and not over 200 special hunt permits are issued annually. Similar protection is afforded the bear by the Canadian Government within its jurisdiction.

In his frozen habitat, the polar bear spends most of his time roaming far and wide in search of seal or other prey such as Arctic ducks and fish.

Because of his wide-ranging habit of covering vast areas over the Arctic ice pack and swimming from ice pan to ice islands in search of seal, his main diet, the polar bear is a difficult animal to locate.

Aircraft are necessary to search for the animal, and planes must range from 100 to 200 miles over the Arctic Ocean. Once the bear is spotted, the hunter and his pilot-guide return to land and then set forth by boat to reach the area where the bear was last sighted. This can prove dangerous at times while dodging icebergs and islands of drifting ice. If hunted entirely by aircraft, two planes are used for safety reasons. Once the bear is sighted, the aircraft containing the pilot-guide and sportsman lands on the nearest safe ice pan strong enough to withstand the weight of the aircraft, and then the bear is stalked. If the first aircraft makes a safe landing the second lands some distance off so that if one aircraft cracks through the ice there is a chance of rescuing survivors. The second plane's crew backs up the stalkers, and assists with the skinning and the loading of gear if the hunter(s) are successful.

It is a dangerous and exciting way to hunt, and there have been disastrous instances with the loss of aircraft and crew. Several hunters have received cold-weather injuries, but were

Camouflage when hunting polar bear is very important for obvious reasons. BEAR
ARCHERY COMPANY

saved through the efforts of the guard plane's crew who were able to fly them to a hospital on the mainland in time.

The Gun The same high-velocity bullet used on brown bear will down the polar bear. Refer to ammunition chart (see Chapter 4).

Rocky Mountain Goat This white goat is a type of antelope, and is a cud-chewer like the mountain sheep. Like the high country sheep, the mountain goat, as his name implies, is a dweller of the dizzy heights and crags, and his distribution is limited to the mountain ranges that offer this type of wilderness terrain. A few goats range the crags of the Olympics, the Rocky Mountains of Colorado, Wyoming, Montana, and Idaho, but they are most plentiful in the northwestern Rockies of British Columbia and Alberta and in Alaska.

Severe weather seldom forces the goat to leave his sky-high peaks for the protection of the forests below. However, in the southern ranges, the goat comes down to the valley meadows to graze during the summer and will be seen in the vicinity of bands of sheep. For safety reasons, he hardly ever strays far from his home of cliffs.

How to Get a Shot at One If this slow-moving billy isn't a difficult animal to hunt, it is because of his remoteness. He is hunted less than other big game. Of course, some are specifically hunted by trophy hunters. In some regions, goats can be found in rough, steep, but relatively small canyons where at times a hunter on horseback, riding along the rim, can spot a lone billy bedded either below or across the narrow canyon. The goat hunter must use caution as to where he shoots his quarry; otherwise a goat

Browning Standard Safari high-power rifle. Browning Magnum Safari high-power rifle. BROWNING ARMS COMPANY

not dropped in his tracks may roll over a sheer cliff and not only damage the horns and pelt, but be impossible to recover.

What Caliber to Use on Goat The Rocky Mountain goat is a heavy-bodied animal, and some fat old billies have weighed up to 300 pounds. The rifle to use should be the same as that mentioned for antelope and caribou—a flat-shooting scoped rifle.

The Big-Horn Sheep It appears as though domestic sheep have taken over most of the summer range of the once wild sheep. However, there is still some good sheep country left. The Rocky Mountain big-horn, the largest of the several species of wild sheep, can still be found in Colorado, Montana, Wyoming, and the northern part of Idaho. Due to good range management, sheep have been re-established in Arizona, Texas, the Dakotas, and parts of New Mexico.

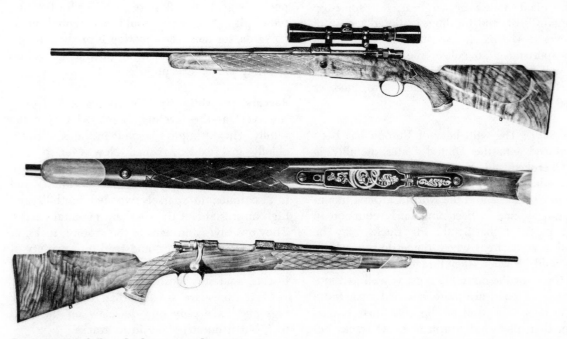

Browning Medallion high-power rifles. BROWNING ARMS COMPANY

The desert sheep is found in Arizona, Nevada, and Mexico. There are a few scattered herds in the southern Sierra Nevada of California. However, the largest herds of mountain sheep are located in western Canada and in Alaska.

This cud-chewer with a four-chambered stomach is related to the antelope, and the goat family. The white Dall and black Stone sheep of northwestern Canada and Alaska are among the most coveted prizes among big-game hunters.

Hunting these nimbled-footed animals remains good in Canada and Alaska, where their future is assured by the overflow from Mt. McKinley National Park, and the famous Canadian national parks to the south.

Sheep are creatures of habit, live most of their lives in one area, and will only migrate in extreme emergency, as when their water supply is cut off or predators have moved in. However, they soon return to their old stamping grounds as soon as conditions return to normal.

Bagging Big-Horns Hunting wild sheep is to many sportsmen the greatest and one of the most difficult of all types of hunting. The hunter must be in excellent health and physical condition to climb the rugged peaks and terrain where these agile creatures live among the clouds.

The giant Alaska brown bear, the spike-top mountain goat, and the huge antlered moose of the North Woods are second-best trophies to most sportsmen. To collect the big-horn sheep you will need a high-velocity bullet with a flat trajectory such as the .264, .284, .270, .308, or .30-06.

Wild Boar The wild boar of Europe has been introduced into the United States, notably in the Cherokee and Nantahala National Forests. It provides excellent hunting for the local sportsmen in Tennessee and the North Carolina mountain ranges, and is becoming fairly common in other parts of the South. Pig tracks may be found in some areas where domestic swine have gone wild, or where they forage in deer country. The tracks of the domestic pigs, as well as those of the wild boar, are more rounded than those of the deer. The trail of the wild boar is narrower than that of the farm hog, the tracks being almost in single file. Those of domestic swine are off-set, forming a single zigzag line or two lines.

The wild boar is of course more agile than the farm pig and can become quite dangerous when cornered. The boar will run or jump up banks and over fences too high for farm-fattened hogs or the wild peccary of the Southwest. Wild boar frequently cross steams by walking across wind-felled trees or logs. They are good jumpers, and will leap over obstacles that other animals would have to go around or under. They are taller than domestic pigs. Therefore, the height that trees are muddied may be evidence of identity.

Another sign to look for is rooted-up areas where pigs have been rooting for plant food, and pig wallows similar to those made by bear. Look for "pig trees," too! A wild boar will rub on trees and stumps, gouging them with its tusks, so look for tell-tale hairs and tracks. When feeding on grass and greens, the pig produces pellets that are comparable to those of elk and moose and at times give the appearance of miniature horse manure.

How They Are Hunted Boar hunting is usually conducted with packs of hounds, and shots are mostly taken at short range. Rifles or shotguns using slugs are used to down the 200- to 300-pound hogs. Deer rifles are excellent for bagging these pigs, but they should be sighted in at 50 yards, for most the shooting is of short range. A 12-gauge smoothbore using rifled slugs will do a better job of execution.

Peccary, the Little Pig The peccary, known in the West as the javelina, is related to the pig family. This little pig's home is in the Southwest, chiefly in Texas, Arizona, New Mexico, and parts of Mexico and south to Central America. It inhabits the mesquite and cactus country and is also found in sparsely wooded foothills and high up in some of the southern mountain areas. They use caves and dens in the ground, rocks, or hollow logs for shelter, and feed on a variety of wild foods, roots, bulbs, wild fruit, nuts, and insects, and any flesh that is available.

Their hoofs are smaller than those of other pigs and have only one dewclaw on the hind feet, but it doesn't show in its tracks.

It is an active little animal, and will leap 6 to

8 feet at a jump. The javelina is a ferocious little bundle of dynamite and weighs in at 40 to 50 pounds of energy, and is fast on the pickup. He will charge at you, but usually turns off when he gets up close. However, when in herds, peccary have been known to attack a person on foot, and their tusks can do considerable damage. They will tree wildcats and run coyotes off and even kill and eat rattlesnakes!

Westerners use Jeeps or other four-wheel-drive vehicles to cover large expanses of the rough, arid country the peccary inhabit rather than stalk them entirely on foot. Horses are also used in hunting them in open country.

Once you have slain a javelina, you should immediately remove the musk gland, located from 6 to 8 inches above its stubby tail between the hips. If this isn't done, the gland's secretions will permeate the whole carcass and the meat will be unfit to eat. If properly dressed out, the meat tastes similar to lean boar or domesticated pig.

Check with the Game Department of the state in which you plan to hunt them, since regulations and seasons change from time to time.

Pig Hunting Hunting these little desert pigs with dogs is not difficult, but can be hazardous for the dogs when a pig is cornered. I have seen a cornered pig give out a squeal and suddenly half a dozen of his desert mates arrived and charged the dogs. Two of my best dogs were slashed so badly that they were not much use the rest of the hunting season.

In pig territory, hunting upwind, the hunter will be able to smell a herd of musk hogs. If he hunts downwind, he might hear the herd take off through the brush, but will seldom see them. It takes a smooth, quiet stalk to get near enough to a herd for a shot.

Caliber? A powerful gun is not needed for these small pigs, and a .44 carbine or rifle in the .222 caliber class is a good bet. I have even bagged them with my .357 magnum revolver. Check your game laws if you use a sidearm. Since peccary are shot at close range, a shotgun using slugs might be considered.

> "The rifle is the free man's weapon. The man that uses it well in the chase shows that he can at need use it also at war with human foes."
>
> THEODORE ROOSEVELT

Buffalo hunting in the Fort Smith area of Canada's Northwest Territories. CANADIAN GOVERNMENT TRAVEL BUREAU

Chapter 13

WILDERNESS FIRST AID AND SURVIVAL TECHNIQUES

The treatment of illness or injuries in a survival situation is necessarily simple. In the back country it is important to be a "do-it-yourself" man. With the exception of snake bite, the cardinal rule is DON'T OVERTREAT! Nature is often kind and, given a chance, cures or helps to cure and heal many illnesses or injuries. The following measures are designed to help nature and to speed healing.

Because most persons entering a wilderness area are ski mountaineers, mountain climbers, big-game hunters, explorers, or fishermen who hike, fly, or canoe into remote regions, they are more likely to be accident-alert. Therefore, they very seldom meet with an accident or become ill.

Who May Need It   Once in a great while something does happen so that they have to render not only first aid to a member of their party but assist someone else who has met with a misfortune along the trail. Usually these incidents, when they do occur, happen far from professional medical aid.

Because specialized help may be miles and even days away, they should have a knowledge of both basic and advanced first aid plus the know-how of backwoods medicine in case of an emergency where the victim may very likely die.

First aid is defined by the American National Red Cross as the immediate and temporary care given the victim of an accident or sudden illness until the services of a physician can be

obtained. This is correct and as it should be. However, the back country poses a more difficult situation. It may be impossible to transport the victim quickly to a hospital or doctor due to distance, lack of communication, breakdown or loss of aircraft, canoe, or boat, or strayed pack animals.

Accidents can happen anywhere, afloat or ashore. On land, it is often possible to get medical aid quickly. However, on a boat or in the bush it is important to be a "do-it-yourself" man. Even seemingly harmless falls, cuts, and bruises should be looked after because of the danger of infection. One caution, though, about first aid: No matter how expert you may be, the cardinal rule to remember is DON'T OVERTREAT!

It is suggested that every licensed packer and guide be required to take the American National Red Cross Standard and Advanced First Aid Instructions Course and be required to carry the needed first aid and medical supplies necessary to handle the average recreational accident that may occur to members of his party in the back country!

First Aid if Injuries Do Occur   1. Give first aid for any injury or illness, however minor!

2. For serious injuries give proper first aid and get medical aid as soon as possible!

General Directions   1. Keep injured person lying down in a comfortable position, his head level with his body, until you know whether the injury is serious.

2. Look for serious bleeding, stoppage of breathing, poisoning, shock, wounds, burns, fractures, and dislocations. Be sure you find all injuries.

REMEMBER: (1) Stoppage of breathing, (2) serious bleeding, and (3) poisoning, in that order, must be treated *immediately*.

3. Keep injured person warm, but not too warm.

4. Send someone to call a physician or get an ambulance.

5. Keep calm and do not be hurried into moving the injured person unless it is absolutely necessary.

6. *Never* give water or other liquids to an unconscious person. The symbols* and** in the following list of injuries indicate: *=*Immediate Action Cases;* **=*Special Care Needed.*

Shock—the Killer On a number of recreation accident and rescue missions involving automobile, aircraft, and boat accidents, I have found several victims dead on my arrival at the scene without a mark on their person. Post-mortem examination revealed no internal injuries. The victims had died from shock!

Any severely injured person will develop shock, and treatment must start immediately, without waiting for symptoms of shock to develop.

SYMPTOMS: Face pale, eyelids droop. Skin cold and clammy. Partly or totally unconscious.

TREATMENT: Have victim lie down. Loosen clothing. Keep patient warm and quiet. Conserve body heat by wrapping person underneath and above with blankets or with whatever warming material you have at hand. In cold regions, keep patient warm by placing him in a double sleeping bag and placing chemical heating pads between his legs and under his arms. Heated rocks or jars filled with hot water will do if hot water bags are not available. These should be wrapped in towels or clothing or other material at hand and placed so they will not cause further injury by burning the patient. Keep victim lying down with feet raised. Place head slightly lower than feet unless head injury or skull fracture is suspected. Fluids may be given by mouth unless patient is unconscious or has an abdominal injury. Water, hot tea, coffee, milk,

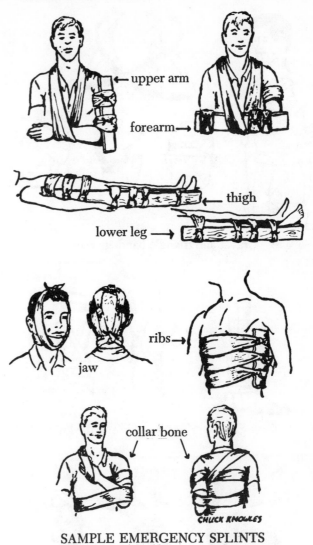

SAMPLE EMERGENCY SPLINTS

Every hunter should be thoroughly familiar with tying emergency splints. COURTESY OF THE AUTHOR

or broth may be given. NEVER TRY TO FORCE LIQUID down an unconscious person's throat! You will just cause him to strangle!

CAUTION: In cases of head or chest injuries, or if face is flushed as in sunstroke, keep patient lying down, but with head higher than feet.

*Wounds with Severe Bleeding 1. Use direct pressure on wound. Place thick layer of gauze on wound and apply firm pressure until bandage can be put on. Also press with finger at arterial pressure point to help stop flow of blood.

2. If direct pressure is difficult to maintain and bleeding is from a limb, a tourniquet may

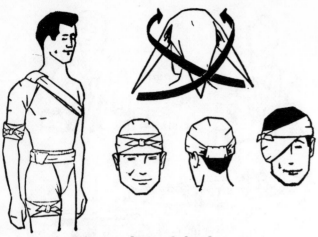

Cravat and triangle bandage uses

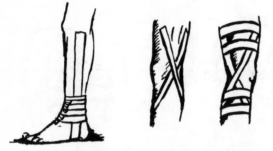

Taping support for the ankle and the knee

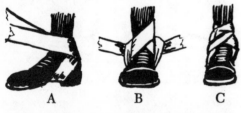

A   B   C

Cravat bandage to support the ankle

Emergency bandage uses. COURTESY OF THE AUTHOR

have to be used. Apply tourniquet at leg or arm tourniquet point. Loosen the tourniquet every 15 to 20 minutes.

WARNING: *A tourniquet is always a dangerous instrument and should not be used if bleeding can be checked readily otherwise.* USE IT ONLY FOR SEVERE LIFE-THREATENING HEMORRHAGE THAT CANNOT BE CONTROLLED BY OTHER MEANS. Once a tourniquet is applied, it should be released only by a physician or medical personnel prepared to control hemorrhage, unless none are available. A tourniquet can be left in place from 1 to 2 hours without damage to a limb, if periodically loosened and replaced.

3. *Treat for shock.

*Overcome by Smoke, Asphyxiation, Stoppage of Breathing 1. Start artificial respiration immediately.

2. Move patient into open or clear air.

3. Loosen clothing.

4. Check for obstructions to breathing in mouth.

5. Check for wounds.

6. Treat for shock.

*Poison—Internal For general first aid, remember two practices:

1. *Dilute.* Give patient large amount of fluid such as soapsuds, salt water, baking soda in water, lukewarm water, or mustard water.

2. *Wash out.* Induce vomiting repeatedly.

3. Continue diluting and washing out the stomach until fluid is as clear as when swallowed.

4. Treat for shock.

**Burns Shock and infection are chief dangers from burns. As a first aider, your duties are to relieve pain, prevent infection, and treat shock.

Burns of Limited Extent Apply sterile petroleum ointment or burn ointment, and cover with sterile gauze. The best-known burn ointment is 50-50 cod-liver oil and Vaseline.

Extensive Burns Extensive burns are very serious. Shock is always present. Remove loose clothing from burned area. If clothing sticks to burn, cut around it and leave for doctor to remove. Dip strips of clean cloth in solution of three tablespoons of baking soda or Epsom salts in one quart of warm water and apply cloth to burned area. Keep patient covered and warm.

**Broken Bones or Dislocations REMEMBER! If in doubt, treat as a fracture. Proper handling of a fracture is essential.

1. Unless absolutely necessary, do not move patient until fracture has been immobilized by a splint.

After painting fang marks and knife blade with antiseptic, make cross incisions over each fang mark.

Incision in fang marks.

Tie tourniquet, just tight enough to dent skin, about 1½ inches above wound.

Applying lymph constrictor.

Apply suction—first moistening mouth of cup and skin surrounding wound.

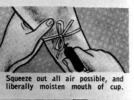

Squeeze out all air possible, and liberally moisten mouth of cup.

Each Cutter Kit contains full directions for continuing emergency treatment if there is delay in getting to a physician.

Showing application of finger cup. Be sure to squeeze out all air possible.

As indicated in the sketches at right, it is a wise precaution to carry several Kits if it is likely that first aid must be continued for any considerable time.

Litho in U.S.A.   527-76-559-130

CUTTER *Laboratories*
BERKELEY 10. CALIFORNIA

Apply all the cups available up to 20. Make plenty of incisions—50 to 120 are not excessive.

Venomous stings and bites. CUTTER LABORATORIES

2. Improvised splinting or immobilization material may be made from boards, wire, blankets, pillows, folded newspapers, folded coats. Pad the splint to make more comfortable.

3. A general rule is to make splint long enough to immobilize both the break and the joints above and below the break.

4. Treat for shock.

A person unconscious or in shock on the trail, suffering a fracture or fractures, requires extra heat to the extremities, particularly the feet, to prevent frostbite and freezing injury if in a cold area or at any high elevations. *NEVER* assume the victim's feet will stay warm because he has "adequate" footwear. His feet may have been at the point of frostbite at the time of injury. *Always* investigate the feet, change to dry socks, and use heating pads or other forms of additional heat IF FEET ARE NOT FROZEN.

The classic signs of fracture are *pain, swelling,* and *point tenderness.* The patient may or may not have heard a snap, he may or may not be reluctant to use the member, and there may or may not be deformity with attendant muscle spasm. *Point tenderness* means that there will be *one specific point* which gives excruciating pain when *gently* pressed. A second test for fracture is to *gently* tap the member in the longitudinal axis of the bone suspected of fracture. This produces mild but sharp pain; e.g., for suspected ankle fracture tap heel *gently* on bottom toward the knee. Or for suspected finger or hand fracture tap *gently* on tip of suspected finger toward the wrist.

SPLINT ALL FRACTURES, ALL DISLOCATIONS, AND ALL SEVERE SPRAINS.

**Sprains A sprain is a twisting or tearing, in greater or lesser degree, of structures which surround and support a joint. Fractures frequently accompany sprains and dislocations.

TREATMENT: Apply a snug (not tight) bandage, preferably an elastic bandage. Elevate the part. Cover with an ice bag or towels wrung out in iced water. Leave the cold applications on for 1 or 2 hours. Leave the gentle compression bandage on for 24 hours. After second day hot soaks are indicated, and after 48 hours these may be followed by gentle massage. A sprained joint should be rested until pain has disappeared. Sometimes in an emergency one can walk a considerable distance on a sprained ankle if a bandage is applied. Splint all badly sprained limbs until proven there are no fractures.

Wounds, Bleeding Not Severe 1. Keep wound clean to prevent germs from entering wound.

2. First the bleeding must be stopped, and this can be accomplished by a pressure dressing or by elevation of the part. Usually you are far from medical aid—somewhere in the back country in a hunting or fishing camp—so you will have to apply second aid by thoroughly washing with soap and water, irrigating with salt solution if grossly contaminated, or washing the wound clean with rubbing alcohol, Zonite, or peroxide.

3. Apply antiseptic such as Tincture of Merthiolate or mild Tincture of Iodine. (Tincture of iodine must dry before bandaging or it will cause a burn and add more injury to the wound.)

4. Cover with sterile dressing, and bandage snugly in place.

5. The wound will heal if held together with a sterile dressing and adhesive tape. Contaminated wounds may require preventive oral sulfa or wide spectrum (Aureomycin) antibiotic therapy. Cuts and abrasions of outdoorsmen living in camps will heal as quickly as any others, providing there is adequate vitamin C, and the wound is kept clean and is properly cared for.

Wilderness Treatment of Venomous Stings and Bites

PREVENTION: Watch where you step, walk, sit, or place your hands. Shake out vigorously all clothing, hats, and boots—there might be a yellowjacket, a wasp, one of the two deadly scorpions found in the Southwest, a centipede, tarantula, black- or brown-widow spider, Gila monster, Mexican beaded lizard, or a pit viper you failed to notice! Sleep up off the ground if possible or in an insect-proof tent.

TREATMENT: The TCS (tourniquet cut-and-suction) method is a rough, tough, and primitive method under adverse sanitary conditions. However, when properly performed, it may be beneficial, especially if the venomous snake was a large one or the injection is in a fibrous pocket.

1. The first step is quick action to prevent rapid absorption of the venom and bacteria into the body.

2. Place a tourniquet, string, shoelace or whatever is handy, just above the swelling. Wash off surface venom if you can do it quickly. Apply an antiseptic if you have it over a 4-inch-square area.

3. Sterilize a sharp knife or razor blade with a match, cigarette lighter, or antiseptic. Carefully make a ¼-inch-deep linear cut parallel with the limb in each fang puncture. (Linear cuts are less apt to cut nerves, veins, or tendons, and they stimulate drainage better than the traditional X cuts.

4. Suction should be applied steadily to the incisions and all successive ones for the first 2 hours. The suction cups should be removed for 10 to 15 minutes each hour thereafter. During this rest period, the wounds should be covered with wet saline or salt packs. If swelling continues on up the limb, it will be necessary to place the constrictor band an inch above the swelling and make a bracelet of linear cuts about 2 inches apart around the limb. Suction should continue 8 to 24 hours, or until the swelling has noticeably subsided. Undertreatment is far more dangerous than overtreatment regarding incision and suction.

ANTIVENIN TREATMENT: If you have an antivenin snake bite kit, follow the instructions carefully! Be extra cautious—sometimes the reaction can be more destructive than the snake bite! Best results may be had by injecting the antivenin into a vein or large muscle, distant from the bite. The hip is a good location. Normally, an antivenin kit contains only one ampule of 10 cc of antivenin. Usually it requires from 4 to 12 ampules (40–120 cc of antivenin) in the case of a bite from a large angry pit viper.

THE L-C METHOD: The L-C technique is the most modern and up-to-date method in treating venomous stings and bites if applied correctly! However, under survival conditions unless you are near a snow or ice patch or glacial stream, you would be unable to use this method.

1. Place a ligature or tight tourniquet on the bitten extremity as near the point of entrance of venom as possible. Generally, the ligature should be placed at the nearest *one-bone* site so that complete "strangulation" can be obtained. If the bite is on a finger or toe, place the ligature at the base of the digit for best constriction results.

2. Hold a piece of ice on the bite while someone prepares a suitable vessel of crushed ice and water. Place the bitten member well above the constriction point in the iced water.

3. After the affected member has been in the iced water for not less than 10 minutes, remove the ligature and continue to keep the hand, arm, foot, or leg in iced water for at least 2 hours.

4. If envenomized member is to be treated for more than 2 to 4 hours, the limb should be protected by placing it in a plastic bag. All air spaces between the covered limb should be eliminated by wrapping excess bag around the limb. The injured limb should again be immersed in iced water or have finely chipped or crushed ice

packed solidly around it. (Covered ice packs are not adequate.)

5. Normally, 2 hours of cryotherapy for poisonous scorpion sting, and from 6 to 12 hours for a Gila monster bite are sufficient. A minimum of 12 hours' treatment should be maintained for even the smallest pit viper bite. The bite from a 2- to 3-foot rattlesnake may require two or more days of continuous cryotherapy, while larger viper bites may require treatment for 4 to 6 days or more. The L-C treatment does not destroy tissue from cold therapy.

6. Keeping the entire limb refrigerated can soon cause the victim to shiver from cold. Keep patient warm by wrapping in blankets or in a sleeping bag. Supplement with an electric blanket or with hot water bags or chemical hot bags to a point of mild perspiration. This will assist the detoxification process by the body, and speed recovery.

7. A warmup period after all cryotherapy has been discontinued is important. This must be carried out gradually. This can be accomplished readily by not replenishing the water with ice. Allow the iced water to come to room temperature. If venom sickness and pain start in again after the warmup period, cryotherapy must be continued.

8. Some outdoorsmen carry a small bottle or cylinder of Frigiderm for emergency use to lower the temperature of the bitten site until they can reach a town where ice can be obtained and the L-C treatment started. In an emergency, the contents from a small carbon dioxide (CO_2) fire extinguisher can be sprayed onto a handkerchief or piece of cloth and placed on the bite and then resprayed on top again. Be sure not to spray directly on the skin or a freeze burn may appear.

9. WARNING: Treat all cases of snake bite for shock. Never administer morphine or Demerol in case of a deadly scorpion sting and neurotoxins. These increase the killing power of the venom! When using the L-C technique, the victim does not experience the usual tissue destruction or sloughing resulting from other types of envenomation treatments, nor is amputation necessary as it occasionally is when some other types of treatment are employed.

Recommended Reading The most complete details on the subject may be obtained by writing for the booklets *Scorpions,* and *The Treatment of Venomous Bites and Stings* by Doctor Herbert L. Stahnke, Director, Poisonous Animals Research Laboratory, Arizona State University, Tempe, Arizona 85281. $1.50 each. A *Summary of Treatment of Venomous Bites and Stings* may also be obtained from the university for 10 cents.

Poison Ivy—Poison Oak—Sumac—Nettles, and Other Plants Poison ivy, poison oak, sumac, nettles, Manzanillo, sandbox, dumb cane, cowhage, and many other plants of this type can cause skin irritation and poisoning on contact with the sap or spines that penetrate the skin. The smoke or steam from burning wood or leaves of these plants is dangerous and is likely to affect the skin and eyes as much as the actual sap or juice.

SYMPTOMS: Red itchy skin with small blisters with swelling. The involved area may increase greatly in size, with swelling and numerous large blisters. Fever may rise high and discomfort become great.

TREATMENT: Wash the part involved with a heavy lather of soap and water. Rinse and then sponge it with rubbing alcohol. Following this cleansing, apply calamine. Wet bicarbonate of soda packs may also be used.

Blisters SYMPTOMS: Small collection of water or blood under the skin. Swelling redness at site of friction causing blister. Soreness.

TREATMENT: If not opened, the fluid will gradually be absorbed by the body. If you decide to open the blister to relieve pressure, wash the part thoroughly with soap and water; then apply an antiseptic to skin. Next sterilize a needle in an open flame and puncture the blister at its edge. Using a sterile gauze pad, apply pressure along the margin of the blister to remove fluid. Place a sterile pad or dressing over the area. If the blister has already burst, wash the part gently with soap and water and apply a sterile dressing. Never puncture a blister unless absolutely necessary since it contains a sterile cushion of serum. Remember that a blister that heals without breaking seldom becomes infected.

Heat Exhaustion SYMPTOMS: Cold, wet skin, dizziness, headache, nausea, cramps.

TREATMENT: Have victim lie down. Loosen clothing. Keep patient cool. Rest is essential. Administer salt water, half a teaspoonful of salt per half-glass of water every 15 minutes until patient has consumed three or four doses.

Heat Stroke SYMPTOMS: Hot, dry skin, fast pulse, dizziness, headache, nausea, and unconsciousness may occur in severe cases.

TREATMENT: Treat the same as for heat exhaustion, but sponge body with lukewarm water. Apply cold packs to head. Sometimes it is necessary to bring high temperature down by placing victim in cool stream if in a wilderness area.

Sunburn SYMPTOMS: Skin red and inflamed, depending on the degree of burn.

TREATMENT: Apply any oil or available fat as for chafing. If skin area is blistered, treat as for blistered foot. If burn area is extensive, apply a pressure bandage.

Snow Blindness SYMPTOMS: Eyes feel gritty and are painful. There is a tendency to rub the eyes. Eyes are inflamed. Sunlight or flame from campfire light are painful to look at.

TREATMENT: It is desirable to give eyes a complete rest for a minimum of three days. In severe cases they must be rested for longer periods. Cover eyes with cold compresses and keep patient out of sun glare. Blindfold the eyes during daylight or against firelight at night, especially if there are considerable pain, redness, and tears present. A drop of mineral oil in the eyes will soothe the gritty feeling.

Prolonged Exposure to Cold When a person is exposed to excessive cold for a long time, he becomes numb, movement is difficult, and irresistible drowsiness overtakes him. He staggers, his eyesight fails, he falls and may become unconscious.

1. If breathing has stopped, begin artificial respiration. Bring the victim into a tent or cabin if one is available. Rewarm him as rapidly as possible by wrapping him in blankets or in sleeping bags. If a canvas bathtub or any other tub is available (which is unlikely in the back country), place him in a tub of warm water 78° to 82° F. but not hot water. When he reacts, give him a hot drink. Dry the body thoroughly if water was used to rewarm him. WARNING: Never rub frostbite or frozen limb with snow.

Heart Attacks There are times out on the trail when one of your party may have a heart attack or you may arrive at a hunting camp where a member has had one. SYMPTOMS include shortness of breath, chest pains, bluish color of the lips and about the fingernails, a chronic cough, and swelling of the ankles. Pain is most often located in the chest, particularly under the sternum, or breastbone, and sometimes down the left arm or into the head and neck. Sometimes the pain in the arm and shoulder is severe. At times pain in the upper abdomen, especially in a person of middle age or older, frequently reflects an acute heart attack. Indigestion manifested by nausea and vomiting is associated with heart attacks. In one type of attack, the patient insists on lying still in a position comfortable to him; such attacks usually subside shortly. In other cases, the pain in the chest or abdomen may be so severe as to induce profuse sweating. The patient insists on walking about rather than lying down.

If the victim has been under medical care, the first-aider should assist in administering prescribed medicine. If medical care hasn't been given previously, advice should be obtained at once if possible, in the meantime deferring transportation. If the patient is faint, the lying-down position is best. Raising the legs may be beneficial.

For shortness of breath, raise the head and chest to a position so that the patient is in the most comfortable position to him. When pain is acute, the lying-down position again is best but the pain may not permit such position at first. This position demands less strain than the upright.

A messenger should be sent to the nearest phone or radio so that medical advice may be obtained and a helicopter sent for to remove the victim to the nearest hospital.

In the meantime, the patient must have absolute rest and quiet. It is best not to show extreme concern, and to avoid reference to the attack as being a heart attack. If oxygen is available from a small oxygen cylinder that is now on the market, use it.

If the helicopter or rescue plane is unable to land close by, it will be necessary to transport the victim on an improvised stretcher. This can be made by cutting two poles approximately 8 feet long and about 1½ inches in diameter. Lay the poles about 2 feet apart and lace ropes or strips of a blanket or canvas between them, back and forth for a distance of 5 to 6 feet. Carefully place the patient on the stretcher in a sleeping bag or wrapped in blankets. The victim's body weight will hold the poles apart.

It is extremely important that the victim remain recumbent during transportation. BE VERY CAREFUL NOT TO TRIP AND FALL! Easy does it!

Rescue Breathing ARTIFICIAL RESPIRATION—USING A RESUSCITATOR. IMPORTANT: ALWAYS HOLD VICTIM'S CHIN UPWARD AND HEAD TILTED BACK.

1. Place victim on back (face up). Clean throat only if necessary; otherwise start with Step 2. If jaw is tightly closed, wedge open with your index finger inserted between cheek and teeth behind wisdom teeth.

2. Take position facing top of victim's head. Tilt his head back, holding his tongue forward with fingers and insert resuscitator tube over tongue. Insert long end for adults, short end for children over three years old. With children invert flange toward short end.

3. Pinch nose with your thumbs, press flange of tube firmly over lips with index fingers. With other fingers hold victim's chin upward and toward you. NEVER LET THE CHIN SAG.

4. Take a deep breath and blow into mouthpiece. When victim's chest rises, take your mouth off to let him exhale, then blow in next breath. Blow rapidly at first, then once every 3 or 4 seconds. Continue until victim breathes naturally. NOTE: For an adult blow forcefully; for a child blow gently. The new Venti-Breather is handier and more sanitary than most mask-and-tube methods.

CONTINUE ARTIFICIAL RESPIRATION UNTIL THE VICTIM BREATHES NATURALLY OR A PHYSICIAN PRONOUNCES HIM DEAD.

There are various effective ways to administer artificial respiration manually, each with its advantages and disadvantages. Mouth-to-mouth rescue breathing has proved far more effective than manual methods. It moves a greater amount of oxygen into the lungs. It is easily learned, and is an approved life-saving method. Two other methods are as follows:

Emergency Oxygen Emergency oxygen kits are now on the market. These small cylinders are used where an oxygen inhalant is indicated for first aid or emergency measures. The cylinder weighs only 24 ounces with face mask and is priced at under $10.00. Directions are simple. The oxygen is inhaled through the mouth or plastic mask furnished with each cylinder. To operate, press and inhale; release and exhale.

CAUTION: Keep away from open flame or inflammables. Do not smoke when using. LIF-O-GEN and other kits can be purchased at most drugstores. It would be an excellent idea to carry one aboard each pleasure boat or plane, and for mountain climbers to have along at high elevation.

Wilderness Camp Medicine Whenever you go into wilderness country where you will be away for days or weeks from quick medical aid, there should be at least one person in the party who is well versed in advanced first aid. This person should also have some knowledge of how to administer a few drugs in an emergency.

Before venturing on a trek of this magnitude, you should consult your family physician and have a physical checkup. Check with your dentist also. Consult your family doctor on the type of first-aid material and drugs to take along; and, of course, get instructions how to use them for various illness that might be contracted on the trip. Be sure he makes out prescriptions for the necessary drugs or you will be unable to secure them from your druggist.

Basic Medical Supplies for a Small Expedition The list of drugs to carry can vary widely, depending on personal needs and perhaps upon your particular boating or land area. Here is furnished a list of medical supplies and equipment for a four-man trek into wilderness country for a period of two or more weeks. The advanced first-aid member of the party must be taught such definitive medical procedures as how to clean and sew up, clip or tape closed a common laceration. Evacuation to definitive medical care should be taken as soon as possible. In any case have a *Master's Manual*, used by lay mariners and explorers for years in successfully treating emergency cases far from regular medical facilities. It is a handy item to have in the kit.

RECOMMENDED: "The Ship's Medicine Chest and First Aid at Sea" by U. S. Public Health Service and War Shipping Administration, Revised 1955 (U. S. Government Printing Office, Washington, D.C. 20402).

2 Morphine sulphate syrettes ½ grain—for combating pain and shock.

6 Morphine sulphate ¼-grain tablets for relief of pain.

6 Codeine sulphate tablets; ½ grain for pain.

50 Aspirin or Bufferin tablets, 5 grains—for headaches and joint pains.

12 Gantrimycin (Roche)—2 to 5 tablets every six hours—for infection or pneumonia and for those allergic to penicillin.

12 Mexipan (Pfizer) or Synsillin (Bristol) —250 mg synthetic penicillin, 400,000 units each oral, and less allergenic than penicillin. One tablet every six hours between meals for *high* fever which must *not* be due to dehydration. If person breaks out with itching "hives" or develops asthmatic breathing (in easy, out hard), discontinue immediately and put patient on Gantrimycin.

1 Zinc oxide ointment; 20-ounce tube to protect nose and face from sunburn.

1 PhisoHex 5-ounce squeeze bottle or bar of Ivory soap for cleansing hands and wounds with copious washings.

1 Bismuth and paregoric, 2 ounces. For diarrhea, one tablespoon after each bowel movement until back to normal.

1 Tr. Merthiolate 1-1000—1-ounce bottle for wound disinfectant.

1 Butyn eye ointment, ¼ ounce. For painful eye, dressing must be worn at least 8 hours after administration. Helps to relieve pain caused by snow blindness and other inflammation.

1 Cod-liver oil-Vaseline ointment (50-50), 1-ounce tube. Excellent for burns.

1 Elixir of terpin hydrate with codeine, 2 ounces. For nagging cough—1 to 2 teaspoonsful at bedtime.

100 Water-purification tablets.

1 Water filter and purifier.* Worth its weight in gold at times. Weight approximately 30 ounces.

50 Bursalina iodine tablets for purifying water.

1 Earache medicine, ¼ ounce—2 or 3 drops on a pledget of cotton and insert into ear.

1 Oil of cloves, ½ ounce—for toothache.

54 Sterilized Q-Tips or swabs for cleansing and applying disinfectant to wounds.

1 First-aid kit (16-unit). Add laxative and vitamins B complex and C in high potency, stress dose, to replenish body needs being drained by a severe accident or illness.

1 Metal fever thermometer (nonbreakable type). Priced at $12.00.

1 Rubberized wide-mouthed ice-pack bag. For headache and to reduce swellings.

1 Rubberized hot water bag. (Chemical bags may be used instead.) For shock. (Water in bag may be used for toilet or for washing dishes in cold country.)

2 Snake bite kits (suction type).

1 Snake bite kit (10 cc, syringe type if in bad snake country).

2 Surgical needles with ligature and needle holder in glass vial.

12 Metal surgical clamps for closing wounds.

2 Artery forceps and clamps. To hold and close an artery.

2 Wire malleable splints.

1 Spool silk ligature thread.

12 Safety pins.

1 Pr. dressing forceps or bandage scissors.

REMEMBER, IT MAY BE YOUR LIFE THAT YOU ARE SAVING.

Cold Weather and General Survival Techniques The problems facing a hunter in regions of heavy snow and extreme cold are among the most hazardous and most severe with which man can come in contact.

Unfortunately, a few hunters enter the wilderness back country improperly prepared and in poor physical condition and health. They become lost, injured, or meet with a fatal accident through carelessness. Some receive burns, that become infected, from their campfires, others

* Sure Pure Co., Inc., Box 164, Ringoes, N.J. 08551. Price $6.95.

Grisly proof that cold weather can be a deadly enemy to the poorly prepared winter sportsman. COURTESY OF THE AUTHOR

blistered feet from not having the proper sock-and-boot combination, others get stung by yellow jackets, snake-bitten, or drown crossing a swift mountain stream. Others become ill from drinking polluted water or hurt themselves stalking when they accidentally slip, trip, or fall onto rocks or over a bluff. Severe sunburn is another danger at high elevations when hunting in snow country—and so is snow blindness! Then again there is the careless hunter who mistakes his father-in-law for a moose or other game!

An example of not being prepared or not having the proper equipment for sudden snowstorms or blizzards is that of the over 3000 elk hunters who became snowbound and marooned in Arizona's Mogollon Rim country several years ago. Six hunters died and many were frostbitten, overexhausted, or had heart attacks when they abandoned their cars and attempted to buck their way out on foot, and others contracted other cold-weather sicknesses or injuries.

The same situation happened again in the state of Washington when a 13-day blizzard caught elk hunters in high country.

Other hunters have been stranded on isolated shores when their outboard motors failed en route to choice hunting grounds along the coast. A few hunters using private aircraft have had to make forced crash-landings in remote wilderness or desert regions.

To survive, you will need the art and skill used by pioneer and experienced woodsmen. You will need to know how to build fires in rain or snow or under other adverse weather conditions. You should know how to build various types of wilderness shelters, how to hunt, fish, snare, and trap animals for food—more so if you lose your firearm crossing a stream or have used up all your ammunition; and, if necessary, find your way safely back to habitation and your family or friends. Your chances for survival are more favorable if you carry a well-equipped survival kit in your aircraft, automobile, or boat.

Here are a few pointers that will be helpful to ease your ordeal:

In any area, you can improvise shelter from parts of your crashed aircraft (if you aren't badly injured), automobile, or pack outfit, or from natural materials in the vicinity.

The type of shelter you make depends on whether you need protection from rain, cold, heat, sunshine, or insects. Also whether your bivouac camp is only for a one-night stand or is to be used for many days.

Pick your emergency campsite carefully. Try to place it near sufficient fuel and water (stream, lake, or spring) to last you until rescued.

Reconnoiter for abandoned cabins or old ranchhouses. You may run across a miner's abandoned cabin or winter snow surveyor's station. Most of the latter will have some food in them and a stove to cook on. Snow-measuring stations are well stocked with food for winter patrols. Finding a ready-made shelter will save you time and labor.

Don't make a shelter camp at the base of steep slopes or in areas where you may run the risk of an avalanche crushing you and your shelter. Avoid snags and timber that might fall on you and your makeshift home. Build in a sheltered location if possible, away from battering winds.

In summer, if you stay with your downed plane, use it for a shelter. In winter you may need a more wind- and snowproof shelter against the cold. You may be able to provide a better-insulated place outdoors in a cave, or tepee made from a tarpaulin or parachute. A warming and cooking fire can be used inside the latter-type shelter.

Keep the front openings of all shelters crosswind. A windbreak of logs, snow, or ice blocks set close together and in front is helpful.

A fine shelter for drizzly weather and protection against insects is a tepee made from a canvas tarpaulin or parachute. In this Indian-type shelter you can cook, eat, sleep, dress, and make signals—all without stepping outside. If you should fall asleep the smoke from your warming fire will be weaving up through the top as a signal.

You can make a simple shelter by hanging a tarp or other cloth material over an aircraft wing (if you haven't sheared the wings off in landing). Anchor the tarp edges down with rocks or earth.

In timberless terrain, make a simple snow cave or burrow by digging into the side of a snowdrift that is well packed, and lining the bottom of the hole with any material handy. Snow caves must be ventilated. So must any airtight shelter when a fire is used inside.

Whatever type of shelter you are able to build, don't sleep directly on the ground or snow. Provide insulation under your sleeping bag or body. Lay a thick bough bed in shingle fashion, or pad the bottom with whatever material you can find. You will be much warmer and sleep much better.

Try and keep your sleeping bag, blankets, or other bedding as clean and dry as possible. Fluff up your sleeping bag to obtain maximum warmth.

To dry a sleeping bag, turn it inside out if it doesn't have a zipper. Beat out any frost that might have collected, and warm it before a fire.

Emergency Shelters A tent, of course, has been found to be the most satisfactory portable shelter for all types of outdoor living. It can be used in the mountains at high elevations, in the desert, jungles, or the Arctic.

Bivouac Sheet A bivouac sheet (poncho, canvas, or plastic sheet) can be used as a ground sheet, roof for your snowhouse, or as a lean-to. It may be the means of saving your life if you are caught out during a severe rain- or snowstorm.

The Lean-to This is a simple type of shelter to make. You can make the frame from downed dead poles or cut green ones. The success in constructing an emergency shelter is taking the time and making the effort to do a good job.

Hole-in-the-Snow or Tree Shelter The only fault with this type is that it is difficult to spot from the air, but it does protect your fire and you from the wind.

Snow Dugout This is a larger, deeper hole excavated into a hard-packed drift or glacial snow. Blocks of snow should be cut and piled around the periphery of the hole. This will give double depth with half the effort. Roof over with branches, tarp, or whatever you have available. Note illustrations.

Desert Hunting and Survival Desert hunting can be exciting and rewarding and a change from mountain and woods hunting. Upland bird hunting for quail and dove near water holes usually proves fruitful. In some areas, desert sheep and deer are there for the sportsman who knows his way around. However, the hunter and the old desert-rat prospector and his "reluctant" burro are being pushed farther and farther into remote desert where, as some city dwellers say, everything "sticks, stings, and stinks (probably they mean that the cacti sticks, scorpions sting, and the shrubs are pungent). However, they are living "high off the hog" with lightweight, quick-freeze, dehydrated foods. Gone are the days of the three "Bs," bacon, beans, and bannock! The desert hunter and inhabitant also will be more apt to be driving a Jeep or a four-wheel-drive vehicle than leading a "desert canary" (burro). In this manner the prospector and hunter can cover larger areas, carry more food and equipment, and stay "out-beyond" for longer periods.

Those with a knowledge of desert lore have found that deserts are not the uninhabitable places that the uninformed believe them to be. There are edible plants, roots, berries, and nuts to be eaten for the taking. There are animals such as deer and mountain sheep. Under emergency conditions, desert animals can be snared, trapped, and even shot if one has the patience. Water can be obtained from desert wells or natural rock tanks and water holes.

Organize and plan your hunting jaunt well in advance. This gives you time to make any changes in route or plans. Study your desert contour map well, since you will be going off the beaten paths. Desert maps may be obtained from local county surveyors and federal agencies. Be sure you have one of these maps before going on a trek into the interior!

When using side or back roads, it is best to use a pickup with four speeds ahead. Four-wheel-drive Jeeps or power wagons are better off-the-pavement vehicles, and negotiate high-crowned desert roads much more easily. If you are driving a conventional vehicle or station wagon, or hauling a small travel trailer or towing a two-wheel utility rig, be sure to inquire at each opportunity regarding the route and road ahead! Here are a few safety pointers that may be helpful:

Your chances for a successful hunt can be improved by contacting the game warden nearest the region you plan to hunt. He will know local game conditions and advise you of the safest and most productive game areas.

Be sure before you take off on your hunting jaunt that you advise your family and friends where you plan to leave the main traveled roads.

Also notify and check out with the local sheriff's substation or Ranger station. Tell them where you plan to go and when you expect to return. Check in again with these officials when you return. This is *IMPORTANT!*

Watch for road and warning signs. They mean what they say. Don't take chances and ignore them.

Beware of water holes that are bare of vegetation and have bird and animal bones lying around or near them. They have been poisoned by minerals or other sources. Under no circumstances drink or cook with the water.

For shelter, use a tent with a sewed-in floor and windows and door flap that has a screened zipper opening to keep out insects, snakes, and desert rodents. (I personally use a jungle hammock where desert shrubbery is handy.)

WARNING: Don't camp in dry washes; they can be death traps during a flash flood from a rainstorm miles from your camp. Camp in the shade of desert shrubs if possible, high on a bank beyond the path of any flash flood. A sudden cloudburst can cause floods that crest better than 30 feet or more at times.

Watch out for rattlesnakes—it is safer to sleep up off the ground, in a jungle hammack or tent with a sewed-in floor with all zippers closed. Putting a hair rope or lariat around your camp will *not* keep rattlesnakes out. It just won't work!

Shake out your shoes, socks, and other clothing—there might be a scorpion or centipede hiding in them. Don't forget to check your hat before putting it on. (There are two deadly scorpions in Arizona and adjacent states according to the Director of Poisonous Animals Laboratory at the University of Arizona.)

Be careful when inspecting abandoned shacks (better to sleep outside). These are excellent hideouts for black-widow and brown-widow spiders. The U. S. Public Health Service claims that the brown-widow spider is more poisonous than the black widow. The little brown spider looks similar to the black; however, it is smaller and has a mandolin-shaped spot on the top of its body. The two poisonous desert lizards are the Gila monster and the Mexican beaded lizard. Leave them alone!

Remember, be careful. You are safer in the back country than you would be crossing a city street!

If You Do Get into a Desert Survival Situation

Your first problem, of course, is to find water. Remember, some desert plants and cacti contain some moisture or juices that will assist in slaking thirst (for instance, the barrel cactus). Cut off the top of the plant and mash in the center pulp and sap will collect. Or you can slice the center pulp in pieces and chew them. This will slake your thirst for a short period.

Willows and cottonwood trees will usually outline a water course. Note the direction birds such as dove and quail are flying in the early morning and evening. They head for water twice a day.

Here is a sure way of obtaining water anywhere, except in the driest desert in the summer: Carry several thin sheets of plastic 6×6 feet in diameter in your hunting outfit. They aren't heavy and might save your life. An average of 12 persons die from thirst every year on the California and Arizona deserts. The use of a plastic well probably would have saved their lives. All you have to do is dig a hole about 30 inches deep and approximately 3 to 4 feet wide, unfold the plastic sheet you have been carrying for this purpose, and spread it over the hole. Weight the edges down with dirt or rocks, then make a dimple or indentation in the center of the sheet for moisture to trickle down and drain into a can or other container placed in the bottom of the hole. (Note illustration.) Approximately a pint of water will collect by condensation overnight in the summer. That's not enough to keep a person alive very long. You need at least a gallon of water per day in summer. However, you can increase this water ration to a life-sustaining 1½ pints per day by lining the hole with desert foliage. This amount can be increased a considerable amount by using several plastic wells some distance apart. The moisture comes from the soil and any moisture that might be in the air by means of condensation and by vaporizing in the hole. (I have used this method on beaches of tidal streams that were contaminated by salt water, and it works there, too.) The Armed Forces teach this method in their survival schools.

Keep out of the direct rays of the sun in summertime during the heat of the day to keep from becoming dehydrated. During midsummer, and sometimes in early fall, the ground surface of the sun-scorched desert averages 140°–150° F., but approximately 18 to 24 inches or so below the surface, the temperature is only 65°–70° F. Dig down to this cooler area in the shade of some desert shrub and lie down and rest until the heat of the day is over.

If it is a case of walking out, it is best to travel at night. However, travel only if the moon is out and it is light enough to see clearly. Be careful. Rattlesnakes travel and feed at night on desert rodents and other small animals.

Stay with your downed aircraft or disabled vehicle. If the machine is water-cooled, use the water from the radiator unless the water has become contaminated with anti-freeze. Remember that a plane or motor vehicle can be seen by rescue search aircraft more quickly than a person standing among mesquite or other desert shrubs.

Lay out three signal fires in a triangle some distance apart so they may show to better advantage. Throw green shrubs on the fire and pour on crankcase oil if you can to produce as much smoke as possible.

Salvage the aircraft or car compass if it isn't damaged. You might use it if you decide you must walk out. Salvage all usable parts that might help in making a shelter from the sun and wind, and for making snares, traps, or deadfalls.

Flowers and buds of most desert plants are safe to eat! Don't become alarmed if you get diarrhea or if your bowels don't move. The abrupt change in diet, plus stress, can cause this discomfort. You will be back to normal as soon as your system gets used to the rough food.

If you are forced by some decision to hike out, and have a map, study it carefully and then lay out the most direct course that the terrain will allow to the nearest road, power line, or railroad. If you come to one of these, look for tracks and follow them. Most power companies patrol their lines every few days by plane, helicopter, or Jeep.

If bitten by a rattlesnake, use standard first aid methods in treating it. Forget all about the old "desert-rat" tales of treating it by cutting the wound open and placing a raw onion or by putting freshly killed game meat on the wound to draw out the venom. It just won't work. Probably the only reason some of these old-timers survived poison snake bite is that the rattler had struck some prey recently and had expended most of its venom. In addition, the old-timer probably had a very strong heart and was also in excellent physical condition, or had been bitten often enough to build up an immunity.

If your desert vehicle is an aircraft, you no doubt filed a flight plan before leaving your home airport, so you should expect a search party if you don't arrive at your designated field within your fuel range. Be patient, for it takes time to get organized, and weather conditions may delay the search crews.

If you are one of the careless pilots who doesn't file a flight plan, you deserve your difficulties, and should be made to pay for the ground and air search—it can really be costly!

If you fly or drive into Mexico or another thinly settled area on a hunting expedition, be sure to carry a good survival and first aid kit, for it can be a long grueling hike out.

If You Become Lost—What to do

Sense of Direction Remember, no person is born with the innate ability to find his way into and back out of wilderness country entirely strange to him. This prowess is acquired only by slowly becoming acquainted with the terrain. There simply is no truth in the notion that some people have a "built-in" sense of direction. Outdoorsmen who seem to arrive where they want to go, do so by being observant. They are guided by nature—the prevailing wind direction, the position of the sun or stars, the lay of the land, and many other natural clues that the inexperienced person would not usually notice.

Lost-in-the-Woods Experience Fear-gripping and agonizing "lost-in-the-woods" experience, common injuries, and camper-caused fires can be avoided by going to your hunting and recreational areas in good physical trim properly prepared and equipped with a good map and compass, ax, shovel, bucket, stout shoes, warm clothing, bedding, and plenty of nourishing food; by determining in advance where the nearest ranger station is located in case of an emergency (help can be obtained without too much lost time); by staying on signed forest roads and trails unless you know how to take care of yourself in isolated territory; and by forming the habit of keeping oriented with the terrain as you move through the woods. The following pointers may save your life sometime:

If you do get mixed up, don't call yourself lost! You may just be confused for a few minutes. Remain calm, sit down, and relax. Have a smoke or chew some gum—think things over—don't panic and worsen the situation!

Get out your map and compass. Study the surrounding terrain. See if you can recognize some object such as a peak. Go over in your mind the route taken and try to reconstruct your course since you left a known point. Try to recall where and about when you lost contact with a peak, rock, snag, stream, lake, or other familiar object.

How to find time and direction by the quickest method. Which way is north? If you have a watch and compass, settle the matter. If you do not have either, use the latest and most accurate means—the Owendoff Method, used by the Armed Forces and the Boy Scouts.

Try to recall which way the prevailing wind was blowing when you left your vehicle or camp; was the sun to your right or left, which side of a stream, river, road, or trail were you on; how many creeks did you cross; how many passes did you hike over, etc.

If you cannot recognize any familiar country, but have a rough idea where camp is or how to reach familiar landscape from observation from a high point, you have three decisions to make: (1) stay where you are until a search party finds you; (2)

stay overnight and start out at daybreak; or (3) start out immediately if you think you can make it to camp before dark.

If darkness has overtaken you, and your camp, car, plane, or boat is a considerable distance away, make as warm and comfortable a bivouac camp as you can. Use any safe natural barrier, rock or log for a windbreak. However, watch out for flash floods in creek bottoms, rockslides, and widow makers (falling dead limbs and snags). Clear the ground where you plan to build your fire of all forest litter down to moist mineral soil for a distance of five feet from the center of your fire—all around it. This can be accomplished by scraping the litter away with a thin rock or by using a limb to dig with.

In cold weather, build a reflector in back of your fire to direct heat into your improvised shelter. You can use a slab of thin rock or green limbs back of the fire to reflect heat, or build the fire against a rock cliff.

Don't forget safety, woodsmanship, and your outdoors manners just because you got yourself into a "jackpot." Keep your fire safe, and keep yourself and camp as clean as possible—you will feel better by doing so.

Your night fire will keep you warm and safe from prowling night animals and may attract a fire lookout or aircraft. If not, a search plane or helicopter pilot may spot your signal smoke in the morning.

If it is still early in the afternoon or light enough, and you feel you can get out of your predicament before dark, do so, but be sure to plan your steps carefully. If you stayed out overnight and still do not know where you are, be sure to put out your fire and try the circle method.

Here is how, the circle method works: Blaze an anchor or base tree at or near your camp on all four sides with your knife, ax or with the edge of a sharp rock. Next, walk in a northerly direction as far as you can in a straight line without losing sight of your anchor tree. You can keep a straight course by lining up trees, rocks, or other objects. Mark another tree in line with your base tree. This should be marked on two sides—outgoing and incoming—so you can find your way back to your emergency camp if you do not find tracks or if you are way out on your first try.

Keep lining up trees and blazing them until you have traveled a quarter or half mile or so. If you haven't cut your original tracks into the area, follow your backtrack blazes to your camp. Next try a northeasterly or northwesterly direction. You may have to travel out from your base camp like the spokes of a wheel before you finally cut your original tracks or trail into the area. If this doesn't work, enlarge your circle.

Remember, search the ground carefully as you hike along. Finally, if this method fails, climb the highest point in the vicinity—you just might spot a prominent peak or object in the distance that you recognize. If you do not, return to your camp and wait for help. Conserve your energy as much as possible, and don't give up!

If you decide to walk out, be sure to leave a note prominently displayed at your camp before you leave. Fasten it to your base tree. In the note should be your name, address, the time you left your camp, the date, your physical condition, and the direction in which you are heading. If you haven't a pencil and something to write the note on, scratch the information on a tree bark or on the ground with a sharp rock.

You can assist searchers by heading in as straight a direction as possible—don't wander around aimlessly. Of course, in canyon country this would be impossible—you would have to go up or down the canyon. Whichever direction you head, select a landmark, tree, rock, peak, or other object in the direction you decide on. Walk toward it, marking your trail with blazes, rock "cairns" (one or more rocks on top of each other), or stones lined out arrow fashion. If no small rocks or stones are handy, scratch arrows on the bare ground. Pieces of cloth tied to brush or tree branches will also help trackers to follow and lead to you. If you use scraps of paper or cloth on the ground, weight them down with earth or stones so they will not blow away.

Making off-sets to avoid obstacles. Due to rough terrain, you may have to make off-sets or detours around swamps, lakes, canyons, large brush, snowfields, etc. This is simple, even though you may not have a compass. Make a 90° turn (as nearly as you can) to the right or left of an obstacle—whichever is the shorter end and easier to get around. Line up some objects so you can travel on a straight course. Count the number of steps needed to clear the upper or lower end of the obstacle in your path. Once cleared, make another 90° turn at this point and take the same number of steps required on the opposite side, and you will be back on line again in the desired direction.

If you run across a trail, logging or fire motorway road, power or phone line or railroad, check carefully for foot tracks and follow them.

Don't travel at night! It is too dangerous, and you may slip, trip, or injure yourself by falling. You might, in the dark, cross or miss a road or trail, thereby lengthening your ordeal and worry for your family.

Generally, you can follow a stream or river downstream and reach a place of habitation. However, in some regions the streams cataract over bluffs and terrain too dangerous to climb down. In this case it is safer to follow game trails along ridgetops.

Don't forget that if the sun is out it will give you a rough east or west direction, depending on the time of day. If you happen to be east or west of a river, road, or power line shown on your map, or that you know runs in a more or less northerly direction, you can head due east or west as the case may be and arrive at one of these landmarks and find your way from there.

If you run across a timber survey metal tag or marker on a tree, you are in luck. On the tag will be printed a TOWNSHIP PLAT marked into 36 sections. Each section (640 acres or a square mile) will be numbered, and a tack positioned to show the relative location of the particular tag and tree. If you have a map, you can now locate your position quickly, since the township and range are identified at the top of the marker. Even without a map or compass, you can still follow survey blazes placed on trees along the quarter section and section lines. You'll soon come to a trail or road. Should the tag be located at other than a section or quarter section, your relative distance from such a surveyed line also will be revealed by the tag's position and numbers at the bottom of the survey marker. Always remember that the numbers used on timber survey tags identify distance in terms of chain length, not feet. So keep in mind "66 feet equal one chain."

The survey markers are also placed at edges of roads and trails where the section or quarter section lines cross. Section "corners" are usually marked with an iron pipe, concrete, or a wooden post. Generally, "witness" trees facing such posts are well blazed, but due to passage of time the blazes heal over and tend to be inconspicuous and are easily overlooked. From section corners the four section lines are marked by trees, each bearing two blazes, one on each side of the tree, to indicate the section boundary line. Along the line you will see an occasional tree blazed just on one side. If so, this merely means that the section line happens to parallel only one particular side of the tree. Very few trees grow exactly on line to use as markers. To sum up, if you can identify and follow a section line, you should have no difficulty getting your bearings or general location.

One more point—when you leave camp in the morning for an all-day hunt, you'll have to start back shortly after noon, if you want to return before dark. Allow return time if you don't want to spend the night in the woods.

Arrangements should be made ahead of time with hunting companions regarding what action members of the party will take if one of the party becomes lost.

Your Survival Fire Fire has been man's friend since the beginning of time; it also has been his enemy when he has let it get out of control. Under survival conditions, it can become one of your greatest comforts and assets. You will need fire for warmth, for keeping dry, for signaling, for cooking, or for purifying water by boiling. The following checklist will tell you where to build your fire, what fuel to use, and how to build it.

1. Prepare the location of your fire carefully. To be safe, build it out on a sandbar, rock, or other safe place. If you build it in the woods, do so away from rotten logs, stumps, brush fields, low, overhanging limbs and other inflammable material. Clear away leaves, pine needles, moss, and dry grass, so that you don't start a grass or forest fire.

If possible, clear a circle 10 feet in diameter down to mineral soil (damp soil) and build your fire in the center. If the fire is to be built on wet or muddy ground, on a swamp or on snow or ice, first build a platform of flat rocks or green logs under it.

2. To get the most warmth and to protect your fire from wind, build it against a rock or wall of green logs which will serve as a reflector to direct the heat into your emergency shelter. Cooking fires should be walled in by logs or rocks, not only to concentrate the heat, but also to provide a platform for your cooking utensils.

3. You will need some easily inflammable kindling to get your fire going. Good natural kindling materials are "squaw" wood such as pine needles, ferns, leaves, dry bark, grass, thin sticks of dry wood, limbs that have been split into small, fine pieces, crumpled paper or waxed ration boxes, etc. You can also whittle several fuzz sticks by leaving the shavings intact on the sticks. Dry twigs from standing dead trees burn quickly.

4. For fuel, use dry standing dead trees or snags and dry dead branches. Dead wood is easy to split. If you do not have an ax, you can break up the wood readily over the edge of a rock into the desired lengths. The inside of fallen tree trunks and large branches may be dry even if the outside is wet; cut into it and use the heart wood. Sometimes you can find a pitch knot in a stump or rotten log. You can make green wood burn if you split it fine enough

and your kindling is dry and there is enough larger dry wood to create sufficient heat.

In treeless areas, you can find other natural fuels, such as dry grass which you can twist into bunches, dead bushes, peat dry enough to burn (found at the top of undercut river banks), dry animal dung, and animal fats. If you have no natural fuels, you can use gasoline from your disabled boat, aircraft, or motor vehicle. Place one to two inches of sand or fine gravel in the bottom of a can or other container and add gasoline, lubricating oil, or a mixture of both. Stand away and toss your lighted match or wick into the container so that the flashing gasoline will not explode in your face. If you do not have a container, dig a hole in the ground, fill it halfway to the top with sand and gravel, and pour your gasoline on it. Protect yourself by standing a safe distance away when you toss your match or burning wick in the container or hole!

5. Be sure to gather wood enough for overnight if you plan on making just a one-night stand; however, if you stay in one spot, be sure to gather sufficient kindling and fuel to last you for several days at a time and for starting signal fires.

6. Your next steps are to decide on what type of fire you want, then to prepare the fireplace so that the draft (breeze) will draw through the front of your fireplace and out the back. You can use rocks or green logs in front of the fire for a damper.

7. Have all your fire-making material and fuel together and handy before you start your fire. Make sure that your matches and fuel are dry. Have enough fuel on hand to keep the fire going. Now arrange a small amount of kindling in a low pyramid, close enough together so flames can lick from one piece to another. Leave a small opening for lighting. Next lay small pieces of wood or other fuel gently on kindling before lighting, or this can be done after kindling begins to burn. Lay on the smaller pieces first, adding larger pieces of fuel as the fire takes hold. *Don't* smother your fire by crushing down kindling with heavy fuel. Don't make your fire larger than your needs call for. Don't waste fuel!

8. If the sun is out and you have a burning glass (magnifying glass), use it and save your matches. You can save matches by using a

candle, if you have one. Light the candle, use the burning match and then the lighted candle to get going. If you have no candle, use a fuzz or "shave stick" or make a faggot of thin, dry twigs, tied loosely together. Shield your match or lighter from wind, and light the candle or other fire starter. Apply to lower windward side of kindling, shielding it from the wind as you do so.

9. If you are out of all lighting or fire starters, but have a fusee signal flare in your survival kit, light it by striking the self-contained flint and steel. Most fusees have printed instructions on them. Follow them carefully, so that you do not burn yourself. Hold away from your body when lighting.

10. You can make a burning glass if you do not have a magnifying glass by using the lens from a rifle scope, binoculars, bifocal eyeglasses, camera lens, etc. (Better practice at home before you get into a survival situation.)

11. The old flint and steel was the standby for our pioneer forefathers. It is a reliable method if you have patience and know-how. If you happen to have one of the military-type match-cases, use the flint on the bottom of the case. If you have no flint, look for a piece of hard rock against which you can strike sparks using a piece of steel. Hold your hands close over the dry tinder; strike flat side with a piece of steel, using a sharp, scraping, downward motion so the sparks fall on the center of the tinder. The addition of a few drops of lighter fluid or gasoline can also assist in starting damp wood. For safety reasons, keep your head to one side.

I personally carry a small aluminum wire welder's torch, weighing only 2 ounces, in my survival kit. This little "gem" will throw more sparks into tinder than any other type of flint-and-steel gadget.

12. I also carry a cigarette lighter with two extra flints—filled and sealed with waterproof tape. The lighter must be of the leakproof type. From it you can obtain from 500 to 800 lights, if you're thrifty with the flame.

13. You can start your fire with firearms. Wiggle the bullet back and forth until it is loose enough to remove. Shake out most of the powder onto your tinder and kindling, then fire the nearly empty cartridge into your tinder from about a foot away.

14. You can start a fire from the old friction methods used by some Boy Scouts. However, this takes considerable energy and lots of patience. The old bow and drill, fire plow, and fire thong methods will work, but remember that flint and steel will give you the same results with a lot less work.

Useful Fire Hints   1. Don't waste your matches trying to light a poorly prepared or constructed fire. Don't waste matches for lighting smokes—get a light from a coal or lighted twig from your campfire, or use your magnifying glass.

2. Collect good dry tinder wherever you find it and carry some of it along with you. Pack it in a waterproof container. If it becomes damp, dry it out on a sunny day. Adding a little powdered charcoal from your campfire will improve your tinder.

3. Dry damp or wet wood near your fire so you can use it later. Save some of your best dry wood for easy fire starting in the morning. Keep firewood dry under shelter; cover with whatever is handy.

4. To make a fire last overnight, place several large logs over it so it will burn into the center of the pile. After a good bed of coals has formed, cover it lightly with ashes and then dry dirt. The fire should still be smoldering in the morning.

5. If your large fuel proves too large and long, you can lay it across your fire star shape and keep pushing the burned ends toward the center of the fire as they burn through. This is a handy method if you do not have a saw or an ax.

6. Never build a fire under a snow-covered tree or limbs—snow may melt and put your fire out.

7. Don't waste fire-making materials. Your very life may depend on being able to start a fire. Use only what is necessary to start your fire and keep it going for the purpose intended.

8. Don't leave your fire unattended! A breeze may spring up and burn your survival camp up. Or it may start a brush or forest fire that could overtake and kill you or damage the country for miles around, killing wildlife and possibly human life in its path.

The Art of Keeping Warm   It is necessary for a survivor to retain body warmth in cold

These hunters wear warm, loose clothing that gives protection and freedom of motion. WISCONSIN CONSERVATION DEPARTMENT

weather, and to keep cool in hot weather; otherwise he can worsen his condition with these extremes. The body burns food to produce heat at various rates, depending on the amount of work involved. Thus, a sleeping man produces very little heat, while a survivor hiking up a steep slope in a deep snow can be producing almost ten times as much heat, with a corresponding loss of energy.

The function of clothing is to regulate the heat loss according to the body's heat production and outside air temperature. The clothing assembly itself can be considered in three layers, each performing a definite function.

Next to the body should be a ventilating layer of wool or thermal knit underwear. When the body cannot lose enough heat by convection from exposed surfaces or through clothing, it uses a more efficient method via water (sweat) and water vapor (insensible perspiration). In fact, the body is always losing some water vapor through the surface of the skin. If this moisture is allowed to soak into the clothing it greatly reduces the clothing's insulating value and a

survivor can freeze to death in subzero weather.

The second layer of clothing provides insulation. This includes the ordinary pants and shirt for summer use and additional insulation thickness (wool shirt, sweater, etc.) for winter. The third layer is the outer shell—a windproof, water-repellent jacket or parka. The amount of insulation against convective heat loss depends on thickness provided and not on materials used to provide it.

To guard against losing heat by conduction through the feet to the ground, lug rubber shoe soles and plastic mesh or felt insoles, to keep wool socks dry and warm, is an effective combination.

CLOTHING DO'S AND DON'TS

1. Keep clothing as clean and dry as possible, to get maximum insulation.

2. Wool shirts and trousers should be washed at least every three months or oftener to maintain insulation properties. (Watch out for shrinkage.)

3. Snow should be brushed from boots and clothing before entering any shelter.

4. Carry extra wool socks, gloves, and inner soles so that your hands and feet can be kept warm if the first pair becomes wet.

The function of clothing is to regulate the heat loss in relation to body heat production and outside air temperature. COURTESY OF THE AUTHOR

The splendors of nature await the hunter who seeks them. U. S. FOREST SERVICE PHOTO

5. Keep clothing loose and free from binding, particularly on the feet. Get wool clothing large enough to allow for shrinkage.

6. When more than one pair of socks is worn from inner to outer layers, the socks must increase progressively in both *width* as well as *length* to prevent constriction or pressure on the feet. Any sock combination *must,* in cold weather, allow free movement of toes, for constant toe and foot exercise when the feet begin to numb to prevent a freezing injury.

7. *Don't sweat.* Keep comfortably cool at all times. Underdress rather than overdress. This entails much time in dressing and undressing en route, but the effort pays off. If you get too warm, take the following steps until comfortably cool: (a) take your mittens off; (b) loosen or remove belt or parka waist tie; (c) open shirt or parka throat; (d) remove hat or throw parka hood back.

How to Keep Warm and Keep Your sleeping Bag Dry

Keep your face outside your bag to keep moisture and frost out.

Sleep in dry "long-john" underwear; even better, sleep in a "sweatsuit."

Don't sleep in a bag having a completely waterproof cover, or moisture will gather and you will become cold. In extremely cold weather, frost will collect and can add approximately one pound or more per day to sleeping bag weight!

Sleeping bags or blankets should be insulated from the ground or snow. Use an air mattress, cot pad, or boughs between the bag and ground.

Air mattresses should be inflated by pump rather than breath to prevent internal moisture or icing which will add weight. Blowing up an air mattress by mouth can sometimes cause severe nosebleed at high elevations.

A ½-inch "Raidoprene" or "Ensolite" blanket next to the bag absorbs moisture and prevents the bag from freezing to the air mattress or ground cloth.

Sleeping bags should be turned wrong side out and exposed to the sun and air whenever possible. Keep the bags fluffed up for maximum warmth and comfort.

For cold weather, hunters and other outdoorsmen have found that placing a pocket warmer or two, a canteen full of hot water, or a hot water bag at the foot of the bag makes entry into the bag most luxurious. Using a hot water bag or canteen in this manner will also ensure drinking and cooking water

in the morning, save on fuel used for melting ice or snow, and save time.

Sleeping bag liners will help keep bags clean, and will prolong the life of the bag.

Zippers should be handled carefully and zipped slowly to prevent bag material from catching. Zippers should be lubricated, if necessary, with soap, Vaseline, or light lubricating oil; apply full length.

If you prefer to sleep in long johns or your underwear, keep a set just for sleeping in, for they must be dry. If you sleep in clothing worn during the day you are apt to sleep cold due to moisture absorbed from your body. Adding one pair of wool socks to your kit just for sleeping use will aid in your comfort. The socks *must* be *clean and dry;* not ones you hunted in all day. A wool stocking cap or watch cap will also help keep your head warm!

Checklist for Cold-Weather Survival
If you travel the northland routes as do commercial fishermen and bush pilots who fly polar bear hunters onto Arctic ice floes or into remote fishing areas, or if you are a prospector or big-game hunter or fisherman who enters the Northwest Territories of Canada and the state of Alaska, you should carry the following articles in your survival kit:

Ammunition, minimum of 200 rounds.

Arctic sleeping bag.

Ax, with 2½-lb. head and 26-inch handle with sheath.

Boots, Barker insulated type.

Compass, Leupold Sportsman type.

Can, leakproof with spout and strainer, 1-gallon size.

Cold-weather survival suit developed for the U. S. Air Force, and now available to the public in limited quantity. (Eventually all aircraft operating in or across Arctic regions will carry vacuum-packed cold-weather survival clothing just as emergency life rafts and rations are now carried on transoceanic flights. The outfit gives protection for living and sleeping at −50° F. It may be secured from Gerry, Incorporated, Boulder, Colorado, makers of lightweight camping and mountaineering equipment. The outfit is called the "Walk-around-Sleeper" and lists for $131.55, and is worth every cent for the peace of mind it gives to those in cold areas.)

Dark glasses or snow goggles with case.

Felt innersoles.

Fire makers: 100 waterproofed matches with a waterproofed match safe; cigarette lighter (filled) wrapped with two flints and an extra wick in waterproof tape; flint and steel with tinder in a waterproof bag; a small magnifying glass; and a welder's sparker lighter. This latter article weighs only 2 ounces, will throw hundreds of sparks downward into tinder, and is much faster than the old flint-and-steel method. It retails at 50 cents, and extra flints may be obtained at 10 cents each.

Firearms: SAC AR-5 U.S.A.F. survival rifle, .22-caliber or its civilian version, the AR-7 Explorer floating model; or better still, the .22-410-gauge over and under rifle/shotgun combination that will shoot .22 Long Rifle hollow point ball ammunition plus .410 birdshot or .410 slugs for larger game.

Insulated or two-piece underwear (Navy cold-weather type).

Knife, B.S.A. combination type with blade, screw-driver, can opener, and leather punch.

Knife, skinning or belt type with sheath.

Map, topographic type, large scale of area.

Mirror, steel type with aiming sight for signaling search planes.

Mittens, wool inners with waterproofed outers.

Pants, smooth weave, wind- and water-repellent. (Also wind pants to wear over regular pants.)

Parka, knee-length, full zipper front, trimmed with wolf, dog, or wolverine fur around the face of the hood.

Pemmican and Pinole emergency rations or Bernard's Kamp-Pack, or other brands.

Rations, dehydrated type. Add vitamins.

Rucksack, Bergan-Meis, or Mountaineer model packsack.

Shovel, aluminum Arctic survival type with ice saw on one edge for cutting ice and snow blocks for making snow shelters, and with a sharp edge on the other side for chopping small branches.

Socks, lightweight wool inners, heavyweight wool outers. (Outers should be ½ size larger than the inner socks.)

Stick, anti-fog for glasses.

Stove, Primus type.

Tent, lightweight Arctic or Mountaineer model.

All equipment should be packed ready to go in a good packsack in case of a forced landing so it will be instantly available and can be tossed into a life raft or boat. Otherwise articles may become scattered or lost.

Chapter 14

OUTDOOR SAFETY, MANNERS, AND ETHICS

Perhaps the most serious difficulty in public use of our national forests, parks, and other recreational land is that created by the guests and visitors using these areas. Complaints are common about vandalism, theft, and thoughtless actions injurious to public and private property and to the general recreation environment.

Vandalism is ever present. Initials have been carved into camp tables, benches, signs, and trees; comfort stations have been left unsightly and filthy, and signs have been split up for kindling. Padlocks have been shot off gates in some closed areas. Holes have been shot into gasoline and diesel storage tanks in logging areas. Logging equipment has been stolen, and some hunters have endangered the lives of loggers operating logging shows by indiscriminately shooting at targets and game nearby.

Any sportsman worth his salt observing acts of this sort should make it his personal duty to report these persons to the nearest law-enforcement officer. Otherwise a few may spoil hunting and camping privileges for many, and owners of private land will start putting up more and more "No Trespassing" signs in self-defense.

Then there is the Litterbug. This person may be a nature-lover, and clean about his own home and property, but he still thoughtlessly throws his film foil and containers on the ground wherever he pauses to snap a picture. The traveler still throws beer cans, gum wrappers, Kleenex and other tissue and debris along our scenic park and forest roads. Some lazy people haven't the energy to lift the lid off from the trash cans—

they just drop their debris alongside and expect someone else to pick it up and deposit it for them. The same thing is happening along our wilderness forest and park trails. Lakes and alpine streams are being littered with bottles, cans, and other debris!

A Few Simple Forest Rules

USE THE FOREST AND HIGH COUNTRY WISELY AND SAFELY!

During the fire season, as declared by the regional forester, a campfire permit is required before building any fire in a national forest, outside an established building. Permits are issued without charge at all forest offices or by forest officers in the field. Observe the rules on your permit before signing, and observe the regulations while camping. (Get your permits during office hours. You can't expect the Ranger to be very happy when you awaken him in the middle of the night for a permit and inquire where the best hunting or fishing is! He gets little enough sleep as it is answering emergencies.)

If camping in the back country use existing campsites and fireplaces where possible. At new fire sites clean an area 10 feet in diameter down to mineral soil; build your fire in the center on level ground away from steep slopes, rotten logs, or overhanging limbs. Keep it small. A small fire is best for both cooking and warming. Never leave your fire unattended. A sudden wind could come up while you are away and blow sparks into dry forest litter! Be certain your fire is DEAD OUT before leaving camp, either temporarily or permanently. Soak it with water, stir dirt into it, and soak again. Feel it with your hands to be SURE THAT IT IS OUT!

*The hunter who uses national forests and wilderness areas for his own pleasure has
a duty to his fellow citizens to protect these lands from vandals and careless hunters.*
U. S. FOREST SERVICE PHOTO

SMOKE SAFELY, only in cleared areas or camps and places of habitation. Break your match in two, crush your cigarettes and pipe heels. Make sure they are out! Do not smoke while hiking or riding.

Keep and leave a clean camp. An experienced camper and woodsman leaves some dry wood for the next camper. Where garbage pits are not provided, burn refuse where possible. Burn and crush cans, and pack out empty cans and bottles to road ends.

Be certain your food is safely stored. (The safest way is to hang it high off the ground from a slender limb away from the trunk, beyond the reach of bears or other climbing animals. Animals in country frequented by people are accustomed to human beings. Food left in a tent or on a forest camp table sooner or later will be raided by deer, bear, squirrels, or other rodents.

Preserve the facilities provided for your comfort—tables, latrines, hitching rails, pastures, and signs.

Pasture pack and saddle stock in areas designated or sufficiently far from campsites to keep them clean and attractive. Graze stock wisely and avoid overuse of meadows. Carry grain or pelletized horse feed.

Keep lakes and streams crystal clear and safe from pollution in any form. Clean game and fish away from water supplies. Bathe and wash dishes away from water supply.

Where no sanitation facilities are provided, dig a deep hole or trench and refill as used. The latrine should be a minimum of 200 feet from any water supply.

Do not dig flowers, plants, ferns, shrubs, or moss without permission from a forest officer. Leave the flowers and plants for others to enjoy. Cutting of green trees, poles, or boughs, or chipping bark on

Use the forest wisely and safely. U. S. FOREST SERVICE PHOTO

trees is not permitted. Do not sink your ax into trees. This starts the sap bleeding and attracts insects that enter and kill the tree. Nails and wire damage trees. Use rope instead!

Dogs are permitted, but be considerate of the other campers and keep your dog quiet and under control. Lead away from camp for sanitation reasons.

Quiet must be maintained in campgrounds. Keep your radio low and quiet after 10 P.M. Keep children from running and screaming through other camps. Be considerate of your neighbor.

Do not shoot firearms within or *near any campground!*

All motorized equipment is prohibited within the wilderness!

Alpine wilderness is in a very delicate state of ecological balance. Careless acts by man will surely result in destruction of such areas in their natural state. It will take nature many years to repair such damage.

Never let it be said and to your shame, that all was beauty before you came.

Suggestions for Safe Boating Do not use gasoline stoves, heaters, or lights on board. Use caution to prevent fires while refueling.

Do not overload your boat.

Observe all boating speed limits and "rules of the road."

Have children wear life jackets. The law requires a life preserver or jacket approved by the U. S. Coast Guard for each person aboard your boat.

Water skiing is permitted on many national forest lakes. Ride with two persons in the boat

CANADIAN GOVERNMENT TRAVEL BUREAU

to maintain a proper lookout, and be sure you are well clear of other boats, swimmers, or obstructions.

Know what to do in case of emergency. In case you capsize, remember that if your boat continues to float, it is best to remain with the craft until assistance comes.

Obey all signs and fish and game hunting laws. If in doubt, ask a Ranger!

Sportsmanship Needed in the Outdoors Each year we get a new crop of campers, hunters, fishermen, water skiers, and camp cruisers in our recreation areas. With this vast army invading our waterways and back country we are meeting with the inexperienced, who enter our recreational areas poorly prepared; this we can cope with—they are willing to learn. What is hard to take and understand is the increasing number of poor sportsmen! These hoodlums, the water skier and boat speeder who cut across the fisherman's trolling line, rocks or swamps his craft; the goof who opens up on incoming ducks before they are in range, spoiling the shooting for everyone else in the nearby blinds. Then, to name a few other woods hoods of this type, there is the campground hog who takes an extra table, leaving none for the adjacent campsite. The thoughtless camper who takes a soapy bath in the stream above camp where you get your drinking and cooking water. The tough-talking character who, when his attention is called to sanitation, fire, or forest infractions, tells the Ranger or game warden off. He boasts of his influential friends at the state capitol or in Washington, D.C., and says that he will see that the officer will lose his job. Then he wonders why he is arrested instead of just given a warning. And I suppose we will always have the poacher and game hog to contend with if our courts are too softhearted with these game thieves.

What has become of the old American idea of sportsmanship? This to-hell-with-you, don't-give-a-damn attitude is on the increase. Perhaps many parents have spared the rod too long with the younger generation and we are paying for it now. Maybe a course in conservation and outdoor manners is needed in our schools. It is probably too late to teach an old dog new tricks, but maybe we can teach our youngsters sportsmanship! You as an outdoorsman and a sportsman need to do something about it! *What?* Perhaps by teaching outdoors ethics and good manners to your children at home, through your clubs and PTAs, and by setting a good example yourself!

KEEP OUR COUNTRY GREEN

APPENDIX

Sources of Emergency Rations and Dehydrated Foods

EMERGENCY RATIONS

Emergency rations may be purchased from the following:

FIREFLY SURVIVAL RATIONS
(Coast Guard Type)
Safety Research & Mfg. Co.
Seattle, Washington 98104

CHUCK WAGON
P. O. Box 66
Newton, Massachusetts 01355

ALL TYPES OF DEHYDRATED FOODS FOR HUNTERS AND CAMPERS

AD SEIDEL
1245 W. Dickens Avenue
Chicago, Illinois 60014

ANN BENEDICT'S
Dri-Lite Foods
11333 Atlantic Avenue
Lynwood, California 90262

ANN'S KITCHEN
1500 Wisconsin Avenue
Washington, D.C. 20000

BERNARD FOOD INDUSTRIES, INC.
(East of Rockies)
217 N. Jefferson Street
Chicago, Illinois 60606
(West of Rockies)
222 South 24th Street
P. O. Box 487
San Jose, California 95103
(Canada)
120 Sunrise Avenue
Toronto, Canada

CHUCK WAGON
Bolton Farms Pkg. Co., Inc.
P. O. Box 66
Newton, Massachusetts 01355

CRAMORE FRUIT PRODUCTS
90 West Broadway
New York, New York 10007

E-Z FOOD PRODUCTS COMPANY
1420 So. Western Avenue
Gardena, California 90247

H & M PACKING CORP.
Life Pack 3-, 8-, 14-Day Kits
915 Ruberta Ave. Glendale, California 91201

LYON'S FOOD SPECIALS
P. O. Box 11215
Los Angeles, California 90011

MEGDEN INDUSTRIES
6808 Marshall Road
Upper Darby, Pa. 19082

SEIDEL TRAIL PACKETS
David Abercrombie Co.
97 Chambers Street
New York, New York 10007

TRAIL MEALS
J. B. Kilsky
1829 N. E. Alberta Street
Portland, Oregon 97211

TRAILWISE SKI HUT
1615 University Avenue
Berkeley, California 94702

TRIP-LITES
S. Gumpert
812 Jersey Avenue
Jersey City, New Jersey 07302

TRIPPEROOS
Hilker & Bletsch
614 Hubbard Street
Chicago, Illinois 60609

YAKIMA CHIEF
709 N. First Street
Yakima, Washington 98901

And don't forget the famous Freeze Dry Armour products or the excellent Wilson dry foods obtainable from sporting goods stores and outfitters.

Outfitters Catalogs for Hunters and Campers.
For companies with an asterisk (*) enclose 25 cents.

ABERCROMBIE, DAVID T., CO.
97 Chambers Street
New York, New York 10007

ABERCROMBIE & FITCH:
Madison Avenue at 45th Street
New York, New York 10017
9 Wabash Street
Chicago, Illinois 60603
220 Post Street
San Francisco, California 94108

ALASKA SLEEPING BAG CO.
334 N. W. 11th Avenue
Portland, Oregon 97209

ALL CAMP, INC.
515 28th Street
Des Moines, Iowa 50312

ALPINE HUT INC.
4725 30th Avenue
Seattle, Washington 98105

AMES-HARRIS-NEVILLE CO.
2800 17th Street
San Francisco, California 94110

BRUN'S SKI SHOP
616 Pennsylvania Avenue
Washington, D.C. 20003

CAMP & TRAIL OUTFITTERS*
112 Chambers Street
New York, New York 10017

CAMPER'S CORNER, INC.
Route 3 Box 203A
Elkhart, Indiana 46514

CANADIAN ALPINE EQUIP. CO.
1315 14th St. N.W.
Calgary, Alberta, Canada

COLUMBIA TENT & AWNING CO.
1314 Rosewood Drive
Columbia, S. Carolina 29201

CORCRAN, INC.
2 Canton Street
Stoughton, Massachusetts 02072

DOLT HUT, Mountain Equipment
2241 Sawtelle Boulevard
West Los Angeles, California 90064

DON GLEASON'S CAMPERS' SUPPLY*
2 Pearl Street
Northampton, Massachusetts 01060

EDDIE BAUER
Expedition Outfitters
417 East Pine
Seattle, Washington 98122

GANDER MOUNTAIN, INC.* ($1)
P. O. Box 248
Wilmot, Wisconsin 53192

GART BROTHERS
Sporting Goods Company
Denver, Colorado 80202

GATEWAY SPORTING GOODS CO.
3177 Mercier Street
Kansas City, Missouri 64111

GERRY, INC. OUTFITTERS
Box 910
Boulder, Colorado 80301

H & M PACKING CORPORATION
915 Ruberta Avenue
Glendale, California 91201

HOLUBAR CAMPING EQUIPMENT
1215 Grandview Avenue
Boulder, Colorado 80301

I. GOLDBERG & COMPANY
429 Market Street
Philadelphia, Pennsylvania 19106

KLEIN'S SPORTING GOODS CO.
227 W. Washington Street
Chicago, Illinois 60606

L. L. BEAN, INCORPORATED
278 Main Street
Freeport, Maine 04032

LAACKE & JOYS COMPANY
1433 North Water Street
Milwaukee, Wisconsin 53202

MORSAN—OUTFITTERS
810 Route 17
Paramus, New Jersey 07652

MOUNTAINEERING SUPPLY CO.
897 St. David's Lane
Schenectady, New York 12302

NORM THOMPSON—OUTFITTER
1805 N. W. Thurman Street
Portland, Oregon 97209

PARKER DISTRIBUTORS OUTFITTERS
40 Industrial Place
New Rochelle, New York 10805

RECREATIONAL EQUIPMENT OUTFITTERS
523 Pike Street
Seattle, Washington 98122

ROD & GUN OUTFITTERS
P. O. Box 6074
Shawnee Mission, Kansas 66206

THE SMILIE COMPANY
30 Jessie Street
San Francisco, California 94105

THOMAS BLACK & SONS*
Camping Equipment
Ogdensburg, New York 13669

THE TRADING POST
3336 M Street
Washington, D.C. 20004

TRAILWISE SKI HUT
1615 University Avenue
Berkeley, California 94702

WIG-WAM, INC.
Route 44
Rehoboth, Massachusetts 02769

WRITE for the Potomac-Appalachian Trail Club's Hiking, Camping, and Mountaineering Equipment catalog. Price, $1.00 plus 10 cents postage. The Potomac-Appalachian Trail Club, 1718 N Street N.W., Washington, D.C. 20036.

Where to Write for Hunting, Camping, and Boating Information

Maps and brochures will be sent without charge. For information on hunting, write to the Game Department at the state capital of the state in which you plan to hunt:

ALABAMA: Division of State Parks, Department of Conservation, Administration Building, Montgomery 36104. Also, Bureau of Publicity and Information, 304 Dexter Avenue, Montgomery 36104.

ALASKA: Department of Economic Development and Planning, Alaska Travel Division,, Box 2391, Juneau 99801.

ARIZONA: Arizona Development Board, 1500 W. Jefferson Street, Phoenix 85007.

ARKANSAS: Arkansas Publicity & Parks Commission, Room 412, State Capitol, Little Rock 72201.

CALIFORNIA: Division of Beaches & Parks, Box 2390, Sacramento 95811.
Sierra Club, 1050 Mills Tower, San Francisco 94104.

COLORADO: Department of Public Relations, Capitol Building, Denver 80203.

CONNECTICUT: State Park & Forest Commission. Also Connecticut Development Commission, State Office Building, Hartford 06115.

DELAWARE: State Park Commission, 3300 Faulkland Road, Wilmington 19808. Delaware State Development, Tourism Division, 45 The Green, Dover 19901.

DISTRICT OF COLUMBIA: National Capitol Region, National Park Service, 1100 Ohio Drive S.W., Washington, D.C. 20242.

FLORIDA: Florida Park Board, 101 West Gaines Street, Tallahassee 32304.

GEORGIA: Georgia Department of Parks, 7 Hunter Street S.W., Atlanta 30334.

HAWAII: Hawaii Visitor Bureau, 2270 Kalakaua Avenue, Honolulu 96815.

IDAHO: Department of Commerce & Development, State House, Boise 83702.

ILLINOIS: Department of Conservation, Division of Parks & Memorials, 100 State Office Building, Springfield 62706.

INDIANA: Department of Natural Resources, Division of State Parks, 616 State Office Building, Indianapolis 46209. Also, Indiana Department of Commerce, Indiana Tourist Division, Room 334, State House, Indianapolis 46209.

IOWA: Public Relations, State Conservation Commission, East 7th & Court, Des Moines 50309.

KANSAS: Department of Economic Development, State Office Building, Topeka 66612.

KENTUCKY: Travel Division, Department of Public Information, Capitol Annex Building, Frankfort 40601.

LOUISIANA: State Parks and Recreation Commission, Old State Capitol Building, Drawer 1111, Baton Rouge 70821.

MAINE: State Park & Recreation Commission, State House, Augusta 04330. Also, Department of Economic Development, State House, Augusta 04330.

MARYLAND: Department of Forests & Parks, State Office Building, Annapolis 21404. Also, Tourist Division, Department of Economic Development, State Office Building, Annapolis 21404.

MASSACHUSETTS: Department of Natural Resources, 15 Ashburton Place, Boston 02108. Also, Department of Commerce & Development, Bureau of Vacation Travel, 100 Cambridge Street, Government Center, Boston 02202.

MICHIGAN: Michigan Tourist Council, Steven T. Mason Building, Lansing 48926.

MINNESOTA: Division of State Parks, 320 Centennial Office Building, St. Paul 55101. Also, Vacation Information Center, 160 State Office Building, St. Paul 55101.

MISSISSIPPI: Mississippi Park System, 1104 Woolfolk Building, Jackson 39201.

MISSOURI: Missouri State Park Board, Box 176, Jefferson City 65102. Also, Division of Commerce and Industrial Development, Travel-Recreation Section, Jefferson Building, Jefferson City 65102.

MONTANA: Advertising Department, Montana Highway Division, State Parks Division, Helena 59601.

NEBRASKA: Nebraskaland, State Capitol, Lincoln 68509.

NEVADA: State Park System, State Capitol, Carson City 90701. Also, Department of Economic Development, Carson City 89701.

NEW HAMPSHIRE: Division of Economic Development, State House Annex, Concord 03301.

NEW JERSEY: Department of Conservation, Forests & Parks Section, Box 1889, Trenton 08625. Also, State Promotion Section, Box 1889, Trenton 08625.

NEW MEXICO: State Park & Recreation Commission, Box 1147, Santa Fe 87501. Also, State Tourist Division, 302 Galiston, Santa Fe 87501.

NEW YORK: Conservation Department, Division of Lands & Forests, Bureau of Forest Recreation, State Campus, Albany 12226. Also, Division of Parks, State Campus Site, Albany 12226 and State Commerce Department, Travel Bureau, 112 State Street, Albany 12207.

NORTH CAROLINA: Travel & Promotion Division, Department of Conservation & Development, Raleigh 27602.

NORTH DAKOTA: Travel Department, North Dakota State Capitol, Bismarck 58501.

OHIO: Ohio Department of Natural Resources, Division of Parks and Recreation, 913 Ohio Departments Building, Columbus 43215. Also, Development Department, Information Center, Room 1007, Ohio Departments Building, Columbus 43215.

OKLAHOMA: Oklahoma Industrial Development & Park Department, Tourist Information, 500 Will Rogers Building, Oklahoma City 73105.

OREGON: Travel Information Division, State Highway Department, Salem 97310.

PENNSYLVANIA: State Department of Forests & Waters, Harrisburg 17120. Also, Travel Development Bureau, Department of Commerce, 113 South Office Building, Harrisburg 17120.

RHODE ISLAND: Division of Parks and Recreation, 100 North Main Street, Providence 02903.

SOUTH CAROLINA: Division of State Parks, Commission of Forestry, Box 357, Columbia 29202. Also, State Development Board, Box 927, Columbia 29202.

SOUTH DAKOTA: Publicity Division, Department of Highways, Pierre 57501.

TENNESSEE: Division of State Parks, 235 Cordell Hull Building, Nashville 37203. Also, Division of Information and Tourist Promotion, Department of Conservation, 2611 West End Avenue, Nashville 37203.

TEXAS: Parks & Wildlife Department, John H. Reagan Building, Austin 78701. Also, Texas Highway Department, Travel and Information Division, Austin 78701.

UTAH: Utah Travel Council, Council Hall, Capitol Hill, Salt Lake City 84114.

VERMONT: Department of Forest & Parks, Montpelier 05602.

VIRGIN ISLANDS: Virgin Islands National Park, Box 1707, Charlotte Amalie, St. Thomas, V.I. U.S.A. 00802.

VIRGINIA: Division of Parks, Suite 403, Southern States Building, 7th & Main Streets, Richmond 23219. Also, Division of Public Relations & Advertising, State Office Building, Richmond 23219.

WASHINGTON: Visitor Information Bureau, General Administration Building, Olympia 98502.

WEST VIRGINIA: Division of Parks and Recreation, Department of Natural Resources, State Office Building, Charleston 25305. Also, West Virginia Department of Commerce, Planning and Research Division, 1591 Washington Street, Charleston 25305.

WISCONSIN: Vacation & Travel Service, Conservation Department, Box 450, Madison 53701.

WYOMING: Wyoming Travel Commission, 2320 Capitol Avenue, Cheyenne 82001.

CANADA

CANADA: Canadian Government Travel Bureau, 150 Kent Street, Ottawa, Ontario. Also write here for information on Northwest Territories.

ALBERTA: Alberta Government Travel Bureau, 331 Highways Building, Edmonton.

BRITISH COLUMBIA: British Columbia Government Travel Bureau, Department of Recreation & Conservation, Parliament Building, Victoria.

MANITOBA: Tourist Development Branch, Department of Industry & Commerce, Legislative Building, Winnipeg.

NEW BRUNSWICK: New Brunswick Travel Bureau, 796 Queen Street, Fredericton.

NEWFOUNDLAND: Newfoundland Tourist Development Office, St. John's.

NOVA SCOTIA: Nova Scotia Travel Bureau, Department of Trade & Industry, Halifax.

ONTARIO: Ontario Department of Tourism & Information, 185 Bloor Street East, Toronto.

PRINCE EDWARD ISLAND: Prince Edward Island Travel Bureau, Box 1087, Charlottetown.

QUEBEC: Department of Tourism, Fish & Game, 12 Ste. Anne Street, Quebec.

SASKATCHEWAN: Tourist Development Branch, Power Building, Regina.

YUKON: Yukon Department of Travel, Box 2703, Whitehorse.

MEXICO

MEXICO: Mexican Government Tourism Department, 630 Fifth Avenue, New York, New York 10020. Also, National Tourist Council, 2 East 55th Street, New York, New York 10022; or Mexican Consulate, in most large cities.

MEXICO: El Secretaria de Agricultura y Formento, Direccion Forestal y de Caza, Mexico, D.F. Also, El Jefe del Depto. de Parques Nacionales, Mexico, D.F., and El Direccion General De Proteccion y Replacion, Mexico, D.F.

UNITED STATES GOVERNMENT

The following publications are available from the Superintendent of Documents, U. S. Government Printing Office, Washington, D.C. 20402 at the prices indicated:

Appalachian Trail, 5 cents.

Backpacking in the National Forest Wilderness, 15 cents.

Boating Regulations in the National Park System, 20 cents.

Camping, 20 cents.

Camping in the National Park System, 15 cents.

National Forest Areas, 15 cents.

National Forest Vacations, 30 cents.

National Park System, 40 cents.

Reclamation's Recreational Opportunities, 15 cents.

Vacationing with Indians, 30 cents.

Wildlife on the Public Lands, 35 cents.